THE TROUBLE WITH CHRISTIANS

The Trouble With Christians

A Fresh Look at the Sermon on the Mount

Jon Jaroszewski

Edited by
Gregg Hakalmazian

RESOURCE *Publications* • Eugene, Oregon

THE TROUBLE WITH CHRISTIANS
A Fresh Look at the Sermon on the Mount

Copyright © 2014 Jon Jaroszewski. All rights reserved. Except for brief quotations in critical publications or reviews, no part of this book may be reproduced in any manner without prior written permission from the publisher. Write: Permissions. Wipf and Stock Publishers, 199 W. 8th Ave., Suite 3, Eugene, OR 97401.

Resource Publications
An Imprint of Wipf and Stock Publishers
199 W. 8th Ave., Suite 3
Eugene, OR 97401

www.wipfandstock.com

ISBN 13: 978-1-4982-0328-9

Manufactured in the U.S.A.   12/03/2014

All scripture quotations, unless otherwise indicated, are taken from the Holy Bible, New International Version®, NIV®. Copyright ©1973, 1978, 1984, 2011 by Biblica, Inc.™ Used by permission of Zondervan. All rights reserved worldwide. www.zondervan.com The "NIV" and "New International Version" are trademarks registered in the United States Patent and Trademark Office by Biblica, Inc.™

NKJV: Scripture taken from the New King James Version®. Copyright © 1982 by Thomas Nelson. Used by permission. All rights reserved.

NASB: "Scripture quotations taken from the New American Standard Bible®, Copyright © 1960, 1962, 1963, 1968, 1971, 1972, 1973, 1975, 1977, 1995 by The Lockman Foundation. Used by permission." (www.Lockman.org)

Scripture quotations marked "KJV" are taken from the Holy Bible, King James Version, Cambridge, 1769.

Contents

Preface | vii
Acknowledgments | ix
Introduction | xi

1. The Verse | 1
2. The Sermon | 12
3. The Poor in Spirit | 19
4. Those Who Mourn | 26
5. The Meek | 34
6. The Righteous and the Merciful | 44
7. The Pure and the Peacemakers | 58
8. The Persecuted | 68
9. Salt and Light | 74
10. Sin and Perfection | 85
11. Our Hidden Father | 99
12. Judgment | 112
13. Two Roads | 128
14. By Their Fruit | 135
15. Re: Rebuke | 143
16. Rebuking Rebuking | 155
17. Honesty | 170
18. Inheriting The Earth | 178

Preface

Years ago Jon brought me the roughs for *The Trouble with Christians*. From the first reading I knew he was onto something special. Arguments ensued over the fresh interpretations Jon brought to the teachings of Jesus. Yes, some of it was hard to swallow and less than easy to digest. However, the work was always compelling and kept me coming back for more.

I recall many mornings driving to work and talking to Jon via the cell-phone about some point I discovered in the previous night's reading. The back and forth was stimulating and eventually we agreed that it would be advantageous for me to assist with editing. What did I get myself into! So here it is, years later, and we both made some compromises. And, that's pretty good considering we both like to get our own way. The teaching is all Jon from his understanding of the Holy Scriptures. My contribution was with style and editing. I may not agree 100 percent with everything in this volume, but the interpretation of what Jesus taught is (in my opinion) right on the money. I am proud and honored to have a part in this book. Enjoy.

Gregg Hakalmazian

Acknowledgments

My deepest gratitude to the people who interceded at crucial points, without whom this book would never have been finished: Gregg, Donna, and Leanne.

My heartfelt thanks and appreciation to those who suffered with me and because of me during the writing process, Linda, Bill, Mom, Logan, and Dave.

Introduction

IMAGINE FOR A MOMENT that you've been diagnosed with a terminal disease. You have young children and they quickly become your primary focus. You can't save yourself but you would love to do anything within your power to help them live a wiser, more abundant life even though you won't be around to offer daily advice. How would you best help them?

I imagine I would videotape a message. In the old days, before video, I would have written the message down and left a copy for each child. Either way, I would use words that the children would have understood at that early stage in their lives, while also attempting to impart concepts that they might not *fully* grasp until they had gained sufficient maturity and life experience to do so. In this way the words would have remained the same but their meanings would blossom along with the child.

This is exactly the scenario Jesus faced as he readied to speak the Sermon on the Mount. His terminal illness was our sin. Yet his love and concern for us overrode any concern he had for himself. Videotape wasn't available to him in the fullness of time and he didn't choose to write down anything we know of other than a line in the dirt. Yet he had Matthew, faithful Matthew, and that was enough.

Jesus used words a child could understand and so we have always understood the Sermon, at least the broad gist of it. But over the ensuing two thousand years Jesus hasn't been passively watching. He has been changing us, growing us; making us capable of greater understanding. When he spoke the words of the Sermon, altruistic agape love was little more than a glimmer in his eye. Now the whole world understands agape to a certain extent, even unbelievers.

But with our greater maturity comes a greater awareness of the concepts Jesus left for us. His words may have been the equivalent of "Share with others" and "Listen to your elders" but if we link his instructions in our minds, something greater emerges. Something like the idea that we must interact well with the people around us. The purpose of this book is to explore those linkages and the newer understanding that blossoms once we acknowledge that such links exist.

There is no doubt that they exist. Jesus used rhetorical devices to clue us in. He begins all his introductory remarks with *Blessed are*. The sermon proper begins with phrases that begin *you are the*. The longest extended section is coalesced around *You have heard it said (but I say to you)* and the final subject is Jesus' various thoughts on judgment.

To look at the Sermon as an interconnected unity is, for some reason, radical and new. The present consensus instead sees the book of Matthew as a collection of aphorisms preserved by the "Matthean community." The idea of community traditions solves some of the discrepancies between the synoptics but I think the solution comes at too high a price. The sermon is less than we have imagined it to be if it is only an accumulation of memorable sayings.

The internal cohesion evident in the sermon should change our view. If it hasn't been noticed or grasped previously, then we can hardly attribute it to clever editing by a more primitive community. It can only be accidental or Divine and I would be hard pressed to differentiate between the two.

The internal cohesion demands we view the words in their fuller context and the fuller context changes the meaning of the individual verses. Jesus wasn't only telling us lust is bad and then teaching that divorce is bad, he is showing us lust may lead to divorce. The words of Jesus become more profound when we can appreciate the profundity with which he has communicated to us in this sermon.

A finer appreciation – and therefore a finer grasp – is the goal of this book. The trouble with Christians is not that we don't attempt to implement what we've been taught, it's that we haven't yet been taught properly. We haven't been taught properly because we've underestimated Jesus and his skills as a communicator, and because we've misunderstood the love with which he spoke. I hope this book is the beginning of a sustained attempt to rectify those shortcomings.

1

The Verse

I HAD A SINGLE verse of Scripture running through my mind for a long time. One verse. Instinctively rather than intellectually, I knew it was important. Jesus expressed it as a command and promised consequences if we didn't obey. Yet I wasn't sure what it meant.

If this had been the Bible's only pronouncement on the subject I wouldn't have hesitated to obey, but it wasn't. Paul wrote extensively on the same subject and seemed to give contradictory advice. Various Old Testament writers did the same. The apparent conflict was a dilemma. Whose directives should I follow? On one side was Jesus (and he offered the same command in more than one way) and on the other side appeared to be a preponderance of biblical evidence. What didn't I understand?

I looked for clarification. The authors of the commentaries I consulted didn't have the same difficulties with the verse that I was having. They simply didn't take Jesus' words at face value. In fact, there was a consensus among them that Jesus meant the opposite of what he said! If they were right, their interpretation would not have been disturbing in and of itself. We often modify our understanding of a passage once we allow for hermeneutics or cultural context, and that's exactly what they did.

However, when we alter the meaning of these particular words, it causes huge relational problems with our unbelieving friends. They also know these words and who said them, and (unlike the commentators) have no qualms about interpreting them literally. It's true; there is a Bible verse that most unbelievers know. The words are from Matthew 7:1.

Do not judge.

Atheists, nominal Christians and anti-theists all see Christianity's proclivity for judgment and can't understand why we ignore this elemental command from the man we say we follow. Read any rant against our faith, and you are likely to find reference to *do not judge*. Pastor Erwin Lutzer of Moody Church said on his daily radio program that it is the Bible's most quoted phrase.

Perhaps unbelievers quote *do not judge* because it dovetails nicely with society's postmodern worldview. Postmodernism postulates that no one has access to Absolute Truth, so no one has the moral authority to declare his or her version of the truth to be truer than any other version of the truth. What is true for you may not be true for me. In this philosophy, *do not judge* becomes a prime modifier rather than a moral imperative. When they interpret *do not judge* literally, it leads to (shudder) tolerance.

Tolerance has become an anathema within conservative Christian circles, and thought to be responsible for all sorts of evils. Could tolerance really be what Jesus meant? Postmodernists love that Jesus said *do not judge* because they interpret it in a way that allows them to ignore Jesus.

Many Christians look at the world's interpretation of *do not judge* with horror. They have determined that the simple and literal interpretation must be incorrect. The conservative Christian's fear of humanist relativism and the anti-Christian agenda it provokes is the basis for this rejection. None of us can imagine that Jesus would suggest that we not witness. Didn't he give us the Great Commission?

The commentaries give us a way out. They remind us that *do not judge* is not a solitary command, but part of a larger passage. Commentators point to the word *measure* in the next verse and say it is a modifier. They say Jesus means we can judge as long as we use the proper measure. By this logic, *do not judge* becomes do judge, but judge carefully.

> *Do not judge, or you too will be judged.*
> *For in the same way you judge others, you will be judged,*
> *and with the measure you use, it will be measured to you.* (Matt 7:1–2)

Not all Christians buy into the proper measure of judgment argument. We seem to fall into one of two camps. Some insist "If Jesus said it, I'm going to follow it. I try not to judge anybody." Others understand we are known and influenced by the company we keep. They can point to the example of Paul telling the believers at Corinth to not even eat with backslidden Christians. We have become so afraid of being *of* the world that we strive to be separate from it. In order to do this properly, we believe we must judge.

A more recent view suggests that Jesus was in the midst of a teaching on hypocrisy and so the command applies only to hypocrites. This rationale falls flat *because* of our love of absolutes. If we believe (and we do) that anyone who commits a sin is a sinner, then any sinner who judges the sin of another is by definition a hypocrite. However, this argument is unnecessary because the underlying assumption is flawed. Even a cursory look at the passage in context shows that hypocrisy is not the main topic, judgment is. Go ahead and read it again, I'll wait. Hypocrisy is mentioned as a supporting point, not vice versa. Jesus wants us to know we are hypocrites *if* we judge, not that we can judge unless we are hypocrites.

Understanding Jesus' words is critical. If we become like the world, we can no longer be salt and light. Yet if we judge when we shouldn't, we erect walls that separate us from the very people we are commanded to reach. The external evidence seems to suggest we are building walls.

Unbelievers look at Christians as judgmental hypocrites in astonishingly large numbers. In a poll by The Barna Group (a Christian polling organization) seven of every eight unbelievers under the age of thirty said judging is our defining characteristic. Almost as many believe we are hypocrites. My guess is that older unbelievers would poll similarly.

Since what the world believes about us affects the credibility of our witness, and since these three little words, *do not judge*, have become a principal battleground; we must come to a proper understanding of what Jesus meant.

Do not judge is from the Sermon on the Mount. The Sermon is Jesus' sustained teaching on how we should live as citizens of his earthly kingdom. In it, Jesus assumes that those not yet in the kingdom are observing us. He is fully aware of the effects of our actions on those around us. In other words, if we are to "be Jesus" to the world, this is how the one who *is* Jesus thinks we should do it. If he really means we shouldn't judge, we had better pay attention.

So how can we know for sure? Postmodernists—and this includes post conservative Christians—would insist that we can't; we bring too much of what we've been taught and too much cultural baggage to the interpretive process.

I sympathize but take a different view. Jesus was a master communicator and his words are divine. These particular words describe reality as seen by the One who invented reality. They are plain and perfectly stated. If we had only the words of Matthew 7, we could come to an absolutely correct conclusion because of the logic Jesus utilizes to clarify his point. The words are self-contained; we don't need to view them through the lens of the rest of Scripture in order to develop a proper interpretation. But we will, because it is important to show the unity of the Word.

If we acknowledge only three things: that Jesus is divine, that Jesus is describing reality, and that reality is logical, then the misinterpretations melt away. Again, the commentaries hang on the word *measure*. They say it is a Roman legal term for meting out the appropriate punishment for a particular infraction. We shouldn't be too harsh but neither should we be too lenient. We shouldn't sentence someone to death for coveting nor should we give a week's house arrest for murder.

This is how *do not judge* gets to mean *do judge*, or more precisely, *judge but judge appropriately*. Although an appropriate penalty seems more reasonable than not judging at all, it doesn't fit with the logic Jesus uses here. His impeccable logic is the key to understanding the passage. He doesn't leave us to interpret as we wish. His rhetoric is clear.

First, Jesus gives us the command and then he immediately gives us a subordinate clause to help explain what he means. When he introduces the consequences of judging, the whole "appropriate measure of judgment" argument falls apart. This is evidenced by the *if. . .then* sequences Jesus sets up. *If* we judge others *then* we will be judged in the same way. Look at it again. *For in the same way you judge others, you too will be judged, and with the measure you use, it will be measured to you. If* we use a certain measure, *then* that same measure will be applied to us.

Our interpretation of judging with the correct measure breaks down if we *consider the inverse of the consequences*. In other words, we could only make the case for judging by proper measure if Jesus had made the command from the positive perspective of "Judge correctly because that's the way you are going to be judged." But he doesn't. He accentuates the negative and adds the negative consequences.

Thus, if the commentators were correct, our God would be a terrible God indeed. Because according to their interpretation of Jesus' logic, *if we* measure judgment incorrectly, *then* judgment will be measured incorrectly to us. *If we* judge unjustly, *then* God will judge us unjustly. *If we* measure our judgment too severely, *then* God will punish us too severely.

Are you buying into this? I can't conceive of God judging us inappropriately. This negative logic followed to its absurd conclusion should clear up any misconceptions about the verse once and for all. This is the reason Jesus presents the consequences as naturally flowing from the act of judgment. *Appropriate* judgment is certainly not what he had in mind. Jesus said, and means, "Do not judge, or you will be judged." It is a warning, not advice about a proper measure of judgment.

If we can agree that God won't judge us inappropriately or punish us too severely, we are still left to wonder exactly what *do not judge* does mean. Part of the reason many of us turn to Christ in the first place is to escape judgment. We've been taught that the blood of Christ covers our sin. The idea is central to our expectation of standing before the Judge someday. I have always thought that we would stand before the Father and plead Jesus and Jesus only. This is not true. Actually, we will stand before Jesus Christ himself to be judged.

> *For we must all appear before the judgment seat of Christ,*
> *that each one may receive what is due him*
> *for the things done while in the body,*
> *whether good or bad* (2 Cor 5:10).

The things done while in the body, whether good or bad may not refer to sin or lack of sin according to some commentators. I'm inclined to agree. They say *good or bad* means *useful for eternal purposes* or *worthless deeds*. The Greek word translated as *bad* in this verse is most often translated as evil, but there is an understanding from many of the passages that instead suggests a meaning of *a wrong outlook* or *a way of thinking that leads to bad results*.

If this is the sense in which Jesus warns us that we will be judged, it is bad enough. It means that judging others is useless and can be harmful to our witness, with eternal consequences. It means we could hear, "In this case you have not done well as a good and faithful servant." That would be judgment enough and crushing indeed. To stand before my Lord and know I missed a chance to further the kingdom would be a sorrowful experience.

So how can we learn not to judge? How can we live our lives without judging? We judge all the time. It is a practical necessity. We wouldn't get married on a first date or let a known murderer rent a room in our home. It is impossible to live successfully without good judgment. Scripture warns us to be careful when selecting friends, when listening to advice and when planning our futures. Don't all these require us to judge?

In my mind this was more than a conundrum; it was a paradox. Jesus commands us to not judge and the rest of the Bible tells us we must judge. Good judgment is one of the innate skills God has created in all of us and one he desires we sharpen. What are the Proverbs but an attempt to impart greater skills of good judgment for better living?

Inherent in the idea of using judgment is the tacit acknowledgment of our free will. Adam and Eve exercised terrible judgment. So has everyone since. Bad judgment means bad choices. Because God knows this, we are commanded to teach good judgment to those over whom we are given responsibility. One of the most important tasks we have as parents, teachers, and leaders, is to develop proper judgment in those we lead.

I meditated on the conflicting biblical teachings about judging for a long time but I couldn't reconcile the apparent discrepancies. I began to believe it was one of the mysteries we are so fond of as Christians, like Jesus being fully God and fully man or the Trinity being three yet one. If this was an antinomy, a paradox, a mystery that was beyond our ability to understand, then I should have been able to let it go and trust the Lord. But I couldn't because there was a difference.

The Godhead three in one was a cognitive dissonance I could embrace because it made no practical difference in the way I lived my life. I can exalt the God I am unable to fully understand and rest in the wondrous knowledge that he fully understands me. But *do not judge* is different. A proper understanding of the passage should make a big difference in my everyday thoughts and actions. It hardly seemed fair that the command could be so vague.

I began to believe the Bible was giving situational advice. Most of the time I needed to judge but in certain situations I would be judged for judging. But which were which? How could I know? This is where I was stuck for months, maybe years. I watched people around me exercise bad judgment with disastrous consequences. I continued to be the victim of my own poor judgment. On the other hand, I watched people open chasms between themselves and others by judging them. Some people would avoid others they thought were judgmental. Others left the church. I even suspect many have left our local church because it wasn't judgmental enough! And if this is what believers were doing to each other, what were we doing to seekers and casual unbelievers? That Barna poll weighed heavily on my mind. If my observations were typical, then maybe our loss of influence in the world and the decline of Christianity itself were due to improper parsing of the texts.

Then one morning, the answer hit me like a thunderbolt. Everything became clear in an instant. There was no paradox, no antinomy. The Bible regained its unity. The conflict had only ever been in my mind.

The command to not judge *was* situational, but in exactly the opposite way I had believed. Here's how it works: we are to judge ourselves, constantly and soberly, but we are not to judge anyone else unless God grants us leave to do so. Brilliantly simple! Naturally I missed it.

There is a difference between using good judgment and the judging that will get us judged. The words are the same but the concepts diverge. Teaching us to use good judgment is one of the major tasks of scripture. There is a way that leads to life and a way that leads to death and it is our responsibility to apply that principle to ourselves. That's good judgment.

Judging others in the same way, however, is wrong. It is the responsibility of others to judge themselves. Will God hold me responsible someday for the sins someone else commits? Of course not. Then why would I decide to take that responsibility upon myself? God tells us a day of judgment is coming. He is the Judge. We usurp his authority when we take the role of judge for ourselves.

This is the great-unwritten rule implied throughout the Bible: we need to monitor our own thoughts and actions very carefully and not worry a single bit about the thoughts and actions of others. It is not our job.

Except when it is.

There is one exception to *do not judge*, but because we don't recognize it as an exception to the rule, it causes confusion. We can judge—no, we *must* judge—if God calls us to the task. And when he does, the call is unmistakable and indisputable.

When God calls us to judge, he doesn't generally do so by a nebulous leading of the Spirit. He knows we tilt toward the physical and tend to misinterpret the leading of the Spirit. So when he calls us, the call is concrete, physical and more importantly, *positional*.

God sometimes calls us to a position of limited authority. Pastors, teachers, government officials and parents are called to exercise authority according to scripture, and these are the people who must judge. They should judge only those God has given them authority over and only for the period he has granted that authority.

The difference between the judgment Jesus warns against and the judgment God calls us to carry out is easy to discern if we keep these authority figures in mind. It comes down to whether or not God has placed us in a position of authority. In contrast, the judgment that will get us judged is executed from an *assumed position of superiority* or *authority that we have not been granted by God*. It's simple; authorities must judge, the rest of us must not; this is the biblical pattern.

God ordained three institutions for the good of humanity: family, government, and the church in their various manifestations. These institutions have authority and authority figures, to teach good judgment and stave off chaos. Judging flows naturally from these positions because *the authority is inherent in the role*. Parents, pastors, civil leaders and teachers must judge.

In contrast, the judgment that Jesus says will get us judged is executed from an assumed position of superiority or authority that we have not been granted by God. We usurp God's role when we think we are smart enough or moral enough to make a proper decision about someone else. The distinction is straightforward. How did I miss it for so long?

Jesus cautions us against peer judgment because he knows we are particularly prone to this way of thinking. In fact, we believe we are wise enough precisely because we have come closer to living according to his precepts.

We see society crumbling around us and know that life would be so much better if only others believed what we believe and did what we do. This feeling of superiority comes from knowing the Bible and being chosen by God. Yet didn't the Jews Jesus was speaking to also feel superior because they knew the Law? Did they not also believe they were God's chosen people?

When Jesus says *do not judge*, he is implying a lot and some of it is in direct opposition to the views we hold as followers. Much of the sermon leading to Matthew 7:1 is an expository on who we really are and how we really think. Much of the sermon after the verse is an explanation of why we aren't capable of the kind of judgment we are so prone to want to execute. Throughout the sermon Jesus is saying we aren't really in the position of superiority compared to those we want to judge, we are only *incrementally* different.

We don't have enough information to judge properly. We don't know the thoughts, motivations, or experiences of those we would judge. We can't understand the consequences of our judgment, either on earth or eternally. Most importantly, we aren't morally justified enough to judge. Our judgment is flawed because we are imperfect creatures. Instead of judging others, we need to work on our own predilection to sin.

Proper judgment flows from relationship. We can judge in vertical relationships but not in horizontal relationships. We must not judge our peers (unless we're appointed to a jury). When God grants the authority to judge, he also attaches additional responsibility and builds in restraints to compensate for our fallen natures. These restraints are missing in peer-to-peer relationships because God doesn't want us to judge our peers.

A civil judge has a mandate to judge. The title is the job description. A judge must judge or the job isn't getting done. However, he must judge fairly, and only those brought before him. He shouldn't judge his brother-in-law's habit of dress or the way his neighbor spends her Sundays. They are beyond the jurisdiction granted him.

If we are blessed with children, we are held responsible for them. It is a responsibility most of us cherish. When God grants the child, he grants the responsibility. Once the child matures, our authority is removed (although our concern remains). We can't ground our thirty-year-old son if his house is messy and neither can we ground his neighbor's children.

Leaders hold power and sway. The kings of Israel and Judah were judged more strenuously for their kingdom's spiritual direction. The same will be true of our presidents and congressmen, our teachers and correctional officers. They are given authority within a certain purview, and for a limited time, and they will answer for what they have done with that authority. They are those meant to judge, and with the measure they use, it will be measured to them.

One last aspect of the authority God grants is most significant. He knows our innate sinfulness, so he builds safeguards into the roles he has ordained. He counterbalances our fallen tendencies with powerful built-in limiters.

Parents need to judge in order to train up a child but God tempers that authority with love. Is there any love quite like our love for our children? Teachers generally teach because they want to make the world a better place. Civil leaders understand there are limits beyond which the populace will rebel. The ability of a churchgoer to leave a local body is a concern for church leaders. Most of the pastors I have known are judicious in their exercise of power. The uncertainty of what lies after death, including the expectation of judgment that God has built into our hearts, should make all leaders more cautious.

Still, the stereotype of corrupt or uncaring judges persists. There are even examples in the Bible. We've all heard of abusive parents, bullying teachers, and despotic rulers. We are, all of us, broken people. God is aware of this, even more than we are:

> *Can a mother forget the baby at her breast*
> *and have no compassion on the child she has borne?*
>
> *Though she may forget, I will not forget you!*
> *See, I have engraved you on the palms of my hands;*
> *your walls are ever before me.* (Isa 49:15–16).

God likens his love for us to the unconditional love of a mother for her child. Then, mid-thought, (as though heinous counterexamples come to mind) he seeks to reassure us that his love is even greater. *Though she may forget, I will not forget you!* He has engraved us on the palm of his hand like a foolish schoolgirl in the throes of puppy love. The walls he speaks of are the limitations we face because we are sinful creatures.

This tempering of authority, together with greater responsibility, is exactly the reason leaders can judge but we shouldn't judge peer-to-peer. We haven't been given any counterbalances in relationships with equals other than civility, and as we see every day on the news, civility is most often the least potent of governors.

So, there are seven characteristics associated with proper judgment:

- The authority to judge is granted by God
- The authority carries an extra measure of responsibility.

- The authority is limited by the definition of the role.
- The role is always vertical.
- The role is given to teach good judgment or to limit those who refuse to learn it.
- The authority is tempered to compensate for our innate sinfulness.
- We will be judged on how well we execute the authority we have been given (as well as the authority we usurp).

I haven't come to these conclusions lightly, or on my own. I think they are clearly spelled out in the text of Jesus' sermon and reinforced by the rest of the Bible. Once we consider whether God has granted the authority to judge, the prophets and apostles come into full agreement with Jesus.

Yet if I didn't think the Holy Spirit was teaching me, I wouldn't have ventured an opinion. But I do think and believe this very thing. Early one morning, before anyone else woke up, my morning devotions again took me back to Matthew chapter 7. But this time the words came alive. I was struck by the thunderbolt of clarity I mentioned earlier. The verses opened up to reveal a new and coherent interpretation. There was an internal consistency throughout the whole chapter that I had not seen before! I began to understand precisely what Jesus was saying.

Teaching us to not judge occupies nearly all of chapter 7; yet it is only part of the sermon. When combined with the two preceding chapters, it forms a cohesive instruction that is so revolutionary and foreign to us that we have never comprehended all of its meaning. We have selected nuggets from the sermon and attempted to live them out; *love your enemies and pray for them* or *hunger and thirst after righteousness*, but we have failed to see the cohesion within the Sermon as a whole. Noting the cohesion is key to a proper interpretation of the Sermon.

We tend to think of Jesus' teachings as many and varied and perhaps not even related to each other except in a general way. This is the major flaw in our thinking. He is not throwing out concept upon unrelated concept, hoping something will stick. Quite to the contrary, Jesus has carefully prepared his message. It seems haphazard to us because we have mistaught so much of it.

There is a gestalt at work here; the whole is greater than the sum of the parts. Jesus logically builds a vision of how we should live, precept by precept, from start to finish. Each thought is related to the one before it and the one after it. We have missed this because we have been taught incorrectly and we have been taught incorrectly because previous expositors approached the text with presuppositions that directed the meaning of the sermon toward what they thought it should mean.

Jesus taught by destroying the foundational beliefs his hearers had built their lives on and then immediately filled the void with a superior way of thinking and living. Our task today is the same, but may be more difficult. We still quote as truth the very "foundational" ideas he sought to destroy because we don't recognize the cohesion. Where Jesus tells us salt and light is love, we think that salt and light is speaking the truth in love. We quote him saying "be perfect as your heavenly Father is perfect" and regard it as a demand for obedience when what he really meant was that we've got no shot at being perfectly obedient so our best strategy is to love like our Father loves. So we must not only chip away at what Jesus chipped away, we must also chip away at our misunderstanding of what he chipped away (whew!).

After an overview of the sermon, we'll begin chipping. As we begin to delve into Jesus' original intent you may at first think me misguided. Please withhold *judgment* until we are finished. Individual concepts may not make as much sense until the Sermon is grasped as a whole.

When that happens, you'll be as amazed as his original audience!

2

The Sermon

The Sermon on the Mount is Jesus' earliest recorded address to a large gathering. He was thirty (or a little older) and he could feel the momentum of his ministry beginning to accelerate. He had turned water into wine. He had been dunked by the Baptist and confirmed by both the Father and the Spirit. He had followed the leading of the Holy Spirit and withstood the temptations of Satan in the desert. He had called some of his disciples and was teaching in the synagogues and in the remote Galilean countryside.

These were the essential events in Jesus' life to this point, but they weren't what attracted the ever-increasing throngs. His growing reputation rested on his ability to heal the sick and cast out demons with the same authority with which he taught. The crowds were attracted to Jesus for the same reason we were first attracted to Jesus; we were intrigued by what he might do for us. But the Sermon wasn't about what he would do for us. Instead, Jesus came to instruct us in what we should do for him, and for each other. The sermon was his call to action and his vision for the future.

On this particular day, the crowds had swelled to the point that he had to take extra care if he was to be heard. He climbed to a higher vantage point so his words could echo down to the audience gathered below. Jesus then delivered some of the most beautiful and poetic words ever spoken . . . and they still echo. Civilization as we know it changed because the early church took his words to heart and put them into practice.

The sermon starts in Matthew 5, but the narrative explaining how he got to the mountain begins at the end of chapter 4:

> *News about him spread all over Syria,*
> *and people brought to him all who were ill with various diseases,*
> *those suffering severe pain, the demon-possessed,*
> *those having seizures, and the paralyzed,*
> *and he healed them.*
> *Large crowds from Galilee, the Decapolis, Jerusalem, Judea,*
> *and the region across the Jordan followed him.*
> *Now when he saw the crowds,*
> *he went up on a mountainside and sat down.*
> *His disciples came to him,*
> *and he began to teach them,*
> *saying:* (Matt 4:23–25—5:1)

Jesus' opening remarks (known as the Beatitudes or blessings) should remind us of the commands his Father had given so many years before. Jesus spoke from the side of a mountain as his Father had spoken from the top of Mount Sinai. Jesus gave a series of commands as enlightening as the Ten Commandments had been in that earlier age. Lest you think the Beatitudes were not commands, we will see later that Jesus referred to them in exactly that way.

The Beatitudes split into two categories: statements about the present and promises for the future. I had never noticed this distinction before, (and the commentaries ignore it) but it is both intentional and important. Jesus is beginning the greatest sermon ever recorded, one that could only be produced by a keen mind. I'm certain the verb-tense changes he makes are not grammatical errors.

The first Beatitude is in the present tense and so I think of it as an assertion about the present state of believers. As we will see, Jesus is not just talking about the present state of believers then, but also the present state of all believers of the age. This includes citizens of the kingdom of heaven today.

The rest of the Beatitudes provide assurances for individual believers and for the future of Christianity. I think of them in this way because Jesus is saying that as believers we are blessed now because of something that will happen in the future. We are blessed in the present tense for reasons that are all in the future. How's that for radical thought?

The Beatitudes hold out hope to a wounded world. When we read them they are calming to the soul, even if we don't fully understand their meanings. There is a rhythm and a cadence to these opening statements that I imagine translates equally well from language to language and dialect to dialect, because the words are divine.

There are also mental images each blessing produces in the hearer's mind, and unlike the universality of the cadence, the images reverberate through each individual's psyche in a slightly different manner. Jesus doesn't seem to be giving us precise rules in the Beatitudes; they read more like poetry. If poems are word pictures, then Jesus offers an impressionist painting rather than a photograph. Just as beauty is in the eye of the beholder, so the Beatitude is in the mind of the hearer. At least . . . that's what I used to think.

We can begin to understand this sermon better by looking at the rules for effective communication. Jesus was a master communicator and even if he didn't write the rules, he surely used them to our great advantage. The rules say

1. Grab people's attention.
2. Tell them *what* you are going to tell them.
3. Tell them.
4. Tell them why you told them.

Also, throw in a little humor, don't talk too long, and end on a rousing and inspirational note. This is exactly what Jesus did. He succeeded spectacularly (of course) at every turn. He grabs our attention, tells us what he is going to talk about, and then explains it all in the heart of the sermon. Finally, he tells us why it is important for us to know these things. The whole sermon lasted only fifteen minutes. Yet it is one of the longest sustained teaching sessions in the Bible, and the longest public address from the mouth of Jesus.

The sermon is Jesus' mission statement. He unfolds his plan for his earthly kingdom and his vision is for us to live a life of mission. The mission is the same as he gives us in other places. In the Great Commission he tells us to go and make disciples, in the Sermon on the Mount he tells us how. In fact, the Beatitudes are the seven-step process Jesus would prefer us to use to bring others to Salvation. The early church was proficient in using this process because God had structured circumstances in such a way that they had no other good choices. Early believers had no power so they had to live out the Beatitudes.

Today we need this seven-step process like never before. Christianity has fallen from the great heights of power it once enjoyed, but we will see that that's a good thing. I can't help but believe that the loss of power is just what God wants. However, we needn't confuse power with influence. Jesus wants us to influence the world. The commands we call the Beatitudes are exactly the way he would have us influence the world—with or without power.

The Beatitudes are also particularly well suited as a means to reach the postmodernists we mentioned in the last chapter. They are suspicious of truth claims but open to the truth when lived consistently. The missing piece of the puzzle is for us to adjust our perception of what the Sermon says to reality as we live it. Jesus goes into great depth and leaves us with no choice but to change the way we think about ourselves, for it isn't our view of the Bible that must change, but our view of ourselves. We are doing mission incorrectly and we have for over a hundred years. It isn't a coincidence that our distortion of our mission dovetails with our loss of influence in postmodern society.

As we walk through the sermon verse-by-verse, our wayward ways will become apparent. It's not that we don't have a heart for the lost; it's more that our hearts are deceitful. Once we realize the interconnectedness of the themes within the sermon, the flow of Jesus' thoughts will lead us to realize there is a better way.

I no longer see any ambiguity in Jesus' words. The sermon is sophisticated beyond a doctoral thesis in words suitable to the common man. Jesus unfolds his vision piece by piece, backtracking for clarity and repeating for emphasis, all the while leading us to an inescapable conclusion.

Although we all recognize the sermon as a masterpiece, it is not what we have supposed it to be. The things I have been taught about it are often wrong or only partially correct. The scholars have missed seeing the message as a cohesive whole. They often miss the jests and always miss the gestalt.

Think about it. Our pastors don't speak on every subject that pops into their heads during a sermon. They have a plan. Some use an outline and some write their message out word for word. Television shows are scripted. Scholarly papers develop a premise. Why would we think Jesus to be an inferior thinker or an inferior communicator?

We haven't completely understood Jesus because none of us is the biblical scholar he surely is. At times, he speaks in a kind of Bible code, referencing passages his original audiences would have known better than we do. Today, with our New Testament emphasis, some of these references have become obscured. This is where the computer has been invaluable to me. (I am indebted to BlueLetterBible.com.) I am not an expert, but when I searched the Old Testament passages Jesus referred to, I began to understand what he was (and is) saying. We know there is unity to scripture and the Sermon on the Mount is the culmination of many Old Testament passages.

The logic Jesus used to build his argument should be the ultimate persuader for a new understanding. His structure is simple and elegant. Jesus intends for us to absorb it with wonder and growing excitement. The Beatitudes were meant to grab his listener's attention. (The first would have rocked their world.) The body of the speech that followed explained and expanded upon his opening remarks, and his summation was meant to inspire them, and us, to change the world.

Jesus spoke of a radical new way of life. After only a quarter of an hour his audience instinctively understood that they had heard true wisdom spoken with an authority that surpassed anything they had experienced. So let's start there, at the end and look at their reaction to Jesus' his words:

> *When Jesus had finished saying these things,*
> *the crowds were amazed at his teaching,*
> *because he taught as one who had authority,*
> *and not as their teachers of the law* (Matt 7:28–29)

Today we accept Jesus' authority but we've lost our sense of amazement. The concepts within the sermon (at least as they have been taught to us) are staid and trite. We've twisted his words century by century until some of the ideas have become unrecognizable. *Do not judge* is one example. We also misinterpret meekness and righteousness. We misunderstand the profundity of mourning and the worth of proper persecution. We miss the quest behind mercy and the simplicity of peace. We've lost God's take on our sinful lives—and especially his opinion of our distorted view of ourselves after salvation.

Our misinterpretation comes partly because no one has ever spoken to us like this before. God's thoughts are not our thoughts, even today. The Sermon, so simple, so beautiful, so profound, is nevertheless a hard teaching. If we are to follow Jesus, it will cost us. The cost may be the most enduring reason we have misunderstood the sermon. We love the beauty, we cherish the concepts insofar as we have understood them, but we think we have misheard the price. Our modern interpretations are often a matter of haggling the price downward.

Yet Jesus allows us to choose whether we will pay or not. He allows it because he wants more than our assent and more than a rote following of a set of rules. He wants us to pay the price he asks, gratefully and enthusiastically—to live out the sermon with all our heart and all our life. Jesus wants us to catch the spirit of his vision.

To do this, we must first comprehend it. This is our task in this book—to look at the vision of Jesus line-by-line and sometimes even word-by-word. The words are plain. He means for us to understand his vision because he wants us to live it.

The crowds were amazed because Jesus didn't teach what their teachers of the Law taught. He didn't sound like their teachers of the Law and he doesn't sound like many of our present day teachers of the law. He was and remains revolutionary. He tears down so many of the premises we hold dear while deeply expanding our understanding of the things he doesn't destroy.

We have lost some of the revolutionary aspects of Jesus' teaching in the mists of time and a less than stellar understanding of the Old Testament. We have removed some of the radicalism, more of it than we have retained. We have explained away his forceful message under the cover of our newer yet very old traditions. He probably saw it coming.

We can't mesh our thoughts and ways with the thoughts and ways Jesus demands we consider. Our precarious reality doesn't fit with the kingdom he calls us to inhabit. The kingdom is foreign to us and so we determine Jesus must have meant something else. Because we so discount Jesus' instructions we are left with a crippled Christianity and a breached kingdom. We often assent to a mutual churchy reality that doesn't connect with the reality of the unsaved world around us and so we don't see that sometimes they have it right and we're the ones who have gotten it wrong. They have assimilated parts of this message better than we have. This is because unbelievers can only view the world as God established it. Whether or not they acknowledge God has no effect on what they see.

Believers look for something else, something unseen. We call it faith. We understand that things work on a level beyond the apparent. This faith begins with faith in Jesus but soon becomes more (or should we say less). It morphs into faith in certain teachings of the church, which can be inferred from a Bible that never spells them out. This is fine provided our inferences are correct.

Because the Bible is so large and our capacity for learning is greater than our ability to systematize such a complex work, we learn a set of assumptions about what the Bible means long before we become familiar with the words themselves. This can lead to reading the words with presuppositions unintended by the original writers. I believe this is what happened to the Sermon on the Mount. The misconceptions we apply have hurt our testimony and damaged our influence. As we have moved further from the lessons Jesus means us to live out, the damage has accelerated.

Two hundred years ago unbelief was regarded as almost a character flaw, and unbelievers were likely to keep their unbelief to themselves. One hundred years ago the world around us still shared the moral views of the church. Some people even joined churches for the prestige and economic advantage membership afforded them. Fifty years ago the outsider's view of the church was still generally favorable. In fact, unregenerate members (as the unsaved infiltrated) were seen as a major problem facing the body.

Today Christians are thought of as irrational and controlling, unloving and unkind, and superior in our own minds. Remember; the vast majority of unbelievers under the age of thirty see us as hypocritical and judgmental. The world's distrust of Christ's body is directly proportional to the suffering we impose. That distrust is increasing.

If we explain away the things Jesus tells us and distort the principles by which he calls us to live, we are asking for trouble. These very rationalizations and distortions are exactly what the world sees with such great clarity; and this is the trouble with Christians.

3

The Poor in Spirit

Blessed are the poor in spirit, for theirs is the kingdom of heaven (Matt 5:1)

BEFORE WE TAKE A more leisurely stroll through this first Beatitude, I would like us to imagine ourselves among the crowd that Jesus addressed that day. This might help us recapture some of his revolutionary spirit. His first sentence was as radical as any the crowd had ever heard. Had Jesus said only this and nothing else, his listeners could have pondered its implications for a long time.

With a single word, the first word, *blessed*, he acknowledged their expectations. They had gathered to witness miracles. Now the man who performed these great works was about to tell them how to be blessed. Yet his very next words puzzled them. It wasn't his audience that was blessed; it was *the poor in spirit*.

Poor in the Greek was an emotionally loaded word. It wasn't "barely scraping by" poor, it was "unable to fend for yourself" poor. Beggar poor, from the Greek verb that meant *to slink around*, most likely because someone this poor and helpless felt that their poverty was due to a deficiency within themselves. Imagine the surprise when the crowd heard that first phrase. Jesus thought someone that desperately *poor in spirit* was blessed.

His listeners would have thought themselves rich in spirit. They had a rich spiritual heritage in the Law and the Prophets. They were God's chosen people. And now they had abandoned the ho-hum of their everyday existence to partake of a new and rich spiritual experience. Could they be spiritually rich yet poor in spirit?

Before they could ponder it, Jesus finished his astonishing statement. The thing he said the poor in spirit already possessed was something called *the kingdom of Heaven*. Those who heard him were already part of a kingdom. They were provincial citizens and subjects of the great Roman Empire. They must have wondered if Jesus was about to counsel sedition. Kingdoms need a king; was Jesus about to proclaim his kingship? Could he be the promised Messiah—Israel's conquering king? He certainly showed signs of God's favor upon him by the miracles he performed. Could this moment be the very beginnings of revolution? Would they be able to tell their grandchildren they were there on the fateful day the Jews began their promised rise to rule the world?

In about five seconds, in one short sentence, he had their complete and focused attention. The emotions stirred by his strange new words must have had their hearts racing in expectation. I imagine that he paused here for a moment to let his words sink . . . and then he was on to the next Beatitude.

We have the luxury of a less hurried consideration of his words. There are two phrases in his opening sentence and, unlike much of the rest of the sermon, we understand both of them better than his original audience did. Let's consider them in reverse order.

When Jesus announced *the kingdom of heaven*, the Jews would have been puzzled at first. They didn't expect to go to heaven when they died, they were destined for Sheol. Heaven was God's dwelling place. If Jesus' audience made the connection between God as their king and a *kingdom of heaven*, then the kingdom could only have been Judea and the king in question would have been the promised Messiah, come to bring peace and justice to the earth, as described in the many Old Testament *Day of the Lord* passages. The Jews awaited their coming Messiah with the same fervor most Christians today show for his second coming. In their minds the Day of the Lord was yet to come, but Jesus spoke of the kingdom of Heaven as a place the poor in spirit already possessed. Theirs *is* the kingdom of Heaven.

Jesus' listeners didn't have time to ponder the new term but we do, and can understand it better because we have the whole New Testament. Jesus spoke of the kingdom of heaven thirty-one times, all in the book of Matthew. It was a major theme. Nine of Christ's parables explain what the kingdom of Heaven is like. Only once does he confirm that it is an earthly kingdom, and already in existence. *From the days of John the Baptist until now, the kingdom of Heaven has been forcefully advancing, and forceful men lay hold of it* (Matthew 11:12). Forceful, as it was commonly used in the Greek, was a poetic term. It doesn't denote violence so much as it does zeal. We must be zealous for the kingdom.

I bring the present existence of the kingdom to the forefront for two reasons. The first is because Jesus mentions it first. The existence of the kingdom is his opening assertion in the sermon. In Jesus' view, the kingdom was an established fact.

The second is to combat an idea that pervades much of conservative Christianity, and weakens us. A prominent school of thought insists the kingdom of Heaven is a future reality. We only achieve it when we die, or perhaps when we are resurrected. The people who believe this tend to speak disparagingly of the *Kingdom Now* movement and associate it with the social gospel.

I hope Matthew 11:12 would persuade us otherwise. The kingdom is almost two thousand years old. We can't let the plans of men discourage us from the Plan of God. The social gospel failed because, although it attempted to put the kingdom of Heaven into practice, it was a kingdom without a proper King. The social gospel movement was led by men rather than God. N. T. Wright, the fine Anglican theologian, reminded us that the very people who promoted the social gospel were often the same people that questioned the historical veracity of Jesus.

We must take both Jesus and his vision seriously. We can't ignore the mission he lays out in the sermon just because humanity has previously attempted it under its own power; and neither can we attempt it without his lordship. The kingdom of Heaven is faith put into practice. This last thought, faith in practice, leads us naturally back to the first puzzling phrase, *poor in spirit*.

Most commentators believe the poor in spirit are those who realize they cannot live this life successfully on their own and so they turn to God. It makes sense. The poor in spirit are those of us that have finally come to the end of pride, at least for one very important moment. The poor in spirit are believers. The Holy Spirit regenerates us and we are then able to see the futility of relying on our own methods or goodness. God has thus worked behind the scenes in our lives, set the circumstances of his plan in motion, and drawn us. In a moment his strength is made perfect in our weakness. In the twinkling of an eye, we become citizens of the Kingdom of Heaven.

With this simple three-word phrase, so foreign to the thought patterns of his original audience, Jesus begins to reorganize us into groups recognizable to God. His thoughts are not our thoughts and neither were his categories their categories. Jesus divided the world, for the first time, into believers and unbelievers. This differentiation is so familiar to us today that we might think it has always existed, but his original audience would have never thought of it. To them, the world was composed of Jews and Gentiles. Jesus' first sentence was earth shaking in ways they didn't understand.

There is great significance in the fact that we can understand *poor in spirit* while those who first heard it didn't. It means Jesus was aware that he was speaking as much to later followers as he was to that original gathering. To those listening, *poor in spirit* was both emotionally charged and puzzling. Today we view the phrase in its proper light as a reference to salvation.

This first Beatitude is in the present tense because the kingdom is ours already. Ours *is* the kingdom of heaven. Salvation must be the starting point. We can't work in the kingdom unless we are first made citizens of the kingdom. Salvation is our naturalization papers.

Salvation is a prerequisite for bringing others to salvation, don't you think? I can't imagine that Marx, Freud or Attila the Hun led anyone to Christ. If the Beatitudes are indeed the seven-step process by which Jesus would have us witness to a lost world, then our own conversion to Christ-follower must be the first step. We can't make disciples unless we are disciples.

We must also *remain* poor in spirit. Blessed *are* (present tense) the poor in spirit *contains the command that must influence all the commands that follow.* Jesus could have used the past tense. "Blessed are those who *were* poor in spirit" but he used the present tense because he knows remaining poor in spirit will be a continual battle in the war to advance the kingdom. Pride is the first enemy, the perpetual enemy, and the deadliest enemy of the kingdom of heaven. This is why Jesus uses the phrase "poor in spirit" instead of "blessed are the repentant" or "blessed are the born-again." Repentance can be occasional and born-again can lead us to believe it is once in a lifetime. The verb "are" is what keeps being *poor in spirit* a continual precept.

Each ensuing verse in the sermon needs to be considered through the lens of remaining poor in spirit. *Blessed are the meek, for they shall inherit the earth*—if they remain poor in spirit. *Blessed are those who hunger and thirst for righteousness, for they will be filled*—if they remain poor in spirit. *Being* poor in spirit (present tense) is first in the sermon because it is both foundational and necessary to our continuing quest. Remaining poor in spirit helps us battle our pride.

Pride is the first obstacle believers overcome; it is the only way to be born-again. Yet pride is the one sin we must all continually battle. Those that have been victorious over every other sin are (ironically enough) the most susceptible to pride. Pride is always the primary sin, because pride attempts to usurp God's rightful place in the cosmos.

Pride caused the rebellion when Satan fell from heaven. Pride caused the second fall when Eve and Adam sought to be as gods. Pride has caused every fall since. Pride causes the fall of Christian leaders and followers even today.

We think we can "handle" a certain level of sin because as believers we understand sin better than we did when we were unbelievers. Or we try to walk on the edge of the rules without breaking them because we know the rules and we understand how finely they are drawn.

But mostly the pride we enjoy as Christians comes from knowing our spirits are made alive in Christ. We contrast our enlightened state with the sad moral state of the world around us and we are proud of the difference. We see how we are now and compare it to how we used to be and we think we have come so far.

And we like to talk about it—how far we've come. We think we are giving God the glory for the changes in our lives but that might not be what our listeners hear. And after all, for whom is our testimony if not the unbeliever?

Being proud in spirit warps our testimony. We unintentionally infer that we are better than they are. Think about it. We tell people we used to be terrible sinners, but Jesus changed us. We don't do the things we used to do before we were saved. Unbelievers might very well hear that we think we used to be like them, but now we are better.

The focus in *our* minds might be on God, but in their minds *they* hear a comparison between them and the new and improved us. This is why Jesus used poor in spirit in the present tense. We must *remain* poor in spirit. Poor in spirit is the effectual difference between solid testimony and bragging.

Pride puts self first. Pride causes prideful people to not recognize they are being prideful. Jesus will give various clues throughout the sermon to help us recognize our own prideful tendencies. The Bible tells us pride causes destruction.

In contrast, Jesus will often ask us to practice mercy because he knows our propensity to pride and the walls it builds. Mercy tears down those walls. Mercy requires empathy and works best when we are grateful for our salvation. Mercy trumps pride.

Just as the Beatitudes are a microcosm of the Sermon on the Mount and the Sermon is a microcosm of Jesus' life and earthly ministry, God gives us a verse in the Old Testament that is a microcosm of the Beatitudes. It is Micah 6:8:

> *He has showed you, O man, what is good.*
> *And what does the Lord require of you?*
> *To act justly*
> *And to love mercy*
> *And to walk humbly with your God.*

In the Sermon, Jesus showed us *what is good*. He told us what is required of us. We must treat others well. We must love mercy. *And to walk humbly with our God* is the best way to remain poor in spirit. Micah had to explain what the Lord required because Israel was complaining about their lack of results after all they were doing for God. Listen to the pride in their complaint.

> *With what shall I come before the Lord*
> *And bow down before the exalted God?*
> *Shall I come before him with burnt offerings, with calves a year old?*
> *Will the Lord be pleased with thousands of rams,*
> *With ten thousand rivers of oil?*
> *Shall I offer my firstborn for my transgression,*
> *The fruit of my body for the sin of my soul?* (Mic 6:6,7).

Can you hear the sarcasm? They started by throwing God's commandments for ritual sacrifice back at him. *Shall I come before him with burnt offerings, with calves a year old?* Then they upped the ante with gross exaggeration: *Will the Lord be pleased with thousands of rams, with ten thousand rivers of oil?*

Oddly enough, they ended their spiritual temper tantrum with God's own solution from before the foundations of the earth. He ignored it as the ludicrous suggestion it was, coming from them instead of from himself. *Shall I offer my firstborn for my transgression, the fruit of my body for the sin of my soul?* God ignored their tantrum and he ignored their sarcasm. Instead, he reasoned with them because this was too important for him to respond with wrath; we are too important to him.

Micah says that the Lord *requires* us to walk humbly. The poor in spirit are uniquely suited to doing that. Pride and humility are almost opposites. I say *almost* opposites because I think the actual opposite of pride is love. The Bible's examples of love and pride can be distilled down to a simple, contrasting definition for each. Love is placing the desires of another above oneself. Pride is placing self above others.

If you've ever fallen in love, try to remember your early thoughts. They were of your beloved. I remember my first love. I wondered what she was doing when we were apart. I wondered what she was thinking. Even when we were together I would ask what she was thinking, and she would often ask the same of me. I put a great deal of thought into what would make her happy, what she liked and disliked. My thoughts were of her and not of myself.

I also remember my thoughts of my wife during our divorce. I wondered why she would do certain things to me. I wondered why she tried so hard to hurt me. I thought about how I suffered because of her actions and how things could be different if only *she* was better. I tried to make her a better person. I tried to get her to see things my way, but she refused.

Do you see the difference? The love paragraph was about her, her, her. The pride paragraph was about me. That is the difference between love and pride.

It may have occurred to you that we were thinking about remaining poor in spirit but now we've digressed into a discussion of love. It's not really a digression and it's unavoidable. The poor in spirit have an outlook that allows them to put others first. But we can't do it unless we can tamp down our pride.

Mercy, our most recent subject, is the tool we would use in the tamping. Mercy is a striking and visible exercise of love, and mercy weakens pride. Pride rightfully says "I know my rights" while mercy forgets it has rights. Mercy is love in action.

There is a Hebrew word, *checed*, that the NIV usually translates as *mercy*. However, the KJV sometimes translates it as *loving kindness*. As in *"surely goodness and loving kindness will follow me all the days of my life, and I will dwell in the house of the Lord forever"* (KJV, from the end of 23rd Psalm). The King James word selection is appropriate. Mercy is the kindness we show when we love. Mercy is the concrete manifestation of Jesus in the world.

Jesus says twice in Matthew, *"I desire mercy, not sacrifice"* (9:13 and 12:7). In both places when he says *sacrifice* he means obedience to the law, yet he desires mercy even more. Both times, he was trying to teach the people who really thought they understood Scripture that it is more important to show loving kindness than it is to compel others to follow his rules or their rules. We would do well to follow Jesus' advice.

In his greatest sermon, the very first words Jesus speaks concern how the poor in spirit are blessed. He will end this sermon with a long treatise about not judging. In between he calls us to mercy and to the tearing down of walls. He has known pride and its effects from before the foundation of the world. He wants us to make *remaining* poor in spirit our continual goal in thought and action. Jesus' true kingdom is filled with those who are poor in spirit . . . and they are blessed.

4

Those Who Mourn

Blessed are those who mourn, for they will be comforted (Matt 5:4)

THIS IS WHERE JESUS changes to the future tense. Mourners aren't comforted now, but *they will be*. He won't return to present tense until the final Beatitude. The future-tense Beatitudes reveal Jesus' vision. He tells us what we can expect from kingdom living, if we do things his way.

This promise is easier to understand than the promises that follow. Those listening that day hadn't *seen God* or *inherited the earth*, but they had experienced a measure of comfort during the mourning process. So have we. Our experience with mourners being comforted lends credence to the ensuing promises.

We don't see the verse in this literal way. The commentators tend to spiritualize it by saying that the mourning is over past sins or a wicked lifestyle. To them, mourning is synonymous with repentance. But if that were the case, why wouldn't Jesus have said, "Blessed are those who repent." The word "repent" was certainly part of his vocabulary. In fact, repentance was a fashionable idea at the time. John was preaching and baptizing not far away and his main instruction was to repent: *Repent, for the kingdom of Heaven is at hand* (Matt 3:2 NKJV). But Jesus has avoided the word "repent" so far in the sermon. Repent was less precise than poor in spirit and it is different than mourn. Therefore, Jesus is *not* telling us that if we continue to feel bad about all the bad things we have done (repentance), we will someday be comforted. The Greek words aren't related and neither are the concepts.

The mention of Greek words reminds me that we should look at the Greek word for blessed, *makarios*. It is the one noun used in every Beatitude.

A few translations use the English word *happy* for it. Strong's Concordance tells us *makarios* can also mean *Oh, how happy*. Blessedness and happiness were related in the Greek mind because the Greeks believed the Fates ruled them. Who could be happier than those upon whom the gods had smiled?

However, I doubt that Jesus was a Hellenist. I know he was a realist, and *happy* doesn't fit with some of the Beatitudes. Although we might be joyful, I doubt that persecution would make any of us happy. *Oh, how happy are those who mourn* doesn't make sense either.

Even if we still believe that *mourn* means "repent of sins," "happy are those who repent of sins" still doesn't seem realistic. I am not happy while repenting. I am apprehensive. I know my own propensity to return to the pig's trough even though my repentance is sincere. *Blessed are those who mourn* doesn't mean, "Happy are those who have already repented" either. Mourn is in the present tense. Jesus doesn't say happy are those who *have* mourned.

The promise of comfort is in the future tense. Jesus doesn't mean we are happy now because we know something is going to happen in the future. *Blessed are those who mourn* is not a resurrection promise. An expectation of something better in the future gives us hope, not happiness. If we are happy now, we should know it. We should clap our hands.

Being blessed means *to be favored by God*. Jesus seeks to reassure us that God is involved in the present circumstances of our lives and even what we see as undesirable holds God's hidden blessings. Thus, we are blessed.

We don't think of mourning as a blessed event. Grief feels like anything but a blessing. That's why we think mourning must mean something else. And it does. Mourning assumes the conjunction of two factors. The first is love.

Who can mourn except one who has loved? Love is indeed a blessing. Love is an attribute of God, part of who he is. Love is also a creation of God, formed in every one of us. It is a blessing he gives to believer and pagan alike, like sunshine and rainfall. When God created us in his own image, he instilled the ability to love. Love provides richness to our lives. Love also fulfills the greatest commandments and that is why Jesus starts the promises with *mourning*.

Jesus is telling us we are blessed because God has given us the ability to love. How great a blessing love truly is! How often we take it for granted. God never takes it for granted. I think he must be particularly happy with the concept of love and the act of loving another human being. I know he is happy when we follow the greatest commandment and love him. It is also not an option to love God without loving our neighbor. He wants all he created to be cherished because he cherishes it.

God honors love throughout Scripture. Love (which again means putting the needs and desires of another above our own) is first shown by his creation of Eve. He had love in mind from the start.

God personifies love in his greatest act: coming down to live as a man and dying on the cross. This is the finest example we have of someone laying down his own rights for the good of another. There are many other ways God personifies love. Year after year and century after century his longsuffering in the face of our sin is matchless. He suppresses his anger, disappointment, and sorrow. He withholds his wrath. He does it all out of concern for us. It is an absolute display of passionate love.

In this same way, God especially prizes romantic love. He sees in that passion all that is best in us. He honors Joseph, the first offspring of Jacob's true love, above his older brothers. He honors Solomon, a child of David and Bathsheba above the older offspring of David's first wives, even though David and Bathsheba began in such dishonor. And look at the description God gives us of Isaac and Rebekah's first meeting. Doesn't it sound like love at first sight?

> *Rebekah also looked up and saw Isaac.*
> *She got down from her camel and asked the servant,*
> *"Who is that man in the field coming to meet us?"*
> *"He is my master," the servant answered.*
> *So she took her veil and covered herself.*
> *Then the servant told Isaac all he had done.*
> *Isaac brought her into the tent of his mother Sarah,*
> *and he married Rebekah.*
> *So she became his wife,*
> and he loved her; and Isaac was comforted *after his mother's death* (Gen 24:62–67)

Speaking of "blessed are those who mourn" and how they will be "comforted," notice how both love and comfort in mourning are there in verse 67.

The idea that mourning is a blessing is profound, among the most profound teachings in the Bible. We have difficulty processing the blessing (and its place in the seven-step process) because the other component of mourning is death.

We need to consider the death component of this Beatitude. But before we do, I would like to make a small detour. It is time to stop and consider what we believe about Jesus and his teachings. I don't mean we should debate his divinity or manhood, or whether his words are the Truth. These beliefs are foundational to our faith. Specifically, I would like to explore the quality of his mind.

I think Jesus was smart. You probably do, too. But I think he was smarter than you think he was. I think he was a genius. This belief colors my interpretation of the Sermon on the Mount. While you may think the Sermon is a wonderful teaching, I believe it is also great literature. It may surprise you, but I don't think you think so. If you and our commentators and teachers believed it is great literature from an extremely fine mind, we wouldn't have the propensity to take his words to be some scatter shot stream of consciousness, touching on whatever ideas popped into his mind. I've already hypothesized a unity and cohesiveness to his words. Now I would like us to keep in mind the subtlety and fluidity he achieved as he taught.

The problem with our present view of the sermon, and our opinion—or lack thereof—of his intellect, is the way it allows us to view the sermon. If we extract juicy little tidbits and make them stand on their own out of context, then when we reinsert them into the text, the context disappears. When the context disappears, so does the subtlety of his point.

I know none of this is clear yet. I hope to make it so by the end of the book, but in the meantime, I want us to begin a habit of giving greater weight and honor to every idea he expounded, every thought he developed, and indeed, to every word he spoke that day. To do that, we must explore the quality of his intellect.

I won't try to prove my point philosophically. That is, I won't flatly state that he is fully God and so, of course he is smarter than anybody ever. I don't need to. The New Testament gives us many examples of the magnitude of his mind.

One incident is representative; the time the Pharisees tried to trap him into either endorsing Caesar's tax or inciting rebellion against it. When he said, "Render to Caesar what is Caesar's and to God what is God's," he confounded them. Their elaborate and premeditated trap was sprung harmlessly by the quickness of his mind.

An even better example is the parable of the Prodigal Son. More than one eminent author has recognized it as the greatest short story ever told. The simple words of the parable establish the mindset and motivation of the characters, the family dynamic and history complete with conflicting purposes and emotions, and all within the context of a larger and much more profound theological and moral lesson. Pastors often need a series of sermons to mine the rich deposits beneath the surface story, and yet Jesus told the parable in a couple of minutes. Every word of the parable is important; not a word was wasted. Just last night, I read additional insights into the parable that I had not considered before. The parable, like the Sermon, is great literature.

There is a reaction to Jesus that runs through the gospels that might be the most convincing proof of all. The people of that day, the people who heard his words as he spoke them, instinctively understood the profundity of his thoughts. After this sermon, Matthew immediately informs us that the crowd was amazed by it.

This wasn't the only time he amazed people. In the very first anecdote we have from his life, when he was not much more than a child, we learn of his capacity to amaze. I refer, of course, to the time he stayed at "his Father's house" while his family frantically searched for him. Although he was only twelve, the learned men of the Temple accommodated his presence and questioning. *After three days they found him in the Temple courts, sitting among the teachers, listening to them and asking them questions* (Luke 2:46). The teachers must have seen something worthwhile in him. They didn't ignore him or send him away. They would have had to feed him for half a week and make sure he had a safe place to sleep. Certainly they saw something extraordinary in him.

In fact, he wasn't only asking questions. He may have even been debating those teachers of the law, for the very next verse says *he* was giving the answers. *Everyone who heard him was amazed at his understanding and his answers* (Luke 2:47). There's that word again, amazed.

This was the first time strangers were amazed by him, but it wouldn't be the last. Of the twenty-three times the Gospels tell us of his ability to amaze others, only eight were in response to some miracle he had performed. The other fifteen occurrences record amazement at the quality of his thoughts. His remarkable mind was one of his most outstanding and observable characteristics.

One of the hallmarks of great literary accomplishment is depth; using simple words to convey deeper truths. When we read Shakespeare or Dostoevsky, we look beyond the surface narrative because we understand there is a purpose beyond the words. There is sophistication to the author's thought processes and he intends that we comprehend it. We look for themes and motifs. We search for the universal in the mundane. We attempt to grasp the author's concept of reality.

Should we expect any less of Jesus Christ? I submit that there is a clarity and literary economy in the Beatitudes equal to the economy he displayed in *render unto Caesar* or the story of the Prodigal. Each word is important. If he meant to communicate effectively with the masses gathered to hear him, or even to us today, I hardly think he would have been deliberately obscure in his word usage.

Clarity in communications is the best argument for the idea that "mourn" doesn't mean mourning over sin or iniquity. It is mourning over the loss of a loved one. The first Beatitude reassures us that we are citizens of the kingdom and subjects with eternal life, the second leads us to think about those who aren't.

Obviously mourning does not only imply love. If it did, Jesus would have said, "blessed are those who love." Mourning also implies death. Jesus is saying that we are blessed because we are mortal. How's that for counter-intuitive? There is an end to all of us. In this second Beatitude, Jesus states and will later explain something we could have never guessed on our own: death is a blessing.

We can only accept this strange and dissonant teaching if we accept the profundity of the teacher. We are about to see the mercy inherent in death as God sees it, as God has put it to our great advantage. God has derived a blessing from the devil's curse of death. Death is our enemy but not ours alone. Death is also God's enemy, and God will overcome it. First Corinthians 15:6 tells us death will be the last enemy to be defeated.

Mortality and its unknown consequences restrain us. The lives of everyone else are better because of our awareness of our own eventual death. Most religions of the world have a concept of life after death and a belief that a man's actions on earth will be recompensed. This was true for the ancient Egyptians and it is true for the non-Christian world today. Calvin, writing in his *Institutes of the Christian Religion* (1536), postulated that we all instinctively understand there is a God but in our fallen state don't comprehend him correctly from nature. He also suggested that we create a distorted image of God and distorted religions as a consequence, and that this is why the special revelation of Scripture is so necessary. Accordingly, the idea of afterlife and judgment are as prevalent in cultures throughout history as the idea of God. (This too, is a gift of God.)

God didn't cut our lifespan from 1000 years to 120 years out of punishment; he did so out of love. He did not turn Adam and Eve mortal to punish them; he did it because he loves us. We will not have to live this wicked life forever.

This may not feel like a comfort to us, but it is to those around us. We live differently in light of death's relative imminence and our uncertainty as to what comes afterward. Mortality enhances morality. It is a quality of life issue and mortality enhances our quality of life. God will choose quality over quantity every time. Isn't it contrary and human of us to want to choose the opposite?

Love is magnificent but God knows death is nearly its equal. Death is the key to heaven's door for those living in the kingdom. Death is also the only ticket to hell (the hottest ticket in town), which is why a works based belief system is so important to unbelievers. To say "I've tried to live a good life" is the only justification an unbeliever can use to combat the uncertainty of what lies beyond the grave. This thought process is the epitome of mortality enhancing morality.

Jesus takes the long view. He knows he has come to grant eternity. He understands what a precious gift this earthly life is as well. And he knows better than anyone does what a hell on earth this present life would be if we lived it forever. Life would lose its sweetness and its blessing. The end must remain in sight for our own good.

The result of this double blessing: love and mortality, is mourning. The world knows love is a blessing. Jesus wants his kingdom to know that death is also a blessing. Then he promises those who are left behind that they will be comforted.

As bad as mourning feels to us, and as far away as comfort might be in those first moments of grief and loss, we can bear it because some part of us knows the pain will change somewhat over time. But we would never mourn had we not first experienced love. Love is sweeter while we love because we know both those we love and we ourselves are mortal. We can read Tennyson's famous line that way, "It is better to have loved and lost than never to have loved at all." Jesus is not as direct as the great poet but (not surprisingly) he is more poetic: *Blessed are those who mourn, for they will be comforted.*

Jesus starts the future tense portion of his treatise of God's blessings with this one because he knows we all know it is true. Our experience lends hope and credibility to the rest of his observations and promises. If we can understand that the mourner will be comforted, we can also take comfort in the assurances that follow.

By stating this promise first, Jesus shows the supremacy of love over all the promises that follow. By using "mourning" instead of "love" he shows us that death is an act of love on the part of God for everyone. By having it follow the "poor in spirit" reference of being born again, he shows us why we should love God above all else; because of the greatness of God's love in moving us past death.

There is one additional reason Jesus spoke here of comfort in mourning. It was a reinforcement of his Messiahship and a call to follow. Do you remember when Jesus made his announcement of his role to the Jews in the synagogue on the Sabbath? He did it through a reading of the beginning of Isaiah 61.

> *The Spirit of the Sovereign LORD is on me,*
> *because the LORD has anointed me to preach good news to the poor.*
> *He has sent me to bind up the brokenhearted, to proclaim freedom for the captives and release from darkness for the prisoners,*
> *to proclaim the year of the Lord's favor*

Here's the next part.

> *and the day of vengeance of our God,*
> *to comfort all who mourn,*
> *and provide for those who grieve in Zion—*
> *to bestow on them a crown of beauty instead of ashes,*
> *the oil of gladness instead of mourning,*
> *and a garment of praise instead of a spirit of despair.*
> *They will be called oaks of righteousness,*
> *a planting of the LORD for the display of his splendor.* (Isa 61:1–3)

The last sentence says *they will be called oaks of righteousness*. We are *they*. The pericope is undoubtedly about Jesus, but the "they" at the end means he will do this, partly, through us. The planting of the Lord is the planting of the Spirit of the Lord within us.

The first Beatitude promised a form of Heaven in the here and now. The second states a problem: not everyone inhabits the kingdom. The rest of the Beatitudes give the solution, the way to get people into the kingdom of Heaven. The remaining Beatitudes explain the Jesus Method of proper witnessing, so that we may see others move from the kingdoms of the earth to God's heavenly kingdom.

As difficult as it was to understand the connection between the first two Beatitudes, it is about to become more difficult still. As strange as blessing from death feels, it is only the first in a series of counterintuitive teachings. Jesus follows *mourning* with the blessedness we all have the most difficulty understanding: meekness.

5

The Meek

Blessed are the meek, for they will inherit the earth (Matt 5:5)

THIS BEATITUDE WAS A puzzle to me. It didn't seem to yield to careful, prayerful thought. Since I thought "meek" meant humble or submissive, it was hard to imagine how the meek would be likely to inherit the earth. I thought perhaps we are to allow people to walk all over us until Jesus comes back and gives us the earth, but that doesn't seem to fit with Jesus' idea that the kingdom has been advancing forcefully.

I went to Blue Letter Bible website and searched the phrase in the NIV. There were no exact matches, but there were instances of *inherit the land*. One verse was almost an exact match. Psalm 37:11 read *but the meek will inherit the land and enjoy great peace*. I clicked through to the verse. The phrase was so close to the Beatitude. I wondered if any other translations used *earth* in the place of *land*, so I hit the Bibles button. Yes, the King James used *earth*, as did the New King James. *But the meek shall inherit the earth; and shall delight themselves in the abundance of peace* (Ps 37:11 KJV).

Hmm. It appeared that Jesus was quoting verse 11a almost verbatim. Yet the distinction between "earth" and "land" was important. God promised the land to Abraham and his seed. Was this another iteration of that promise? If so, then Jesus' promise wasn't something new for those listening.

Then I realized Jesus wasn't quoting from either translation. He was most likely quoting from the version familiar to his audience, the Septuagint. He quoted from the Septuagint in other places. So did Paul. So did the writer of Hebrews, extensively. I went to The Septuagint Bible Online. In its translation into English, it used the word "earth." Progress, I thought. The internet can be a wonderful place.

Then I realized the Greek word in the Septuagint was *"ge."* I already knew that word. We get words like "geography" from it. *Ge* was just as likely to mean "land" as it was "earth." I went back to the Hebrew for clarification but I didn't get it. The Hebrew word was *"eretz."* I knew that word also. It's in the very first verse in the Bible, *In the beginning God created the heavens and the earth.* It could mean "land" or "earth," but it could also refer to the soil. "The meek shall inherit the dirt" didn't seem like such a grandiose statement. *"Ge"* was a good equivalent for *"eretz,"* right down to the multiple meanings, but which did David mean in the Psalm? Which did Jesus mean in the sermon?

Inspiration struck. Maybe prayer *was* paying off. I switched to the King James and searched the phrase again. "Inherit the earth" is used only five other times in Scripture. All five are in the Old Testament and three are concentrated in Psalm 37. The King Jameses stood alone in using "earth" rather than "land." I wondered why. Both *"ge"* and *"eretz"* are translated *land* much more often than they are translated *earth*, even in the KJV.

Then it hit me. My mind went back to Genesis 1:1. We would never translate it *God created the heavens and the land* or *the heavens and the dirt*. Context determined the translation choice. I looked at the five verses from the KJV again. They all promised *"eretz"* to the Jews *when they were already in possession of the land! Eretz* had to mean "earth" in this context, or else the promises were meaningless redundancies. The same is true for *"ge."* For generations, the Jews in the crowd had been inheriting the "land," but Jesus promised they would inherit the "earth."

Jesus' audience probably knew *the meek shall inherit the earth* from Psalm 37 as well as some New Testament passages are known to us today. It was after all, quite a promise. They had the land, but someday they would inherit the whole earth.

The more learned among them may have known that three usages of *inherit the earth* are concentrated in Psalm 37. That's our proof text. The Beatitude was Jesus' deliberate reference, a kind of biblical shorthand. He could have stopped and recited the pertinent parts of the Psalm, but that would have interrupted the exquisite rhythm of his introductory remarks.

Despite my not-quite-scholarly research, I think the conclusion is sound. Especially when we consider that all five mentions of inheriting the earth are also tied to meekness. The linking of the two words is not a coincidence. Meekness is the vehicle of inheritance.

Once I saw the solid connection between meekness and the future inheritance, it became clear that our misunderstanding of the Beatitude came from an improper concept of meekness. Our definition was fuzzy.

Leave it to Jesus to make the definition clearer. He knew there were five other instances of the catchphrase "inherit the earth." He knew all five were connected to meekness. And he knew that we only had to read them in context to form a proper definition of "meek."

Meekness is clearly defined in Psalm 37. Meekness isn't humility and it isn't submissiveness, either. Meekness is *an intentional and active passivity, executed as a long term strategy*. The psalm not only defines the strategy, it also explains why it is necessary—God, in his infinite and intimate understanding of human nature, doesn't want us to mess things up.

The theme of David's psalm is instruction in how to deal with wicked people. How do we deal with the worldly? How does the kingdom of heaven "deal" with the wicked? David's advice is to not even worry about them, but instead to leave them to the Lord. He starts the Psalm with *Do not fret because of evil men*.

Three times in this psalm God gives us some variation of this "do not fret" advice. All three are near the beginning of the psalm, in the first eight verses. That's why I think it is the theme. If you'll grant this preliminary conclusion we can discuss *why* we shouldn't worry about the evil of others. The plain answer is right there in verse 8.

Do not fret—it leads only to evil. Other translations say *it only causes harm*. It is so like God in his wisdom to know that our very response to evil could *itself* be evil. What a nugget of wisdom hidden in the middle of a psalm! Leave it to Jesus to show it to us. The clause is definitive. Verse 8 doesn't say *it might* lead to evil or *it could* cause harm, it says *it only* leads to evil. We have to be very careful then, if even *worrying* about evil in others will lead us to do evil.

Psalm 37 gives us an alternative strategy. David tells us to stay focused on our relationship with God. *Trust in the Lord and do good* (37:3). *Delight yourself in the Lord* (verse 4). *Commit your way to the Lord* and *trust in him* (verse 5). *Be still before the Lord and wait patiently for him* (verse 7). Are you beginning to see his plan? Don't worry at all about anyone else. Leave it all to the Lord.

Meek is actually the opposite of proactive. Wait on the Lord to take care of the things he tells us are his job. Don't react to the moral decay in the world around you because you might just increase the evil that abounds. Evil has always abounded. Wait.

What will be the result of not worrying about evil, of doing good instead, and resting in the Lord? Those who do so will inherit the earth:

Do not fret because of evildoers,
Nor be envious of the workers of iniquity.
For they shall soon be cut down like the grass,
And wither as the green herb.
Trust in the LORD, and do good;
Dwell in the land, and feed on His faithfulness.
Delight yourself also in the LORD,
And He shall give you the desires of your heart.
Commit your way to the LORD, Trust also in Him,
And He shall bring [it] to pass.
He shall bring forth your righteousness as the light,
And your justice as the noonday.
Rest in the LORD, and wait patiently for Him;
Do not fret because of him who prospers in his way,
Because of the man who brings wicked schemes to pass.
Cease from anger, and forsake wrath;
Do not fret—[it] only [causes] harm.
For evildoers shall be cut off;
But those who wait on the LORD,
They shall inherit the earth (Ps 37:1–9 NKJV).

This is exactly what we don't do as Christians. We want to take matters into our own hands. We fret about evildoers. We complain about the wicked world around us. We protest at abortion clinics and campaign against same-sex marriage.

Could this be the wrong approach? Certainly we must fight against the things the Lord abhors! Surely we must work to shape a society that we can be confident and comfortable living in, right? Psalm 37 says no. It says to be still and wait patiently for the Lord. *He* will make the justice of our cause shine like the noonday sun.

There is a difference between our methods and the Lord's method. Conventional wisdom dictates that we can change the world for the better by taking away evil choices. The idea is an outgrowth of our responsibility as citizens in whatever society we co-inhabit. We've instituted penalties for murder, rape, and other mayhem. We do not allow the choice of harming others physically.

But then we try to take it a step further. We believe we should stop others from harming our society spiritually. This is where we err. Let's look at gay marriage. We believe that homosexual marriage is harmful, not necessarily to the individual participants, but to society as a whole. A large part of our society believes that oppressing homosexuals by denying their choices or speaking against their lifestyle is a necessary evil against their evil. The result is a passionate but evil impasse.

God's method emanates from a far superior level of knowledge, experience, and wisdom. He understands we cannot change people's minds. We can only change their hearts. He shows us that this cannot happen across society as a whole. True and lasting change can only happen one soul at a time. God is lobbying not for a change in laws but for a change in our methods. He desires a loving witness as his agent for change. The early believers used God's method and look how they impacted the world!

The early church had no power base with which to effect change. In fact, they lived in societies that would make us cringe. Yet they changed those societies and then the world. The more they were oppressed, the greater the change they effected. They did it through meekness and love, a method far more effective than our "Christianistic" fight for our "rights." Meekness calls us to change society one person at a time by refusing to build a wall. The only lasting change is a change of the heart.

Look at your own life and see if this holds true. It does for me. Before I was saved I thought abortion was a compassionate alternative. I thought abortion stopped unwanted children from being relegated to dismal and unloving destinies. I also thought any other choice an intelligent adult could make was valid as long as it didn't harm other people.

I wasn't slowly disabused of these notions on an intellectual basis leading to my salvation. No, exactly the opposite occurred. The Lord saved me from myself and only then did my views begin to come into agreement with God's views. This was and still is God's way; change the heart and the mind will follow. It is absurd to think we can change the actions and the mind will follow.

In totalitarian societies actions are indeed changed but heart and mind remain unrepentant. In the former Soviet Union twelve to fifteen million spies were employed to quell secret murmuring, but it only caused the murmuring to become more secretive.

God understands that there is only one path to true change and it is a narrow one. It is a heart turned to him. That is the value of meekness; it can widen the path to him by removing obstacles. The obstacles are the opinions about believers held by the unsaved and vice versa. This is a major part of the trouble with Christians. We try to mold the unconverted by force rather than through meekness. Force will not lead to us inheriting the earth.

> *For yet a little while and the wicked [shall be] no [more]*
> *Indeed, you will look carefully for his place,*
> *But it [shall be] no [more].*

> *But* the meek shall inherit the earth,
> *And shall delight themselves in the abundance of peace* (Ps 37:10, 11 NKJV).

> *The wicked borrows and does not repay,*
> *But the righteous shows mercy and gives.*
> *For [those] blessed by Him* shall inherit the earth,
> *But [those] cursed by Him shall be cut off.*
> *The steps of a [good] man are ordered by the LORD,*
> *And He delights in his way.*
> *Though he fall, he shall not be utterly cast down;*
> *For the LORD upholds [him with] His hand* (Psalm 37:21, 22 NKJV).

This triple theme could not be iterated in the psalm more often without becoming monotonous. It carries through all forty verses.

- Rest in the Lord.
- Don't worry about the wicked.
- Wait on the Lord and he will bless you (and you will inherit the earth).

Let's look at another reference. In Psalm 25, David begins by talking about trusting in God. Then he talks about how God is the God of salvation and how he (David) will wait on the Lord. He talks about God's mercies and loving kindness and then he talks about inheriting the earth. So how will they inherit the earth?

> *The* meek *will he guide in judgment:*
> *And* the meek *will he teach his way.*
> *All the paths of the LORD [are] mercy and truth*
> *unto such as keep his covenant and his testimonies.*
> *For thy name's sake, O LORD, pardon mine iniquity; for it [is] great.*
> *What man [is] he that feareth the LORD?*
> *Him shall he teach in the way [that] he shall choose.*
> *His soul shall dwell at ease; and* his seed shall inherit the earth
> (Psalm 25:9–13 KJV).

There it is again, meekness! Twice for emphasis! Notice how the tenses of the final line synchs with the Beatitude. *And his seed shall inherit the earth* is a future event and so is *they will inherit the earth*. If we are meek now, it doesn't mean we will see results now. That's the tough part. We need enough faith to believe God knows what he's asking.

I think a preponderance of Christians not fretting about others will have the effect of attracting unbelievers. This is a battle we can win but the victory won't be immediately apparent. This is a strategy for the long run, a matter of momentum. First we must change the opinion of this generation.

We cannot do this by being judgmental. We can't do it by taking away choices. When we are meek, we allow Christ to change hearts. Year upon year of meekness, generation after generation of quiet strength, will have the effect Jesus intends.

I can think of so many times when well-meaning people have increased the evil in the world by worrying about the evil in others instead of working on their own problems. It is almost like the natural order of things. We have the truth and it makes us glad but we can't impose it on other, less enlightened souls. To do so is evil, but we don't recognize it as such. We think we have things figured out so well in our own lives that we can legislate the choices of others. That's why I've argued that pride is the root cause of evil.

The overriding principle is freedom of choice. We think we can enhance the lives of everyone by taking certain choices away from certain people. Yet giving us a choice is one of the major premises of God throughout the Bible. Adam and Eve got the first choice and the last choices are made in Revelation.

When God knew Cain was contemplating the murder of his brother, he didn't stop him. He didn't take away Cain's choice. He told him, *Sin is crouching at your door. You must master it.* Cain didn't master it. He was left to make a choice and he had to suffer the consequences of that choice and unfortunately, so did Abel. By counseling meekness Jesus is asking us to live by that same Godly principle. We have to allow others their freedom of choice. They have to suffer the consequences of those choices. We might suffer for their choices as well but we aren't given the privilege of taking their choices away. We are only allowed the opportunity to change their hearts with our attitudes. If we take away their choices we can only further harden their hearts.

Think of this; gays would never have the prominence they enjoy in society today if we didn't persecute them. For over two thousand years homosexuality has existed as a covert subculture. In self-defense against persecution by the police, gays first began to band together in the early 1960s. First politically and now even to affect scientific and societal opinion.

It is only natural that gays should act in self-defense when facing persecution. Political action was their only available form of defense. You or I would react in the same way if we faced jail or beatings for being Christians. It is only natural, yet the New Testament calls us to what is spiritual, not what is natural. That's why David says, *do not fret—it only leads to evil.*

I know this idea seems wrong to us. We think so differently. After all, we know our rights! Our country was founded on Christian principles. People fleeing persecution have populated this country. But . . .

If you saw someone being beat up, wouldn't you want to stop it? What if the persecutors informed you that the victim was gay, would you still stand up for the oppressed? I hope we would all answer in the affirmative. What if the victim had worked on Sunday instead of being gay? What if the victim was instead a known adulteress? I know what Jesus did in that situation.

The first scenario, the beating of gay men, is exactly the situation that sparked the gay rights movement. Police officers in New York City would periodically raid a gay dance club and arrest or beat the people inside. I could only hope I would have sided with the oppressed had I been a witness. The gay rights movement spread from there.

We have this crazy notion, a meme we repeat *ad naseum* that insists Christians in America are being oppressed. Yet oppression isn't the proper word for what we experience because we are the majority and we still hold the most influence. A majority is more likely attacked (or counterattacked) than oppressed. We claim persecution when we aren't getting our own way. We sometimes have a worldview temper tantrum. It's human nature to see lack and human to complain.

If five gay couples in Iowa get married today, will it oppress you? Will you even be aware of it? Will you think, *man, if only three gay couples got married in Iowa, I'd be having a much better day*? Oppression is when my life is violated. If the law forced me to marry a gay man (or even a gay woman) *that* would be oppression.

While I defend their right to choose, I am not defending the gay agenda of today. I'm trying to show how fretting about the evil of others can only lead to evil. Gays are forcibly foisting their views upon us in much the manner that they hated when it was used against them in the 1960s. The minor difference is that gay rights can't rise to the level of oppression. Both the gay rights agenda and the conservative Christian opposition are worldly attempts to foist opinions on someone else. They both only lead to evil.

Meekness is so different from the way we have been taught to think. We continue to abide in a works based belief system. We think stopping somebody from sinning is a good work. It isn't. Stopping another person from sinning won't change their eternal fate.

Jesus will use a good part of this sermon to explain good works so we will have the occasion to learn their meaning in greater depth. The examples he gives involve showing God's *attributes* to those around us. Sinlessness isn't a realistic option and neither is keeping another from sinning.

The godly responsibilities God reserves for Himself are judgment and retribution. Taking away a sinner's choice falls into neither of these categories. God doesn't take away choice. Neither should we. We need to leave the things of God to God. So many evils of the modern world have been perpetrated at the hands of do-gooders. More accurately, so much evil occurs as a reaction to do-gooders taking choices away from other sinners. We should really begin to learn our lesson.

Another example is born of the Temperance Movement of the late nineteenth and early twentieth centuries. These people clearly saw the evils and effects of alcohol and legislated away the choice to consume it. Was it effective or did it lead to greater evil?

The immediate effect of the law was an increase in moonshine, bathtub gin, and "patent medicines." Rich and powerful underworlds sprang up to produce and distribute the illicit liquids. What was formerly legal was made illegal. People didn't change, the law did, and formerly law-abiding citizens were by the stroke of a pen legislated into booze imbibing criminals. As they tried to justify their actions (as people are wont to do under any circumstance), they began to view the laws as unjust rather than themselves as unlawful. This occurred in all classes of society. Even policeman, prosecutors, and judges were now criminals. This led to a breakdown of respect for the law.

It was only a matter of time until the loss of respect for governmental laws spread to include moral laws. The Roaring Twenties roared because the lawbreakers tended to congregate in higher concentrations to drink than they had needed to when liquor was ubiquitous. Because everyone who drank was already a "criminal" that did not respect the law, it was just a matter of time before morality became a casualty on the same slippery slope of disrespect.

Gambling moved from behind the closed doors of the speakeasy to become acceptable on a larger scale. This socially acceptable form of gambling was called buying on margin and it was done through the New York Stock Exchange. The rapid unraveling of this form of betting led to the great crash ten years after the beginning of Prohibition and that crash began the Great Depression. This is another example of unintended side effects. I could even argue that the worldwide depression created such dismal conditions in Germany that it allowed the rise of Hitler, which led to World War II.

Meekness as a discipline is spiritual judo. Practicing judo involves using an opponent's reactions against them. To achieve the goal of bringing an opponent close enough to attack, we would first push them away from us. Then, when they naturally reacted by pushing toward us, we would use their own momentum to achieve our purpose. If we are combative and strive to take away the choices of another, we drive them away or we cause them to counterattack in reaction. If we are meek instead, we might attract them.

Choice is God's way. He always lays before us a blessing and a curse. He clearly establishes the consequences of good and evil but always leaves the choice to us. Choice is the whole point of life, our ability to choose, our propensity to choose incorrectly, and our rarer acts of choosing what is right. Remember the two trees in the Garden of Eden? Did you ever wonder why the second tree, the "Tree of Life" was there? Adam and Eve were already (if fleetingly) immortal. They had nothing to gain by eating its fruit. In fact, they were never prohibited from partaking of that particular tree. It was placed there as the symbolic first instance of choice: the Tree of Life or the Tree of the Knowledge of Good and Evil. God was showing us how he has established things. Choice is always a choice between a blessing and a curse, and the blessing is never prohibited or eradicated until we choose the curse. At that point the blessing sometimes becomes unavailable.

Our job is to work on the evil in our own lives. Everything else smacks of pride. Everything else comes from not being poor enough in spirit to realize that *we* are all we can handle. There is no time or energy left to "handle" anybody else.

That is the point of being meek. If we stopped legislating away choice for others, perhaps evil would not react and gain prominence. Evil prefers the cover of darkness. We prefer our own evils remain covered in darkness. Evil only chooses visibility when oppression backs it into a corner.

If we were meek, that could change. Let's leave evil to the Lord. We need to wait for him and rest in him. We need to work out our own salvation; the one Jesus has obtained for us by his magnificent and magnanimous sacrifice.

We need to remain poor in spirit and become meek. We need to add these to the lessons Jesus is yet to present, living in mercy and love and peace. Then the walls can come down. Then our attraction will be real. Then many will be added.

Then . . . we will have a world worth inheriting.

6

The Righteous and the Merciful

Blessed are those who hunger and thirst for righteousness, for they will be filled(Matt 5:6)

THE JUXTAPOSITION OF THIS verse with the last provides contrast as well as cohesion. Fretting about others can't advance the kingdom. We can only advance the kingdom through our pursuit of righteousness. Even though we are not to impose our sense of righteousness on others, we certainly must pursue righteousness for ourselves.

Jesus says this pursuit should be a primary motivation. It needs to be satisfied daily just as we satisfy our hunger for food. More, we must quench it many times a day like our thirst. Righteousness should sustain us.

While we must pursue righteousness like a basic need, it is important to remember that we cannot attain it as a continual state. This is another of Jesus' future tense Beatitudes and so it contains a promise yet to be fulfilled. We can however, be blessed by the quest.

We can't properly pursue righteousness until we know exactly what it is. Righteousness, like judgment, is a word with more than one meaning. Theologians speak of the righteousness *of* God and the righteousness *from* God.

The righteousness *from* God is what our pastors mean when they tell us Jesus is our Righteousness. Another term for this is "imputed" righteousness. When Jesus took away our sins, imputed righteousness is what he left in their place. The righteousness of Jesus becomes ours through a mystical exchange at the cross. However, this is not the righteousness Jesus is speaking about.

I did a word search on (of all things) thirst. I was surprised to find immediate clarification between the two types of righteousness in another thirst analogy, one that points to imputed righteousness. We can contrast it with this Beatitude to better understand the difference between the two.

Jesus told the Samaritan woman at the well, "*Whoever drinks the water I give him will never thirst. Indeed, the water I give him will become in him a spring of water welling up to eternal life*" (John 4:14).

We drink of the water of eternal life (imputed righteousness) once and *never thirst* again. The beatitudinal righteousness must be thirsted after repeatedly. Imputed righteousness is given to us (*the water I give him*) rather than sought after.

So we have three differences between imputed righteousness and the righteousness of Matthew 5. One we receive and one we must pursue. One is an act of God while the other is our responsibility. One needs daily renewal while the other is once for a lifetime.

Understanding the differences helps us rule out imputed righteousness but doesn't leave us with a firm concept of what we *are* to pursue. We haven't deciphered what this righteousness is, but now we know what it is not.

While righteousness is not part of a distinctive phrase like *inherit the earth* or a new concept coined for the kingdom like *poor in spirit*, it was nevertheless easy to define. The ease comes from its prominence throughout Scripture, from beginning to end.

The pertinent definition of this type of righteousness lies in a recurrent theme that spans both Testaments. It comes to us from an Old Testament verse and concept that is cited many times in the New. Jesus referred to it when debating the Pharisees. James quoted the verse in his letter. Paul even made it the basis of an entire theological argument, quoting it again and again in Romans.

We start with the very first use of the word "righteousness" in the Bible, way back in Genesis 15:6. *Abram believed the Lord and he credited to him as righteousness.* The principle of first mention would make the verse important even without the numerous New Testament citations. Abram's belief led him to become the father of many nations and the father of our faith.

The verse says Abram did one thing. He believed the Lord. His belief doesn't seem so special as to warrant the special place it has in our theology. Didn't Melchizedek believe God? And Lot? Even Abram's father believed God enough to leave the comforts of civilization when God told him to leave.

What was it that Abram believed? More to our point, what made this instance of belief different from the *other* times he believed God and unique as an instance of belief?

He believed the Lord would give him a son as an heir and that through this son his seed would be as numerous as the stars in the sky. That's it. Abram believed that God could and would do this, and his belief was a defining moment in his relationship with God and an equally defining moment in the history of humanity. The belief that God could and would do it was credited to him as righteousness.

We can tell that Abram's belief in the Promise was the critical moment not only because of the many New Testament citations of Genesis 15:6, but also because of what followed in the narrative. It preceded a legal agreement between Abraham and God. Immediately after this believing and "crediting" to Abram's account, the Lord instructed him to gather a sacrifice to seal what we now call the Abrahamic Covenant.

The Abrahamic Covenant is an everlasting covenant and it is unilateral. Most covenants are bilateral. They depend on the choices made by human participants. We choose a path and our actions result in a blessing or a curse.

This is not the case with the Abrahamic Covenant. God promised to bless Abram through his descendants and added no stipulations. Abram had already fulfilled his part when he believed God. Abram wasn't even conscious when the agreement was ratified. God made the covenant with Abram while Abram was in a deep sleep, probably snoring away as old folks often do. The Hebrew word for deep sleep is *tardemah*. It generally denotes a sleep caused by God; the same sleep God caused in Adam in order to extract Eve from his side.

God put Abram to sleep *before* he made the covenant with him. It was God's dramatic representation to Abram that he would keep his word regardless of Abram's future conduct. God made a promise but Abram promised nothing. While Abram was still asleep, God also expanded his vow. He promised the land to Abram's descendants.

The close chronology of events—the belief being credited, the credit being the impetus for the Covenant, and then the unilateral manner of the Covenant's execution, signal this moment of belief on Abram's part as qualitatively different from all the other times Abram had believed God. If we can find what was different about this belief, we will understand righteousness as God credits it. If we can understand the distinctive qualities of this righteousness, we can better thirst and hunger after it.

The other instances in which Abram believed God seem more impressive than the moment immortalized in Genesis 15:6. Abram had to be truly committed to God in those other instances while in this one his *actions* were insignificant, only his belief mattered.

It is interesting that God could be pleased by mere belief when today we tend to belittle it. Many people say they believe in Jesus and we wonder if they believe enough. We value faith in action. We reference James 2:19 and think, "Yes, but even the demons believe in Jesus and shudder." Yet, in Genesis 15:6, God valued a belief above almost unbelievable actions we would think of as being "sold out" for God.

If Jesus called you to pack up and move your family to a strange and distant country to become a missionary, your church family would be impressed. If one of your children faced death and you could yet praise God without doubting, *everyone* would be impressed. However, these hypothetical situations mirror episodes in Abraham's life in which God did *not* credit righteousness to him.

Abraham believed God when God told him to pack up his family and journey to a place he would show him. He put a lot more on the line obeying that first command than simple belief. He left his father and his prosperous and comfortable way of life. He subjected his wife, family, and servants to unknown dangers on the way to an unknown destination. He had to trust God with everything he had. Talk about faith in action! It was an act of faith rarely equaled in the world today. Today's missionaries know where they are going and prepare for it in advance. However, this impressive act of faith wasn't credited to Abram as righteousness. It didn't result in the Covenant.

Abraham took Isaac to the mountain to offer him in sacrifice as God commanded. Had God not stopped him, he would have killed the very son God had told him would be used to bless the world. Abraham could only even think of obeying if he had enough faith to believe God would either stop him or resurrect Isaac. Yet God did not wait for Abraham to pass this test and then credit it to him as righteousness.

God chalked one up in the righteousness column because Abram believed *something*. This belief was different from the belief that God could make him a new home in a foreign land or even the belief that God could save his son from death. In order to believe he would father a son in his old age, Abram had to believe *something different about God*. He had to believe something different about God than the pagans believed about their gods.

In the Ancient Near Eastern culture from which Abram was called, people generally believed in a pantheon of gods. They believed in Ba'al but they also believed in El, one of the names the Bible uses to refer to our God. They believed that there were gods who controlled the weather, gods who could make them strong in battle and gods who could ensure an abundant crop. There were gods of the forest, gods of the valleys, and gods of the mountains. There were the gods of their land and the gods of the neighboring tribes.

The Jews have a tradition (which doesn't make it untrue) that Abram's father, Terah, crafted idols in their homeland of Ur. As the story goes, Abram as a child wondered how these graven images could be worthy of worship when he had watched his dad craft them. One night when he was about twelve years old, Abram broke one of the idols after his family had gone to sleep. He waited for cosmic repercussions but none came. That's when inspiration struck. Surely all he saw around him had been created, but there was one God, the Creator, who had made it all.

Maimonides (an influential Jewish thinker from the twelfth century) claimed in *The Guide for the Perplexed* that he had seen a version of the story in a now lost book called the Nabatean Book of Agriculture. The book said that the next night Abram destroyed all of the images in his father's workshop and began telling of a Creator whose essence could not be captured in wood or stone. He was jailed briefly to stop him from witnessing, and when he continued to speak, Terah and his family were banished. If the story is true, Abraham founded the scientific method as well as monotheism.

If the story is close to true, we now have Abram believing two things about God that the pagans didn't believe about their gods. He was all-powerful and he was One. But it was God, not Abram, who left us with an even more precise understanding of himself. He did this when he told Abram that he would have a son and his descendants would be as numerous as the stars in the sky.

To keep his promise, Abram's God would have to be steadfast, for steadfastness was needed if the promise of countless descendants was to be achieved. Abram's God had to be more powerful than other gods if Abram was to have a son, for none of the pagans gods could accomplish fatherhood so late in a woman's life. Believing God could accomplish these things entailed something new and different, a revolutionary concept.

Believing God's promise meant believing *God was a God who worked in history, that he cared for Abram in a special way, and that he imbued Abram's life with a purpose beyond simple existence.*

The righteous men of the Bible all believed these things about God. Jesus, Noah, David, Joseph, and Job all bought into the idea of a loving God who gave us purpose. However, it is first clearly delineated in the story we have studied from Genesis 15.

Abram's great belief had three parts:

- God had a Plan
- The plan was good because God is good and
- God was powerful enough to bring it to pass.

This simple faith in *God's ability to bring a good plan to fruition* is what was credited to Abram as righteousness! Let's look at the pertinent verses:

> *Then the word of the Lord came to him:*
> *"This man will not be your heir,*
> *but a son coming from your own body will be your heir."*
> *He took him outside and said,*
> *"Look up at the heavens and count the stars—if indeed you can count them."*
> *Then he said to him, "So shall your offspring be."*
> Abram believed the Lord,
> *and he credited* it *to him as righteousness* (Gen 15:4-6).

According to Jesus this belief made Abraham the father of our faith. Paul repeatedly quoted this scripture in his extended argument on the power of faith alone to obtain salvation.

Believing in God's goodness seems like Theology 101 to us today. Of course God is good. But it was a revelation to Abram. The pagans knew nothing of a god's motivations. They only hoped to placate the gods to improve their chances for survival.

God was different. He would be faithful in fulfilling his promise for generations into the future. He was not fickle. He was also the God of all circumstances. He could renew Sarah's fertility and he could ensure the safety of the seed. God promised to be good to Abram, and not Abram only, but through him to all the nations of the earth. To fulfill this worldwide and multi-generational plan, to keep this promise, the Lord would have to have unequaled power. No man, no tribe, no nation, and no other god could thwart him. Abram believed God possessed this greatness.

God showed Abram the broad outline of a plan for the future and Abram bought into it. He was the first convert to kingdom living. God didn't make up the plan based on anything Abram did or was. The plan was already in effect. God only included Abram based on Abram's belief in the plan and his belief in God's ability to carry it out.

Belief in the greatness of God and the goodness of his Plan is the biblical definition of righteousness. Righteousness initially has nothing to do with actions. Some of Abraham's actions, both before and after the covenant, were despicable. He also did great things that weren't credited in this special way and Hebrews 11 suggests he died without seeing his efforts come to fruition. By his actions he accomplished nothing. Abram was an alien carving out a life in the wilderness in which he died. But by believing in the goodness and greatness of God he became the father of many nations and changed the world.

> *For he was looking forward to the city with foundations,*
> *whose architect and builder is God.*
> *By faith Abraham,*
> *even though he was past age—and Sarah herself was barren –*
> *was enabled to become a father*
> *because he considered him faithful who had made the promise.*
> *And so from this one man, and he as good as dead,*
> *came descendants as numerous as the stars in the sky and*
> *as countless as the sand on the seashore.* (Heb 11:10–12).

This definition of righteousness may be the most important correction I have made to my own thinking. Now, some passages in the Bible make good sense in a different way. I used to think righteousness had to do with sinning less. Understanding its more precise meaning lets me off the hook to a certain extent, but it also ratchets up my responsibility. I can believe in God's goodness and greatness, but I also need to show that I believe it. I need to hunger and thirst after it. Pursuing righteousness is not living without sin, not even Abraham could do that. Righteousness is living in a manner that shows belief in God's goodness and greatness.

God fulfills his plan in stages. Abraham's descendants *are* as numerous as the stars in the sky. All nations of the world *have been* blessed, because through Isaac, God began the task of establishing a nation as his people. That nation unknowingly fulfilled part of that task by fostering the proper milieu for the birth of Jesus in the fullness of time.

In this roundabout way, Abraham was one of the first to believe in Jesus. He didn't know Jesus' name. He couldn't have understood Jesus' central role in history. The Assyrians hadn't yet invented death by crucifixion. All Abraham really knew was that God was good, God had a plan, and God was mighty enough to bring his good plan to fruition.

Sometimes we wonder why God is taking so long. We need to understand that how long the plan takes is also part of the plan. Although living by faith seems like it should be a simple concept, it is part of an extraordinarily complex plan. The plan is as complex as the human psyche multiplied by all the events in human history. I say this because the plan advances in spite of free will. In fact, God built free will into his plan. Someday, God's plan will become our deliberate choice. The merger of the two will be the culmination of the Kingdom of Heaven. This will be when the meek inherit the earth.

We can even argue that the plan is not for believers only, but for all in every age. All of the nations of the earth have been blessed by the plan regardless of their belief. Not all of Abraham's descendants were believers, but they were promised to Abraham nonetheless.

Our part in this new phase of the plan was exactly what Jesus was talking about in the sermon. God's plan wouldn't stop at the cross, so Jesus filled us in on the Father's vision for how we should live after his death. As believers, we know enough to want to represent and glorify God as best we can. Righteousness is how we do this.

I used to think righteousness came from sinning less. How better to glorify God than by clean living. But righteousness is more than clean living. If it were clean living, Abraham would have lost his righteousness later, when he lied to Abimelek's men about Sarah. A righteous life encompasses a desire to sin less, but there is more to it than that.

Paul deals with the nebulous quality of righteousness that is so difficult for us to grasp. In his extensive treatise on righteousness from Romans chapters 3 and 4, Paul works to move us beyond our assumptions. He makes his point (although we often miss it) in chapter 3. In the midst of explaining that it is faith (not works) that leads to righteousness, he uses examples to explain his point. Many of the examples given are sins, and so we'd miss his subtle point if we take the passage out of its natural context.

The context is defined by bracketing phrases. At the start of Romans 3 Paul begins by telling us none are righteous but God. Later, in Romans 3:23, he tells us *all have sinned and fallen short of the glory of God*. In between he gives many examples of unrighteousness, and they mostly look like sin.

> *As it is written:*
> *"There is no one righteous, not even one;*
> *there is no one who understands,*
> *no one who seeks God.*
> *All have turned away, they have together become worthless*
> *There is no one who does good,*
> *not even one."*
> *"Their throats are open graves;*
> *their tongues practice deceit."*
> *"The poison of vipers is on their lips."*
> *"Their mouths are full of cursing and bitterness."*
> *"Their feet are swift to shed blood*
> *Ruin and misery mark their ways, and the way of peace they do not know."*
> *"There is no fear of God before their eyes"* (Rom 3:10–18).

Why would Paul use examples of sin, in the midst of explaining that it is faith, not actions, that are important? Because refraining from sin is part of righteousness. It is only not all of righteousness.

In this passage, Paul cobbles together various quotes from the Old Testament to show us what the opposite of righteousness looks like. Notice, it is not just the act of sinning; it is also a lack of understanding and regard for God. Half of the quotes Paul uses do not refer to sin. Instead, they refer to lack of relationship, lack of faith in God's goodness and greatness. This lack of understanding makes it easier to sin, especially to sin not merely selfishly, but viciously. Unrighteousness does not follow from sin, but it can cause sin.

Certainly sin is a big part of the problem as Paul sees it here. But the examples of sin follow the quotes about our relationship with God. No one understands God and no one seeks God. Sin then becomes the natural result. And so Paul links lack of faith, (remember, faith is his primary subject) to lack of relationship and lack of regard for the preciousness of others. Disregard for God and his creation—and so his plan to redeem creation—causes disruption and it is manifested as unrighteousness.

We may be so programmed to see righteousness as a lack of sinning that we can only see the sin in Paul's examples. We don't see the part about *understanding, seeking God* and *fearing God*. Yet, that is the way the passage begins and the way it closes.

The difference between sin and unrighteousness is small but significant. When we sin we are being unrighteous, but that doesn't make the two synonymous. Conversely, just because we *aren't* sinning doesn't mean we *are* being righteous. Righteousness is more than that. We can see from verse 12, *All have turned away, they have together become worthless; There is no one who does good, not even one*. In addition to not sinning, we have to *do good*. Later in the sermon, Jesus will define what he means by doing good in an extended passage.

We have confused righteousness with sinlessness because refraining from sin is *part* God's plan. Sin hurts his Creation. Sin also hurts the sinner, who is part of his Creation. He tells us not to do certain things because they disrupt his plans for us. Avoiding "bad" *and* doing good put together is a large part of the righteousness God of desires.

I am trying to define good and bad the way Jesus does in the sermon. The desire to see the world through his eyes is a gift God gives. That's the righteousness *from* God, the desire for a new viewpoint. God bestows it upon us when we are reborn. How we use it is our choice. Hungering and thirsting after righteousness is living everyday as if God has a plan and wants us to do our part to make it a reality.

Look at the big picture. God has had a view of how his creation should be since before the Beginning. He had established it on earth with Adam and Eve. There was a "rightness" about the earth before the Fall. This *rightness* was meant to exist on earth from the beginning and it did at first because it was inherent in the Creation. That is why God was able to look at all he had created and say it was *very good*. *Rightness* was a characteristic of creation because it was a characteristic of our Creator.

God also values choice and free will as we saw when we talked about meekness. God possesses free will and choice and he instilled them in us when he created us in his image. Someday all choices will be righteous. That is God's ultimate plan. It is the whole idea of swords turned into plows and lions lying down with calves (or lions lying down with lambs, as we like to paraphrase it for it alliteration). We can delay the culmination of this plan but we cannot thwart it forever.

Abraham believed in the power and rightness of God's plan and tried to live it out. When he allowed Lot to choose the prime real estate, he knew that God was powerful enough to bless his flocks and herds even though they had to graze the mountains instead of the fertile plains. In the long run, the mountainous regions were easier to defend against attack both for Abraham and for the generations of Israelites to come. The choice lowlands led Lot to a life of leisure (how's that for alliteration?) that caused him trouble and ultimately cost him his wife.

When Abraham tithed to God's priest, Melchizedek, and returned his family's portion of the plunder after his great victory against the kings allied against him, he was practicing kingdom living. Conversely, when he kept Abimelek's bounteous gifts for almost taking Sarah, (even though he had gained them by a deceit) he was accepting that God's blessing wasn't due to his own good conduct. It was an admission of the rightness of God's plan in the midst of his sin and faithlessness. If he had had a greater trust in God, he wouldn't have told Abimelek that Sarah was his sister. Yet God's plan advanced despite Abraham's sin.

Abraham's successes and failures occurred during his attempts to live out his belief. He was motivated by his faith. The plan didn't depend on Abraham's sin or lack of sin because the plan was God's plan and was in God's hands. Jesus is saying we are blessed when we pursue God's goals.

Righteousness is striving to live out the belief that God has a plan for something better and we are part of this plan. It could manifest itself in many ways, through action or even inaction. Jesus called it taking up our cross daily. Jesus going to the cross for us was his part of God's plan. Jesus' was the ultimate act of self-denial; and he accomplished it without defending or avenging himself. It wasn't his act of self-denial that was righteous, it was the understanding that his Father was both good and great, and so was his Father's plan.

Hungering and thirsting after righteousness is living everyday as if God has a plan and wants us to do our part to make it a reality. Jesus says we are blessed when we pursue this. He also says we *will be filled*.

When Jesus speaks in the future tense of being filled, he means that the filling will be permanent. We are filled now when we hunger and thirst for righteousness, but for now the filling is always temporary. Jesus is telling us that God's ultimate plan for the kingdom will come to fruition and then the "filling" will be permanent. The resurrection of Jesus Christ is the most important element for restoring the universe to the state God had planned for us all along. Jesus brought us out from under the thumb of sin and death but did not immediately take us up to heaven. He leaves us here to help the plan progress. Our job is not to bring other people to salvation. Our job is to live righteously, which *in turn* will lead people to salvation. The kingdom of heaven is built in this manner and it all starts with one person at a time becoming poor in spirit and then living the *right* way.

Inherent in the plan was and is God's provision for our propensity to choose incorrectly as well as his propensity to save us from ourselves. He knew we would fall because he gave the angels choice and so many of them chose poorly. Angels could choose only once and were then destined to follow their resultant path for all time, and *still* they chose badly. But God built repeated chances into his plan for us. He lures us with blessings but gives us a way out when we choose the curse. He desires to work together with us (as well as in spite of us) to bring about idyllic communion.

It is important to note that God has never given up on us. Look back even further to the days of Noah, when God had so despaired of us that he contemplated our total destruction. In the midst of the great wickedness of that time God found someone who believed in his plan. Genesis 6:9 says, *This is the account of Noah. Noah was a* righteous *man, blameless among the people of his time, and he walked with God.* Noah worked for decades to carry out God's plan.

After the great flood of Noah's day, God promised to never again destroy the earth by water. Instead he provided an alternative method for executing his plan. The method was separation. Separation was God's primary approach for the remainder of the Old Testament. He gave us different languages at the tower of Babel to separate us culturally and then he scattered us to separate us geographically. Then God separated Terah from his countrymen by calling him from the culture of Ur. Then he separated Terah's son, Abram, from Terah geographically as well. God's covenant with Abram was to separate his seed for God's glory.

Many of the laws God gave at Sinai were meant to emphasize separation. The Israelites couldn't wear two different fibers at the same time. They couldn't eat different animal products at one meal or plow with different animals harnessed together. They couldn't even plant two different crops in the same field.

So much of Israel's troubles throughout its existence came from a lack of separation. Taking wives of the surrounding tribes and then worshiping their foreign gods was a recurring problem. We shouldn't surmise that the surrounding tribes were inferior. Some, such as Nineveh, had also been called by God and repented. But God didn't want a mix of the cultures. He didn't want a dilution of his plan.

The Jews finally began to get it right with the rebuilding of Jerusalem and the Temple in the times of Nehemiah and Ezra. The people divorced their foreign wives. They built a society based on the Law as given to Moses. Although they were no longer sovereigns in their own land, the time from Nehemiah to the coming of Jesus was the longest period without idol worship in their long history. Separation had finally accomplished its task. It had laid the groundwork for a world into which Jesus could be born. They had achieved the "fullness of time."

And now with the Sermon on the Mount, Jesus initiates a new phase and method. Separation had finally accomplished what God wanted it to accomplish. The Jews of Jesus' day had their more limited understanding of righteousness down cold. They thought it was clean living, just as many do today, but clean living wasn't enough. We'll see this shortly, when Jesus warns that our righteousness needs to exceed that of the Pharisees.

Separation had accomplished its task. It was time for more sophisticated narratives to show God to the world. The world was ready for a greater subtlety. The time for separation was over. Jesus was explicit in his parable that the wheat should remain among the tares until the harvest.

Upright and uptight Jews were naturally suspicious and tried to discredit Jesus. A thousand years of instruction and tradition were being dismantled in the twinkling of Jesus' eye. He was deliberate in his rejection of separation. He worked on the Sabbath—a day separated for rest. He touched lepers and the dead although there were admonitions in the Law against it. As the walls of separation began to fall in society, they began to fall between God and man as well. The veil separating us from God in the Temple was torn at last when Jesus died.

The dissolving of separation continued after Christ's death. Peter received instruction from the Holy Spirit overturning the dietary laws. Until then, these laws had been a prime method of distinction and separation for the Jews. Then Paul attacked the social fabric of distinction and separation when he said there is no longer a difference between Jew and Greek, male and female. In this same spirit Jesus announced the new phase with a new phrase: the Kingdom of Heaven is *among* us.

If the Kingdom of Heaven is among us, we should be conscious of the fact throughout the day as we hunger and thirst after righteousness. This is different from the Jewish custom of prayer thrice a day at set times. The set times tended to separate prayer from real life. The habit could compartmentalize God.

Jesus suggests that his disciples should call on God many times a day, while doing ordinary things like stopping for a handful of grapes along the road or slowing their pace for a drink of water from a skin. Jesus wants us to be mindful of him naturally *throughout* the day. Nearly all prayers should end without "amen." This closeness to Lord Jesus is what will keep us poor in spirit, and meek, and forgiving. Pursuing God's plan (rather than our own) is the best work we can do to build the kingdom.

Blessed are the merciful, for they will be shown mercy (Matt 5:7)

If you recall, we've already discussed how newer Bible translations use "mercy" in places the King James Bible sometimes uses "loving-kindness." So mercy is loving-kindness. And we've defined love as the putting of another's wants and needs ahead of our own. Now let's continue to break down loving-kindness and look at kindness.

"Kindness" in loving-kindness means mercy is categorically *not* tough love. Mercy is not allowing someone to suffer the consequences of bad choices. Mercy is the irrational kindness felt and shown against all odds; love beyond reason. In fact, it conquers reason. Mercy is forgiveness where none is appropriate.

Mercy is one of the great themes of the Sermon on the Mount. Mercy has appeared so frequently in the many other passages we've referenced that I've stopped pointing them out. While judgment is the Lord's and being born a second time also comes from above, mercy is our responsibility. Jesus is so adamant in establishing this as our responsibility that he attaches a consequence to it. Just as those who judge will be judged, the merciful will be shown mercy.

Mercy is love in action. Love without mercy is dead in the same way that James tells us faith without works is dead. Until we live out our faith, no one knows about it but us. Unless we show mercy, no one will notice our love. Mercy is the most visible component of love.

Inherent in the promise, *Blessed are the merciful, for they will be shown mercy,* is the realization that a most important reason to show mercy is because we need mercy. The best way to remember how much we need mercy is for us to remain *poor in spirit*. The proud man, unable to recognize his own sin, cannot easily forgive sin in another. The "blameless" man cannot be merciful. Only a blameless God is capable of the mercy we need.

Not only do *we* need mercy; every single person we will meet today needs mercy. Everyone we will meet tomorrow will need mercy. The need for mercy is the bond we share with the unbeliever. We have all sinned; we have all erred and missed the mark, so we all need mercy. A common bond is a natural antidote to the barriers we erect between unbelievers and ourselves.

So *blessed* (now) *are the merciful, for they will receive mercy.* If we remember nothing else from the whole sermon this almost could be enough. Show love to everyone—for God is love. *He who is forgiven much, loves much* (Luke 7:47). Show kindness to everyone, for the Lord has been kinder to us than we could ever deserve.

> *He has showed you, O man, what is good.*
> *And what does the Lord require of you?*
> *To act justly and*
> *to* love mercy *and*
> *to walk humbly with your God.*

These things are required of us.

7

The Pure and the Peacemakers

Blessed are the pure in heart, for they will see God (Matt 5:8)

THEY WILL SEE GOD. Now that is quite a promise! Since *No one has ever seen God* (1 John 4:12) Jesus must be talking about getting to heaven. That's where we will see God. All we have to do is be *pure in heart*.

Ugh, I certainly don't qualify. I'm the person God was thinking about when he said, "*the heart is deceitful above all things and desperately wicked*" (Jeremiah 17:9 KJV). In truth, isn't this all of us? Jeremiah spoke to the human condition. So how do we get from a *desperately wicked* heart to *pure in heart*?

Since *pure in heart* was the sticking point, I thought I'd start there. I searched the phrase in the Bible Jesus read. There were no exact matches for *pure in heart*, but there were a few verses that contained both *pure* and *heart*. The first was in Psalm 24. It seemed to confirm what Jesus is saying. A pure heart gets us up the holy hill; it gets us to heaven.

> *Who may ascend the hill of the Lord?*
> *Who may stand in his holy place?*
> *He who has clean hands and a* pure heart,
> *who does not lift up his soul to an idol or swear by what is false.*
> *He will receive blessing from the Lord and vindication from God his Savior* (Ps 24:3 -5).

If it takes clean hands and a pure heart, I *am* in trouble. A second reference, Proverbs 20:9 seemed to taunt me. *Who can say, "I have kept my heart pure; I am clean and without sin?"* The question assumes its answer.

Perhaps some of us can claim our heart is presently pure, but none of us can claim we have *kept* our heart pure. If we stitch the questions together, they state our conundrum.

> *Who may ascend the hill of the Lord?*
> *Who may stand in his holy place?*
> *He who has clean hands and a* pure heart, *but*
> *Who can say, "I have kept my heart pure; I am clean and without sin?"*

The answer is obvious. No one has kept his or her heart pure, no one is clean and without sin, so no one may ascend the hill of the Lord and stand in his holy place.

Even if there isn't a way for us to keep clean, there is a way for us to get clean, and I guess, pure. Our natural inclination would be to reference First John. *If we confess our sins, he is faithful and just and will forgive us our sins and purify us from all unrighteousness* (1 John 1:9). But this would still be an incomplete understanding of the Beatitude. Jesus didn't mean *blessed are those who repent and confess their sin*. Let me show you why.

First, let's present the logic of those who believe this is exactly what Jesus meant. They diligently point to the Greek word for *pure* in Matthew 5:7. The word is *katharos*, and we get the word catharsis from it. According to the dictionary, catharsis is a purge that brings spiritual release and purification. After such a purge, we are *pure in heart*. This is logical in the way of dictionary definitions but it is incomplete in our application of Jesus' teaching. The release of catharsis may come from our confession, but God must accomplish the purification.

Psalm 51, Jesus' last possible reference point for *pure heart* in the Old Testament, seems to bear this out. Look at David's lament after he was confronted about his sin with Bathsheba. The psalm starts with the required confession and repentance (which should be enough based on our reading of First John 1:9), and then,

> *Hide your face from my sins and blot out all my iniquity.*
> *Create in me a pure heart, O God, and renew a steadfast spirit within me.*
> *Do not cast me from your presence or take your Holy Spirit from me.*
> *Restore to me the joy of your salvation and*
> *Grant me a willing spirit, to sustain me* (Ps 51:9–12).

David pleads with the Lord to create a pure heart within him in verse 10 even though he has already repented and confessed his sin in the first part of the psalm. The purity David desires is not a natural consequence of his confession, his repentance, or God's forgiveness. *God must perform the purification.*

The sequence is not peculiar to this situation, either. God's cleansing is not dependent on our repentance. Neither is God's purifying automatic. If it were, we would be the true god because God would have to do as we please. First John 1:9 tells us God is faithful and just to forgive us, but the concept of God's sovereignty dictates that the decision must be his. Only he has the authority to forgive.

Jesus may desire that we confess our sins often, but the problem with thinking this is the meaning of the Beatitude lies in the opposite unspoken logical conclusion: *Christians who don't confess their sins often enough will not see God*. Does it seem right that Jesus died to save me but I might not have confessed my sin recently enough to see God? This form of Resurrection Roulette takes Jesus out of the equation. The cross is no longer sufficient and Christ's atonement is incomplete. We would be our own saviors through confession and repentance; our faith would require works. As usual, we need to dig deeper.

The Hebrew word for "*pure*" in the *holy hill* passage of Psalm 24 is *bar*, which can mean clean, pure, or sincere. The word for *pure* in David's Psalm 51 confession is *Howrah* (pronounced *ta-hore'*). It means the same thing as *bar*. Which adjective is used in the Hebrew most often depends on the object being described. Actually there are three words in Hebrew for *pure*, and we'll come to the third one in a moment.

Jesus would have known the Greek *katharos* could have been used for any of the words in the Hebrew. All mean essentially the same thing. The noun they describe dictates their use. *Bar* is used as an adjective directed primarily toward people. *Tahowr* is normally used to describe ore as in *pure gold* or *pure silver* and comes from the root word for ceremonially clean (*taher*). Sometimes *tahowr* and *taher* were used interchangeably.

When an object was ceremonially clean, it was acceptable to God in some way we can't quite fathom. Halibut was clean but shrimp was not. Beef was clean but pork was not. There is a theory that God put these laws into place to protect the Israelites from unsanitary conditions and the spread of disease.

Leviticus 10:10 equates "clean" with holy and "unclean" with unholy. *So that you can distinguish between the holy and the common, between the unclean and the clean* (Leviticus 10:10). The verse was a definitive reference in the Jewish mind in Jesus' day. Unclean didn't exactly equate to sinful but an unclean person most often required cleansing and a small sacrifice to be restored to cleanness. Moldy walls in a house or tent were not *taher* and required cleaning. If the mold didn't return in eight days, the inhabitants could move back in after they offered the proscribed sacrifice.

Zak, the third Hebrew word for *pure*, was used to show oils or incense had been refined in the same way *tahowr* was used to show that ore was refined. Both of these words show purity as a result of the refining process. Moreover, the process was inflexible. If the process wasn't followed precisely, the desired purity couldn't be achieved. The desired result was especially important when the object was part of the Temple worship, because the holiness of the Temple was thought of as emanating from God. Just earlier in the same chapter of Leviticus, two of Aaron's sons were killed for bringing "strange fire" into the Temple. Most commentators believe strange fire might have been an unauthorized form of incense. The Temple incense required in the Law had to be refined in a way that achieved the required level of purity.

So all three words demonstrate the idea that purity is the result of *process*, either by refining or by bringing an appropriate sacrifice. It seems that God was a bit obsessed with purity if Hebrew contains so many words to describe it, much like we used to think the Inuit had many different words for snow. No wonder Jesus addresses *pure* in the Beatitude. We will keep all of the definitions in mind because Jesus could have meant any or all of them. However, since two of the words are primarily used to modify inanimate objects (ore and oil), let's go back to the word that was the most often used for humans.

A fuller understanding of the word *bar* can come from a study of its Hebrew root word. Unlike examples we are used to seeing in English, the root word is longer than its derivative. The root is *barar*, and it can mean to purify or cleanse, or even to purge. Other meanings are determined by how it is used in a sentence. *Barar* can mean to test or to prove, or even to polish arrows. To polish arrows?

Here's my little theory about *pure in heart*. (It might be immediately apparent where I'm going with this.) Most Christians know the meaning behind the word *sin*. Sin most often means to miss the mark in both Hebrew and Greek. Maybe a polished arrow misses the mark less often.

Imperfections are removed from an arrowhead in the polishing process, increasing the arrow's accuracy by improving its aerodynamics. I'm not suggesting that a decrease in sin is an outcome of better accuracy on our part. I'm suggesting that less sin would be due to God having tested the Christian in a way that purifies him. (Don't forget *barar* also means to test or prove.) God is the polisher; we are the polished.

This polishing process sounds suspiciously like sanctification. We know God refines us to improve our Christian walk. He doesn't leave us as he finds us at salvation. Our sins are taken away but God isn't finished with us. To ignore our continuing sin would make a mockery of Jesus' sacrifice. God works to move us beyond our predilections. Those he loves, he chastises.

But there is more to this polishing process than chastisement. This is the key to the passage and I bet you've experienced it in your own life. God uses adversity to make us more fit for service. Sarah and Abram suffered but it prepared them for their roles in God's plan. Their lives have been a template for everyone who would be used by God. The oppressive reality of barrenness was especially a trial for Sarah, since Hagar had already bore Abram a son. Perhaps Sarah's longsuffering made her a better parent. Rebekah and Hannah were also barren, and their kids turned out pretty well. We know Hannah was so grateful to finally bear a son that she dedicated him for Temple service. I would guess that gratitude also shaped the way Rebekah and Sarah molded their children's character. The wait made their children seem even more precious. The results (Joseph, Samuel, and Isaac) were worth the ordeal.

Speaking of Joseph, was there anyone who suffered longer to make him fit for the task set before him? The more he did exactly what he believed God required of him, the more he suffered. The polishing seemed evil, but God meant it for good.

We consider Jesus to have lived a good and perfect life. Yet even he was prepared for his ministry by forty days of fasting and the temptations in the desert. And Hebrews tells us (more than once) that Jesus was *perfected* through his final sufferings on our behalf. He didn't need sanctification, but he suffered to make himself fit for service.

I called "suffering as preparation" a template because the process holds true today. I heard a radio preacher discuss the principle. He acknowledged both the validity and the necessity of the process, and then he was honest enough to tell of his prayer as he prepared for ministry. It ran along the lines of "Lord, I know you call us to endure trials to make us fit, but can't you skip them just this once?" He then described some of what he went through next. The answer was no, not even just this once.

We need to embrace the concept of suffering. I don't know how, but we have to learn to consider it all joy. Trials make us capable. The natural talents and spiritual gifts God has given us are honed in this way. If we don't recognize God's methods, we'll think every trial is a chastisement for sin when the reality might be that God is building our character. He refines us until our hands are clean and polishes us until our hearts are pure.

If this is what Jesus meant by *pure in heart*, then the promise (*for they will see God*) is a reassurance and an encouragement. Suffering to eliminate future sin sanctifies us. Suffering while living righteously makes us fit for service, and hey, don't forget that someday we will see God!

Blessed are the pure in heart, for they will see God would mean *don't feel as if every problem you face is a chastisement. God may instead use circumstances to make you fit for kingdom work. One day you'll stand before him and agree that it was worth it.*

Could this be what Jesus meant? Could he have been encouraging rather than threatening? Let's try to confirm this hypothesis; back to Psalm 24. Who will see God?

> *He who has clean hands and a pure heart,*
> *who does not lift up his soul to an idol or swear by what is false.*
> *He will receive blessing from the Lord and vindication from God his Savior.*

The psalm can be interpreted in this way. The person with clean hands and a pure heart is the person who *does not* lift up his soul to an idol (present tense). The verse doesn't necessarily describe a person who has never lifted his soul to an idol or sworn falsely, only one who doesn't do it presently. The Refiner's fire has purified the heart. Since the heart in question has not necessarily always been pure, Psalm 24 no longer contradicts Psalm 20. *Who can say, "I have* kept *my heart pure; I am clean and without sin?"* None of us has kept our heart pure but we can all have a clean heart after God has made us ready to see God.

God refines and polishes us through the circumstances of our lives. Poor harvests, plagues, and floods were the economic meltdowns of Jesus' day. Similar challenges can make or break us yet today. If our response to calamity is to hedge our bets by also worshiping other gods, we fail. If we trust in our 401k, or worse, if we rely on cheating or lies, we are trusting in what is false. He who passes the test is he who trusts in God and his gifts.

We *ascend his holy hill* because *he* vindicates us. *He* is our *Savior*. Our part is to stick with him, and that is faith. If we are tested and refined, we will receive blessing from the Lord. The sequence plays out frequently in scripture. Abraham was tested by God's command to sacrifice Isaac even though he had become the father of our faith years earlier. Our task, like Abraham's, is the proper response to whatever circumstances God sets before us. We are not to turn aside from following him because to follow another path would be to *lift up our souls to idols*.

Idols were the ancient's attempt to influence circumstances. Idols were stone or wooden representations of the heavenly bodies thought to influence conditions here on earth. They knew the moon influenced the tides and menstrual cycles and the sun made it warmer. People were trying to "change their luck" by appealing to other heavenly bodies, other gods.

The Israelites believed in YHWH, but they were hedging their bets by bringing sacrifices to other gods as well. The strategy was an entirely human attempt to cover all the bases. The Israelites didn't *trust in God alone* and were prone to this dubious strategy until God excised it during the exile. We are not so very different if we think the Beatitude means we must be saved *and* confess our sins often.

David is really saying in Psalm 24 to forget about trying to change your luck. Instead we should cast our lot with God no matter what happens, because he will save and vindicate us. Our Father in heaven is well aware of our circumstances. Either he created those circumstances to refine us or he is allowing us to go through circumstances in order to make us fit for duty. Having *clean hands and a pure heart* means one has been tested and has learned not to split his loyalties.

If Jesus is again using the Beatitude as a culmination of an Old Testament teaching, it is confirmed (as usual) by New Testament exposition. Here is a verse that shows a good conscience is something different from a pure heart, because both are necessary to show proper love: *The goal of this command is love, which comes from a* pure heart *and a good conscience and a sincere faith* (1 Tim 1:5).

Paul says love comes from a combination of three distinct things. A good conscience would be the result of confessing our sin often, but a pure heart is something different. He also said we must have a sincere faith. Without it, who can ascend God's holy hill? And without sincere faith we wouldn't have what it takes to go through the purification process. Faith, purity, and a good conscience are related but they are three separate things.

When Paul instructs Timothy in this verse that *the goal of this command is love*, he isn't using *command* in its sense of receiving an order. The command he is talking about is Timothy's *position* as pastor of a church. A command is the position given to a commander. Paul means the goal of being a pastor is love. The goal isn't to instruct the faithful. It isn't to save the lost. It is to love. If Timothy loves, those other things will follow.

Love is God's most accessible tool. It was designed to fit our hands. Timothy could pursue the lost but without the work of the Holy Spirit, they would remain lost. Should the Holy Spirit draw them, Timothy's responsibility becomes to not repel them.

A good conscience would allow Timothy to love without obstruction. A sincere faith would help Timothy love God's way. A pure heart would leave Timothy free to love without an agenda.

Sometimes I hear about a strategy to reach the lost that worries me in its arrogance. I have heard the advice that we should love people into the kingdom. Although trying to love them into the kingdom is probably better than attempting to shame them in or scare them in, it is equally futile. All three methods smack of an inferred superiority, manipulation and ulterior motives. They all look to usurp the Spirit's job and authority.

We all have built-in sensors for these situations. We can sense when someone feels we are inferior and we can sense when we are being manipulated. We weigh the words of others for ulterior motives before we decide their validity. Love must be pure. It cannot be tinged with strategy. We must love for love's sake and love for God's sake.

Our job is to *not repel* those who are drawn. Hence the goal of the command is to love. We can't love anyone into the kingdom—we can only love them. This is the goal and it is a goal unto itself. God takes care of the rest.

We have a final Beatitude to explore. There are two more actually (since Beatitude comes from the Latin for *blessed be* and there are two more phrases that begin with *blessed*) but many commentators don't think the last is truly intended to be one of the Beatitudes. Instead they think it is an explanation of what will happen if we follow the others. I agree. The Beatitudes are the seven parameters of kingdom living. The eighth is a transition into the next phase of the sermon, which explains and expands upon these stated principles. Since Jesus explains the last one himself, he saves us the trouble. See that? Jesus saves! Let's look at this last step in the vision Jesus has for kingdom living.

> *Blessed are the peacemakers, for they will be called sons of God* (Matt 5:9)

I think Jesus' selection of the word *peacemakers* is magnificent. I can't imagine a better word choice. Peacemakers is used only once in the Bible, right here, because Jesus made it up by putting the words "peace" and "maker" together.

The Bible uses peace to describe harmony between nations but Jesus isn't talking about that kind of peace. The peace Jesus desires us to make is both smaller and greater than peace among nations. Peace is the goal of the sermon. The Beatitudes are steps in a process meant to lead to peace and this is the last step. With this in mind I looked for other passages in which peace was the goal.

Here are a few definitive biblical references for peace. The first verse gives us a summary headline, with peace last. The steps leading to this peace are then explained in greater detail, and they sound like the Beatitudes.

> *Love and faithfulness meet together; righteousness and* peace *kiss each other.*

> *Faithfulness springs forth from the earth,*
> *and righteousness looks down from heaven.*
> *The Lord will indeed give what is good, and our land will yield its harvest.*
> *Righteousness goes before him and prepares the way for his steps* (Ps 85:10–13).

Righteousness looks down from Heaven. We know Who that is. I love the idea of *love and faithfulness* meeting together. It is an exact representation of Jesus coming down to earth, isn't it? Then, *Faithfulness springs forth from the earth.* "Faithfulness" would be us trying to be like Jesus. Our job is to be faithful.

The Hebrew word for love here is our old friend *checed*; mercy, loving kindness, or steadfast love. In context, this is God's love for us. Faithfulness is ours since it comes from the earth. The love of God and the faith of a man met together at the advent of Christ.

I also love *righteousness and peace* kissing. They are intimately acquainted throughout the Bible. If we live the *right way* it will lead to peace. In fact, our living in the *right* way helps to prepare the hearts of the unsaved for the message of Jesus. *Righteousness goes before him and prepares the way for his steps*. Steps. Love, faithfulness, and righteousness are the steps that lead to the harvest.

Our land yielding *its harvest* has to be the spread of the Gospel. Jesus often uses the analogy of seeding, harvest and reaping to reference salvation. What a marvelous prophetic Gospel message in just a few verses in the middle of a psalm! This isn't considered one of the messianic prophecies but I think the passage prophesies what was begun at the Sermon on the Mount.

Did you notice the parallels to the Beatitudes? Love, faithfulness, righteousness and peace are the main topics of both the Sermon and this passage from Psalms. Remember that righteousness is God's plan for putting the world right and Jesus is the embodiment of that plan on earth. Our method is love and our responsibility is faithfulness. Love and faithfulness yield peace. Children of God are those who spread the gospel of peace.

Here's a tasty morsel from Isaiah:

> *till the Spirit is poured upon us from on high,*
> *and the desert becomes a fertile field,*
> *and the fertile field seems like a forest* (Isa 32:15).

Beginning with Pentecost (when the Spirit was first poured upon us) it immediately became easier for us to be saved. The book of Acts tells us the early church grew quickly. Isaiah forecast the change seven hundred years in advance. The spiritual desert became a fertile field and the field grew so quickly it seemed like a forest. The blooming of Christianity was (and is) a work of the Spirit but the kingdom grew through the acts of the apostles. So what are our responsibilities today—how do we make peace? You know it's going to involve righteousness, don't you? Let's continue with Isaiah's prophecy.

> *Justice will dwell in the desert and righteousness live in the fertile field.*
> *The fruit of righteousness will be* peace;
> *the effect of righteousness will be quietness and confidence forever*
> (Isa 32:16,17).

I love the poetic description of salvation in the last line, *quietness and confidence forever*. We can be confident because our savior is our Savior. Quietness is most likely the calmness that comes from no longer warring with God. Peace.

The last two lines are a couplet. Couplets are commonly used in Hebrew poetry. Hebrew poetry often states (as it does here) an important idea in two slightly different ways. The fruit of righteousness is peace and the effect of righteousness is confidence forever. Both peace and quiet confidence are salvation. Salvation is spread through righteousness. God makes peace with us and we can spread that peace by living with God's plan in mind.

Being born again (poor in spirit) is the first Beatitude and helping others to get born again (peacemaking) is the last. In between are the effective steps in the process that we have called the Jesus Method. Not surprisingly, the Jesus Method is nothing short of proper Kingdom Living. It is Jesus' forever strategy.

We know acting meekly will lead to peace in the normal sense of the word. How can there be anything but peace if we don't react with aggression? If we walk an extra mile and turn the other cheek, we leave no room for retaliation. No one is upping the ante. The cycle of violence is broken.

Let's move forward to the New Testament and let Paul weigh in on the subject. He says we serve Christ *and* are approved by men if we make every effort at what leads to peace and building each other up:

> *For the kingdom of God is not a matter of eating and drinking,* (keeping the law)
> *but of righteousness,* peace *and joy in the Holy Spirit,*
> *because anyone who serves Christ in this way is pleasing to God*
> *and approved by men.*
> *Let us therefore make every effort to do what leads to* peace
> *and to mutual edification* (Rom 14:18–19).

Paul wrote about both kinds of peace here. Peace and joy in the Holy Spirit is salvation, and peace and mutual edification are peace with humanity. The first peace is *pleasing to God* and the second peace is *approved by men*. The peace accompanying salvation comes from faith, and Hebrews 11 tells us without faith it is impossible to please God.

The other peace is the lack of conflict. This peace is discernible, for it must be to be *approved by men*. Paul doesn't say approved by our brothers, he says approved by men. We think being approved by the world is the antithesis of being approved by our Lord and in many cases this may be true. Peace however, is the sure exception.

The first event in Jesus' life was an announcement by the angels that we would have peace on earth and good will to men. The last word goes to Jesus: *"My peace I give to you. I do not give to you as the world gives* (John 14:27). I'm thankful he doesn't.

Bringing his peace to others will get us called sons of God.

8

The Persecuted

We are at a transition point in the Sermon. Peacemaking is the last of seven steps designed to bring others to Christ. Yet we have eight Beatitudes. The eighth is not a step but a signpost that confirms the right path. It isn't a command we must follow or an act of volition. It is a consequence.

This final Beatitude begins the body of the sermon. Jesus makes the transition back to the present tense with a phrase that sounds like a warning, but is also a reassurance—ours *is* the kingdom of heaven.

> *Blessed are those who are persecuted because of righteousness,*
> *for theirs is the kingdom of heaven* (Matt 5:10)

The other Beatitudes are Jesus' vision for the future, but he isn't a starry-eyed idealist. He knows kingdom living will cost us. It should cost us. In fact, it should probably cost us a lot more than it does, for the kingdom is valuable beyond anything else we possess.

Many of the troubles facing Christianity today can be traced to our unwillingness to pay. We hesitate because the costs are unexpected, and they are unexpected because we weren't warned about them in the witness that led to our salvation. We were told to expect a great big, delicious, calorie-free cherry pie in the sky.

The problem with our verbal witness lies in the innate sinfulness of the people doing the witnessing. Like masterful salespeople, we accentuate the benefits and minimize the costs. We extol the joys of the free gift of salvation and a life more abundant. We got our pitch from Jesus, for he was the first to make these promises, but he was careful not to leave us with unrealistic expectations.

With this verse Jesus goes beyond the common calamities of life. We have an extra burden to bear: persecution. And why are we blessed when we are persecuted? *For ours is the kingdom of Heaven.* That's the message of this Beatitude, the kingdom of Heaven is worth it. The kingdom of Heaven is the great treasure hidden in a field. Should we find it, we should be willing to sell all we have to buy the field. That's what Jesus thought.

Paul thought persecution to be a privilege. Jesus considered the kingdom of Heaven to be worth more than the very life of God. They were unafraid to discuss the downside of believing, but we omit it from our sales pitch. Then, when troubles come, we're puzzled because we weren't warned. I was puzzled for years. I wanted a life of Christian ease because I heard a witness in Christianese.

Now I can look back to all the troubles and consider the advancing kingdom to be worth it. I have come to appreciate (to a certain degree) God's shaping of my character. Someday I hope to look at my trials and like Paul, consider them an honor. That's Jesus' message here. Our troubles, trials, chastisements, and even the persecutions are worth it, because ours *is* the kingdom of Heaven.

The beauty of a well-lived kingdom life is that it makes no false claims. Unbelievers can see us face trials with joy and trouble with élan. Jesus promised that each day would have trouble enough of its own. The manner in which we bear up under the slings and arrows should be a prime attraction to those not yet of the kingdom. How we live is second only to how we love.

Persecute is one of those interesting words in the Greek that can have nearly opposite meanings. It can mean *to suffer* or *to flee hostility*, but it can also mean *to pursue eagerly* or *earnestly seek to acquire*. The King James translates it as having to do with persecution thirty-one times but associates it with following or pursuing ten times. Leave it to Jesus to pick the perfect word. *Choosing* persecution increases our value to the kingdom. That's right, especially in America today, we must choose it.

The early church is our finest example. Those early believers regularly faced loss of livelihood, social ostracism, imprisonment, and even death. We praise them and their remarkable effect on the world, but the effect was so pronounced because they were so thoroughly persecuted.

Jesus was fair and just to warn us of the consequences, but he didn't ask for more than he was willing to endure himself. His persecution and death was the first of many in the New Kingdom.

Paul calls us to suffer even today. *Therefore do not be ashamed of the testimony of our Lord or of me His prisoner, but join with {me} in suffering for the gospel according to the power of God* (2 Tim 1:8 NASB). Suffering for the gospel displays the power of God like nothing else we can do. Suffering has always been our firmest witness.

In my Sunday school class, we have discussed our hypothetical response if we were ever faced with a life or death decision for Christ. These discussions miss the point. Jesus will always present opportunities to suffer for our faith even if we never face death because of it. We face the challenge of denying ourselves purposefully for the good of others. This is the meaning of taking up our cross daily.

The suffering might be a mild social ostracism for our "foolish" beliefs or it might be some small economic privation for refusing to lie, cheat, or steal. Jesus might call us to give a larger gift to our church which means we will have to spend a week's vacation at home. Perhaps we will have to give up season tickets for our local NFL team to become faithful in our church attendance. Whatever the test may be, it most certainly will come often, and its significance will not be determined by the degree of our suffering. The significance will be determined by our eagerness to suffer.

Today in America, we have to go out of our way in order to suffer for Jesus. *We almost need to persecute ourselves.* We don't face death for our belief, or persecution of any serious consequence. This is because we live under the lasting effects of the advancing kingdom. America's Judeo-Christian heritage means we are not subject to historic barbarisms like prison or beheading.

We think otherwise. We've been taught otherwise. We are told we are victims of an increasingly hostile government, the liberal media, wicked Hollywood, and the gay agenda. It may be true that individuals within these institutions oppose us, but the opposition is not persecution. Most likely, the opposition is in reaction to our lack of meekness.

Back to our gay Iowan example, when a gay couple in Iowa gets married, we aren't persecuted by it. We can't feel it. We don't even know when it happens. Maybe five gay couples got married there yesterday, but I didn't suffer for it. If I have to turn off a TV show because it took a sinful turn, it isn't persecution. It is fleeing from sin. If my wife were to watch many shows like that and then divorce me because of the dissatisfaction the shows planted in her heart, it still wouldn't be persecution. It would be suffering because of sin. We all, believer or not, suffer because of sin.

If we blithely roll along, counting the times we've been sinned against as persecution, we aren't going to make kingdom progress. Humanity has always suffered at the hands of other sinners so it isn't peculiar to the kingdom of Heaven. Moreover, if we begin to count the times we refrain from sin as persecution, our self-righteousness will become prominent and the kingdom will begin to *regress.*

Jesus said we are blessed when we are persecuted for *righteousness*. Only when we suffer because we attempt to live out God's plan can we anticipate blessing. We have to pursue the righteousness and hope the persecution follows. I know, the idea seems strange to me, too.

It is important that we understand that Jesus is calling us to suffer *for him* when we are *persecuted because of righteousness* rather than being persecuted because of our own righteousness. He immediately explains this in the following verse.

> *Blessed are you when people insult you,*
> *persecute you*
> *and falsely say all kinds of evil against you*
> *because of me.*
> *Rejoice and be glad, because great is your reward in heaven,*
> *for in the same way they persecuted the prophets who were before you.*
> (Matt 5:11–12)

"Because of me" dictates we be insulted or slandered for the proper reason. The evil must be because people are angry at *his* message and not because we are acting boorishly.

We might think it a good thing if we get a beer poured on our head for holding up a John 3:16 sign at a football game. However, if that same beer is not an unbeliever's gospel commentary but instead a protest because we repeatedly blocked his view, then we are getting in the way of the message as much as we are getting in the way of the game. The kingdom is not advanced and we deserve the beer shampoo.

The John 3:16 sign may be an example of an external witness that does not flow naturally from the events of our life. It may be valuable and necessary, *but only when we are called to it*. This is the baseline criterion. We should be prompted by the Holy Spirit to witness verbally and his call should be *unmistakable*. I've come to this conclusion because Jesus devotes so much attention to living witness as a function of kingdom living and relatively little time to overt witness.

Look at the example of the prophets mentioned by Jesus in that last verse. They are our best models for verbal witness. They could no more not speak the message than not take their next breath. Jeremiah admits as much.

> *But if I say, "I will not mention him* (the Lord) *or speak any more in his name,"*
> *his word is in my heart like a fire, a fire shut up in my bones.*
> *I am weary of holding it in;*
> *indeed, I cannot* (Jer 20:9).

Later in the Sermon Jesus will explain when to witness verbally and what to do if we are persecuted for it. For now it is enough to realize the Spirit must be urging us to witness like God urged the prophets to speak. Usually, we are given a clue by circumstance. Our witness should flow naturally because it is God's job to draw the unbeliever.

If the Spirit does not so intervene with promptings or by arranging circumstances, we must be confident and competent in our alternate strategy. However, if we're doing what he asks, nothing more and nothing less, and still we are persecuted for it, then we are blessed because ours *is* the kingdom of heaven, and great will be our heavenly reward.

Jesus warns us that even though God is blessing us by these things it doesn't mean we're going to have an easy time of it. Nothing worthwhile is easy. We are not necessarily going to be happy. However, even if we're not happy we can be joyous, and we can live with purpose and a sense of significance. If we practice kingdom living, our cup will be filled with blessedness.

This is the essence of kingdom living: a life well lived. The process is so much simpler than we want to make it. Like all of God's principles, the ideas are simple and the execution is difficult. The execution is difficult because we are sinners.

In case we still don't get it, Jesus will spend the majority of the rest of the sermon explaining these simple concepts in more detail. He'll give examples. He'll tell us why we need to live this way and he will end the sermon with the results we will achieve if we heed his call.

Jesus himself lived this way. He knew we needed the example of his life, but he also lived this way because it was the right way to live. His every action was consistent with the principles in his sermon. Every speech and every parable further explains these simple concepts.

The only exceptions were his teachings related to his coming death and resurrection. He omitted these because the multitudes were not ready to grasp them. Yet all the rest is here. If we didn't have the whole Bible, if we only had the Sermon on the Mount, the death on the cross, and the resurrection, it would be enough.

Early in this book, we considered the problems of effective witness and our loss of influence in a postmodern world. The Jesus Method as he lays it out in the Beatitudes is the proper solution to those problems. We don't need to tell the world we have the Truth (not because we don't but because it implies that *they* don't), we only need to tell them we have Jesus. Then we need to live out that truth for the world to see, in the manner Jesus proscribes in the verses we've just studied. Persecution, or perhaps self-deprivation for the good of others to the glory of God, is the cement that holds the seven steps together. If we can suffer, even just a little, it shows we are convinced and it shows the courage of our convictions. That is the best way for others to be convinced.

The Jesus Method can be effective in this wary, postmodern world. In fact, it is the perfect method for any and every age.

9

Salt and Light

You are the salt of the earth.
But if the salt loses its saltiness, how can it be made salty again?
It is no longer good for anything,
Except to be thrown out and trampled by men. (Matt 5:13)

JESUS BEGINS TO EXPAND on the Beatitudes by giving the reason for kingdom living. He states explicitly what until now had only been implied: people are watching. We are the salt of the earth and the light of the world. How we live is important.

Salt is characterized by how it enhances other foods. It doesn't change other flavors; it adds its own. Salt fits into salt-shaped taste buds in the mouth, which then send a signal to the brain. The signal reaches the brain at the same time as another food's flavor signal reaches the brain. The pleasure is in the symbiotic nature of the contrast; the added sensation of more taste receptors being stimulated. That is our role—to add a contrasting yet pleasing flavor to the societies we cohabit. If we become like everyone else, Jesus says we lose our saltiness. The contrast is gone.

Salt is also a preservative, but preservation wasn't Jesus' point. Jesus wasn't trying to preserve the *status quo*, he was urging us to see things anew. This becomes apparent as soon as Jesus moves beyond *salt* to *saltiness*. Saltiness denotes flavor. If salt did not taste salty, it would still be a preservative because of its chemical properties. If it did not have those chemical properties, it wouldn't be salt. If it retains those chemical properties (if it is salt) but doesn't taste salty, then it wouldn't be any good at enhancing flavor. If it didn't do the job we expected when it came out of the shaker, we would throw it out.

If we can agree that *saltiness* refers to flavor, we need to determine the flavor of salt. What did Jesus mean when he said we must be salty? What is the quintessential characteristic, the thing we must add to the world? Most of us would say it is clean living. At the very least, we would say it is cleaner living than we exhibited before we came under Jesus' lordship.

By now you've read long enough to know I'm going to take a different point of view. I base this on logical conclusions drawn from the text. I think it means something different for two reasons.

The first reason becomes apparent from the clause, *how can it be made salty again?* If by *salt* Jesus means cleaner living, then once we revert to worldliness we could no longer live cleanly. We couldn't become salty again. Jesus would mean backsliding is permanent after a certain period or level of bad behavior. This mistaken conclusion would be amplified by the next sentence. *It is no longer good for anything, except to be thrown out and trampled by men.*

Could Jesus really mean backslidden Christians are *no longer good for anything*, worthless ever after? My pastor says Jesus is the God of the second chance and God of the hundredth chance. Mercifully, that is my experience also and I would guess that it is yours as well. Could I be fooling myself? Could I think I am doing my best while long ago Jesus deemed me useless, fit only *to be thrown out and trampled by men*? That is the logical conclusion if saltiness is clean living.

This brings me to the second point. Remember my theory that the sermon was delivered in a logical progression? As usual, I don't think Jesus is changing the subject. I think he is building on his previous point. We are blessed when we are persecuted for his name's sake, therefore we are blessed we when we live in the proper manner.

If the proper prescription for an effective witness is one that emphasizes the Beatitudinal qualities of love and mercy, meekness and living with God's great plan in mind; then that's what Jesus means by salt. If after exhibiting these qualities we become judgmental and critical, there may indeed be no going back. The salt would have lost its savor. Our witness would have lost its Savior.

Look at how well this fits the spirit of the analogy. Once we have wounded a person by judging them for their sin or even subconsciously exhibiting an air of moral superiority, we may have effectively destroyed our credibility as a love witness with that person forever.

Think about it. If we are loving and peaceable and then suddenly we are critical—even if we later revert to loving and peaceable—the last revision won't be trustworthy in the eyes of those who have seen us in both states. People will remember we were salty before and then we changed. Even if we become salty again, they will understand we have the capacity to deliver an unsavory experience. Those persons would have to take every new interaction with (gag!) a grain of salt.

This makes much more sense than our conventional view that we are no longer capable of clean living once we fall into sin. Our propensity to sin is a common bond we share with the world. We are all sinners. We should all hope for the possibility for redemption every time we fall. Saltiness is the subtle, unspoken witness of kingdom living. Saltiness is the Jesus Method, the whole seven-step process.

We can also move to the other end of the spectrum and over-salt. You know how food tastes when it's over salted. Going beyond kingdom living into the realm of overt witness (unless we're asked, specifically called by the Spirit, or gifted as an evangelist) is over salting. Too much salt is what causes us to be *trampled by men*. Later in the sermon, in a section about verbal witnessing, Jesus will return to the subject of being *trampled* in more detail.

I am a Facebook friend with a man who posts a different Scripture passage four or five times a day. Some would say he's on fire for the Lord, but I think he's a little too salty. He rarely gives anything of his own life. I don't know if he likes to fish or golf. I don't know if he's married or has a girlfriend. He doesn't use scripture to speak to people; he uses it to speak at people. I love God's word, and when someone gives me a verse I tend to savor it because it can tell me as much about where they are in life as it does about God. Not so with this man's posts. All I can deduce from his posts is that he is saved and we're not, so we better get saved because God says so. I scroll past his entries as quickly as I can.

If we misspeak (or should I say verbally miswitness) we may be trampled by men. To be trampled is the opposite consequence in the battle for souls. If our actions do the talking: *blessed are the feet of the messenger who brings the gospel of peace*. The verse is from the Old Testament and quoted in the New, and it pointedly doesn't say, "blessed are the *lips* of the messenger who brings the gospel of peace" although logically we would pay attention to a messenger's lips rather than his feet. Our feet (actions) are more effective than the words of our mouth.

While logic confirms that saltiness is showing the positive side of Christianity, the extrapolation against overt witness might seem more tenuous. The conclusion should become more apparent once we see the way the next section describes the proper witnessing sequence.

The passage begins *you are the light of the world* and so it parallels *you are the salt of the earth*. They both start with "*you are the*" as a grammatical construct to signal they are to be viewed as a single subject. Jesus often used rhetorical flourishes to unite his thoughts into a theme. Matthew 5:14–16 elaborates on the saltiness metaphor:

> *You are the light of the world.*
> *A city on a hill cannot be hidden.*
> *Neither do people light a lamp and put it under a bowl.*
> *Instead they put it on its stand,*
> *And it gives light to everyone in the house.*
> *In the same way, let your light shine before men,*
> *That they may see your good deeds*
> *And praise your Father in heaven.* (Matt 5:14–16)

Jesus starts out on the same societal scale, salt of the *earth* and light of the *world*. Then he zooms in to show it in its proper structure. The light first illuminates a house and then all the lights in all the houses together cast the light of a city on a hill. People need something visible and it is all of the lights from all of the houses together. Jesus is painting a word picture.

Each of us is a light on a stand. We should give light to everyone in our house, believer or not. Again, this shows that *light* is not overt witness. We don't give the gospel to the members of our household every evening after sundown. We give it once, or a few times and then we let our actions continue to witness. Jesus' illustration makes it clear that the *actions* of kingdom living are the light we bring to our home.

We asked what the quintessential characteristic of salt might be and now we can ask the same question of light. Because they are parallel passages, when Jesus answers the one, he answers both. He is specific. The light in question is a light that shines on our good deeds to our Father's glory. *Let your light shine before men, that they may see your good deeds and praise your Father in heaven.*

Jesus is talking about positive contributions. Good deeds should be apparent to others. People will see them, realize we are doing them because we are Christians, and give praise to our Father in heaven. First we *declare* our allegiance to Jesus and our Father and then we let our living do the talking.

Can you see how we so often we turn Jesus' words inside out? Our concept of salt and light is like that. Jesus talks about doing good deeds and we change his words to mean keeping other people and ourselves from doing bad deeds. In fact, the idea of salt being a responsibility to keep others from doing bad deeds is particularly prevalent in Christianity today. I bought into the concept wholeheartedly before I understood this sermon better.

For example, acquaintances that curse in our hearing may offend us, (or at least, cursing offends me) so we try to stop them. We say to ourselves that we are being salt, giving the world little reminders of how God thinks they should act. That's not being salt at all; it is us trying to impose our will upon them. God doesn't impose his will on them. He gives them a choice. In the same way, we shouldn't impose our will on that acquaintance. We need instead to show him our good deeds. The pertinent good deed here would be to exhibit meekness. We need not fret about the evil in other men.

The deeds Jesus is talking about are the little ones as well as the big ones. We so rarely get to do the big things, but little deeds are put in our path more often than we notice. Small deeds accumulate. Small deeds are the point of kingdom living. Salt is used in small quantities. We don't use a teaspoon of salt with each teaspoon of food. The light of each flickering lamp accumulates to illuminate a whole city. Small deeds are the basis of kingdom living.

Do you leave a tract with your tip after dinner? If so, make sure it accompanies a generous tip. Otherwise the wait staff will think you are serving Mammon instead of God. You might think the tract is a good thing but the world thinks a 20% tip is a good thing. This command isn't about God seeing what we do and praising us, it is about the world seeing what we do and praising our Father in heaven.

I don't leave a gospel tract, but I bow for prayer before eating. I feel that if I don't leave a decent tip I am in a small way contributing to Christians losing their saltiness. If I don't have money for a nice tip, I'll go to Wendy's or eat at home. It's that important.

We need to declare ourselves. How else can others know Whom to thank for our good deeds? Christian deeds display the salt and light of which Jesus speaks. Unless we change the way we think, we will display badly. It is the plight of fallen humanity. Since we know we are incapable of always behaving in a godly manner we must pay special attention to the good deeds concept.

Good deeds so others might praise our Father in heaven ought to be a default position in our lives because it compensates for our all-too-human failures. God gave us the Law a few thousand years into human history because we had become so proficient at ignoring what he had written on our consciences. The written codes removed any excuses we had for acting badly.

Today we remain equally proficient at searing our consciences when it is expedient, with or without the codes. We understand much of the Law and we understand our newer freedoms in Jesus, but we don't realize that this freedom extends only to our relationship with God. The rules for human interaction remain valid. This is because the character of humanity changes slowly. None of the rules that address how we think and act toward others have been repudiated.

The two greatest commandments are to love God with everything we've got and then love our neighbor as our self. Amazingly, Jesus is about to turn them upside down. At times we must exhibit a special discernment with our visible actions. We may find it better in certain situations to put our love for our neighbor first. This won't signal to them that we love them more than we love God, it will be so they can see our good deeds (toward them) and *praise our Father in heaven*. This is the idea in the parable of the Good Samaritan.

Jesus also showed us with his life that the rules are not inflexible. We are allowed to break the lesser rule to fulfill the greater. That was his point when he healed on the Sabbath or counseled us to drop our stones unless we were sinless ourselves. Healing on the Sabbath broke a commandment, yet Jesus remained sinless. Not stoning an adulteress broke a command, and yet Jesus was not leading them into a sin of omission.

If our neighbor is in need, yet we won't help them because we are leaving for church, we are fulfilling the greatest commandments in the proper order but our neighbor will remain unimpressed. If we take the time to help them, they may very well see our good deed and praise our Father in heaven.

God has a vision for how we are to think about and treat each other. The Law is the Official Rulebook, given for our benefit. But we've come to care more for the rules than for God's vision. The fact that the rules have changed but God's vision is unchanging is the best proof we have that the two are not the same. Jesus will address this momentarily but first I would like to think about the rules themselves using his teaching on judgment. Not judging implies that we should heed the rules for ourselves rather than impose them on others.

We think it can't be helped if we cause suffering in the implementation of the rules. Yet it isn't our job to implement the rules. God implements the rules he wrote; he's the Referee. We're participants in the game. We can't call fouls on the other team. We only need to make sure our own conduct is within the rules.

Jesus said doing unto others sums up the Law and the Prophets (Matthew 7:12). He said the Law and the Prophets depend on loving God more than we love ourselves; and loving everyone else as much as ourselves. If we can love in that manner we can throw the Rulebook out because we would have *fulfilled* everything the Law and the Prophets require of us. Jesus loved in this manner.

> *Do not think that I have come to abolish the Law and the Prophets;*
> *I have not come to abolish them but to fulfill them.*
> *I tell you the truth, until heaven and earth disappear,*
> *not the smallest letter, not the least stroke of the pen,*
> *will by any means disappear from the Law until everything is accomplished.* (Matt 5:17–18)

The Law is here to stay because there is still much to be accomplished.

Yet some of the Law *has* disappeared. We no longer perform the Temple sacrifices. We aren't bound by the dietary or separation restrictions. We don't observe the Hebrew festivals or Holy Days. Jesus promised that *not the least stroke of the pen* (I love *jot or tittle* from the KJV) will disappear but it seems as though we've erased huge swaths.

Even orthodox Jews don't make thrice-yearly pilgrimages to the Temple for the required sacrifices, so it seems a few jots and tittles have disappeared. We need to reconcile the reality with these verses in Matthew. Did Jesus get it wrong? Do I need to fly to Jerusalem and buy a couple of doves for sacrifice?

No and, no. Doves are safe around me and Jesus didn't get it wrong. He was being ever so subtle. This passage is one of the rare instances where he means the opposite of what he seems to have said. I realize I sound like I'm being inconsistent. I'm the guy who thinks do not judge means we shouldn't judge. Now I'm about to argue that the Law that will by no means pass away is passing away.

If we look closely, we'll see that Jesus doesn't say here that none of the Law will pass away. He says none of it will pass away until one of two things happen. He gives us two situations in which jots and tittles will disappear.

- When Heaven and earth disappear
- When everything pertaining to a law is accomplished.

We think we don't need to worry about the first scenario. If Heaven and earth aren't here, we won't be either. The book of Revelation tells us Heaven and earth will indeed flee from before the presence of the Lord at judgment. In the new Heaven on earth, we won't need a single jot.

The second is easier to explain with examples. Jesus' once-and-for-all sacrifice eliminated the need for the Temple sacrifice. Peter's dream removed the dietary restrictions because the kingdom of Heaven is now among us. Paul said it is up to the individual conscience (the new province of the Holy Spirit) to determine whether or not we observe the Holy Days. Jesus accomplished more at the cross than we realize.

You might argue that Jesus said *none* of it would disappear until *everything* is accomplished. He might not have. When I looked up *pas* in the

Strong's the first definition is not *all* or *everything*, it is *each*. This would better describe reality as we observe it, as God ordained it. The jots and tittles have disappeared as *each* thing has been *accomplished*.

The last six commandments describe the ideal in our human relationships, and so they have not passed away. The first four commandments described the ideal relationship with God. They *have* changed, because Jesus brought about a better means of relationship. We are no longer separated from God, the veil to the Holy of Holies has been ripped asunder, and so the Laws of separation have passed away, every jot and tittle. Better things have replaced them.

Maybe it should surprise us that God changeth not, but the rules of engagement have. The first century Jews were more than surprised, they were shocked. That's why God had to take the Temple away. They were still using it for the daily sacrifices and the need for such sacrifices had passed away.

A funny thing happened to Judaism after 70 CE. It evolved to become much closer to kingdom living. Jewish thought replaced the Temple sacrifice with *mitzvahs*, good deeds. The sacrifice inherent in a *mitzvah* is self-denial. Denial of self: so others might *see our good deeds and praise our Father in Heaven*. Sound familiar?

The change in our day of rest is a bit trickier. The traditional Sabbath was on the seventh day of the week to commemorate God's seven-day creation. Our new observance is on the first day of each new week to show that Jesus did something new when he rose from the dead.

Jesus replaced old rules with new ones because we misinterpreted the old rules. The Sabbath commandment had to change because instead of freeing the Jews for rest and worship, it had become a burden. The commandments were meant for our good, but the religious powers perverted them. They took the Sabbath as an outward sign of our vassalage to God, so Jesus had to explain that *the Sabbath was made for man, not man for the Sabbath* (Mark 2:27).

We tend to miss the point as well. A common meme for us today is that "the New Testament confirms all of the Ten Commandments except for the Sabbath regulation." God didn't abolish the Sabbath; he changed it to a new day with new meaning. Had he abolished it, we would no longer have a day that *was made for man*. All the laws were made for us. We know this. They were instituted for our good. God changed the laws because Christ radically changed things, and the Holy Spirit changes us as a result.

All of us have been changed, believer or not. The Spirit changes us and the rest of the world is changed by our example. Western civilization is a far different place than it might have been without Christ, and the east is catching up. The early church taught us the value of an individual life, the dignity of all people regardless of stature, and the supreme value of agape love. Believer or not, we are all better for these changes. John Lennon could have never written *All You Need is Love* without the influence begun in the early church. It would have never occurred to him.

Love is the greatest part of God's plan and he expects us to advance his plan zealously. We are making progress in carrying it out. Today, even the wicked world around us understands agape love. That wasn't true twenty centuries ago. The world doesn't live it out very well sometimes, but then neither do we.

If and when we can love that well, we can throw away the Rulebook, for we too will have fulfilled the commandments. The way we can love that well is spelled out in the Beatitudes. They are a modification of the commandments given at Sinai in the same way Sunday is the new Sabbath.

> *Anyone who breaks one of the least of these commandments*
> *And teaches others to do the same*
> *Will be called least in the kingdom of heaven,*
> *But whoever practices and teaches these commands*
> *Will be called great in the kingdom of heaven.*
> *For I tell you that unless your righteousness surpasses that of the Pharisees and the teachers of the law,*
> *you will certainly not enter the kingdom of heaven.* (Matt 5:19)

The above verses are pivotal to the Sermon. We will refer to them repeatedly because the whole remainder of the sermon explains exactly how our righteousness can exceed that of the Pharisees and why it is important.

We misinterpret the *commandments* and *commands* in verse 19. We illogically insert the Ten Commandments. The sermon isn't about keeping the Ten Commandments. *The Pharisees and the teachers of the law* worked to keep the Ten Commandments and hundreds of others. Yet, our righteousness needs to surpass their righteousness.

When Jesus says *one of the least of* these *commandments*, he means the Beatitudes. The Seven Beatitudes are the proper implementation of the Ten Commandments. This is how our righteousness can surpass the righteousness of the Pharisees and teachers of the Law. Do you remember our new meaning for righteousness? Proper righteousness is living with God's great plan in mind even when it is to our earthly detriment. Yet, even with all of these textual clues, we jump to the conclusion that the commandments we must not break are the big Ten. I have heard many sermons that make this mistaken point.

The pastors who make this error are opposing a teaching of Jesus, but at least (according to this passage) they will still get to remain in the kingdom.

However, they will be called the *least in the kingdom*. We shouldn't make the same mistake. This should confirm that God's rules are not the same as God's vision.

Are you beginning to see how terribly we misread Jesus? We so badly misinterpret his tone because we underestimate his love. We can't feel how every word is *drenched* with love because we are unaccustomed to it. It is beyond the normal human experience. No one has ever spoken to us like this before. This love is what made Jesus perfect. His sinlessness was a result of his flawless ability to love. This is why he could break the Sabbath commandment and yet remain sinless. He broke the commandment to show love.

Our misunderstandings drastically change meanings. We think Jesus is saying, "Don't think I came here to get rid of the law. No siree, the law is here until the end of time and you better start getting it right. If you get it right and teach others to get it right then we'll give you praise, but if you get it wrong . . . In fact, you've got to do a lot better than the Pharisees if you want to see heaven."

Jesus is actually saying, "I have fulfilled the law. I love my Father with all my heart. I love him with all my mind. I love him with all of my life. I love each and every one of you at least as much as I love myself. Even though I have personally fulfilled the law by doing this, it is not passing away yet. Before I get rid of the law, you will have to fulfill it as I have. Love as I do. Love is how you will fulfill the Law and the Prophets. When you all love like that, the law will pass away. Teach others to love and we'll call you great. This is how we fulfill our Father's commandments because this is how we fulfill his plan. This is your work and our Father's will."

Jesus stood in opposition to the Pharisees because they didn't view Scripture through the hermeneutic of love. They had missed the point and this is what made them hypocritical. Like us, they searched for meaning and application for their lives in the pages of Scripture. The tassels with portions of the Law that they would hang from their wrists and foreheads were the cultural equivalent of the tracts some of us carry today, part of their witness.

I don't view the Pharisees as such a bad bunch of guys. I think of them as being a lot like you and me (or at least a lot like me). They weren't priests and they usually weren't even Levites so they had no priestly authority. The Pharisees were men who loved God and studied his word. Pharisees were like Jesus.

The Pharisees imparted rules—they were zealous for God's rules—instead of doing what imparts life. They were zealous for the rules but missed the love. We are zealous for the rules even today. We are zealous for a slightly different set of rules, but the rules nevertheless remain paramount in our minds.

Kingdom living isn't about following the Law. I'll remind you of the quote from Paul: *For if a law had been given that could impart life, then righteousness would certainly have come by the law* (Gal 3:21b). Righteousness doesn't come by the Law, but by running after love, kindness, and peace through the faith Jesus gives us. Paul confirms it here by equating righteousness with imparting life.

As the Pharisees grew more numerous they became more powerful. They were granted seats in the Sanhedrin. As they gained influence, they began to use their power to extrapolate new laws from their interpretations. Where before they had tried their best to follow God, now they were trying their best to make others follow God. Unfortunately, they weren't meek. Their ability to love had succumbed to the rules.

We have to exceed that old idea of righteousness. Jesus wants us to value life and pursue meekness and kindness. If the Beatitudes are the commandments Jesus says we can't teach others to break, then we must be teaching the importance of love over the rest of the law. This is key. Love is greater than the Law. There is a hierarchy to the commandments and love is preeminent. We can sin with love as our motivation and recognize that the "sin" is not sin.

Let me give a concrete illustration. Let's imagine we lived in occupied Poland during World War II and were harboring Jews from persecution. If Nazis came to our door and asked if there were Jews living with us, wouldn't we lie? We've been taught lying is a sin but in this example *not lying* would be the sin.

Our example is cut and dried but in more mundane circumstances we have difficulty applying this idea that love is the primary commandment. In John (because Jesus saw that the disciples just weren't grasping it) he put it a different way. He said, *A new command I give you. Love one another* (John 13:34).

10

Sin and Perfection

Now, finally, Jesus is ready to talk about sin.

Although he doesn't miss the opportunity to tell us how terrible sin is, and how harmful, it isn't his major theme. Jesus wants to teach us something altogether different. He shakes us from our complacency and makes confront the assumptions of our deceitful and wicked hearts. His message here is so revolutionary in fact, that we have to depart from the narrative methods we have used so far in this book. Rather than teasing the message from the text gradually, I feel we must start with the conclusion and then show how he makes it.

Jesus makes one point in this extended passage, one shocking and inescapable point. He makes it repeatedly to make sure we grasp it and embeds it within a structure that should keep us from any other conclusion. He doesn't want us to rationalize it away or spin it to mean something different. He wants us to realize it is true and change how we think about ourselves.

Jesus' point is this: *we sin more than we care to admit and there's not a lot we can do about it.* That's how he sees us. He doesn't admonish us for sinning, at least not here. He doesn't tell us to go and sin no more. His one point of emphasis is how sinful we truly are. The kingdom can't advance forcefully until we understand this very basic idea. We still sin, we still sin a lot, and we need to stop taking comfort in the idea that some people are worse than we are.

You know what we've done with the passage. We've spun it like a top. We've taken Jesus' grim description of our mindset and turned it into a pat on the back for achieving some new, higher standard. Jesus would be spinning in his grave if he were still in his grave.

Understanding the interconnectedness of Jesus' thoughts begins to pay real dividends in this pericope. He repeats certain phrases as a verbal glue to make sure we don't break his thoughts into its component parts because to understand his point we have to see the passage as a whole.

Jesus uses a rhetorical structure that is sublime. He contrasts our common sin with more serious transgressions. He does this to establish our natural mindset. We tend to minimize our lesser sins by comparing them to the things we don't do. Jesus plays with our tendency, for it was also the tendency of the Pharisees (whose righteousness, don't forget, we are learning to exceed). He starts with the worst sin we can think of, murder. Each subsequent sin on his list is slightly less heinous. It's a descending scale.

At the same time, the contrasting examples (the things we *do* do) ascend on an altogether separate scale. Each subsequent example shows a greater measure of pride. By time he gets to his last example, it should begin to dawn on us. Jesus wasn't teaching about sin so much as pride.

There can be no way around his point. Our pride makes us think we are making progress on our sin problem, but we're not, and we can't, because pride is also at the root of our sin problem. Our pride deceives us. That's what makes it such a formidable enemy; pride works both ends of the human condition. Pride leads to sin and lessening sin lead to pride.

Let me repeat Jesus' premise so we can keep it in mind as we study the passage. *We sin more than we know and there's not a lot we can do about it.* It is an alarming conclusion, but it needn't depress us if we remember the love with which he spoke. I know *there's not a lot we can do about it* probably raises some hackles but I won't backpedal on the statement. And really, if we could do something about it, would Jesus have had to go to the cross?

> "You have heard that it was said to the people long ago,
> 'Do not murder, and anyone who murders will be subject to judgment.'
> But I tell you that anyone who is angry with his brother
> will be subject to judgment. (Matt 5:21)

Jesus contrasts murder with anger. We do the same thing, all the time, but from an opposite perspective. We might think, "Sure I got angry, but it's not like I killed someone." We contrast our lesser sin with the greater sins of others and it makes us feel better. We compare and think, "Hey, I'm not so bad." Jesus thinks, "You haven't killed anyone, but look at the hurt your anger causes."

Jesus points out that we can destroy others with bitterness, rage, judgment, or a sense of superiority. These are lesser degrees of the same sin. Jesus says, "Murderers deserve judgment, but so do people who call other people stupid. Do you still think you're not so bad?"

Implicit in his leading phrase for each example (*you have heard that it was said*) was the Pharisees' knowledge of the Law and their sense of superiority as they tried to live it out. The Pharisees didn't commit murder or adultery. They didn't get into shouting matches with their brothers. Even their vitriolic interactions with Jesus were couched in measured and pious arguments. They were well mannered and reasonable.

Most of the Christians I know are well mannered, and a great many of them are also reasonable. These traits may have more to do with how we would prefer to be perceived than with how we are inside. We shouldn't be surprised that Jesus was less well-mannered than the Pharisees. Civility is important, but not a worthwhile life goal. Jesus didn't say, "Blessed are the well-mannered and reasonable, for they will avoid Hell."

Jesus doesn't concede our abject condition. Throughout the Bible he calls us to battle against our natural predilections. However, he doesn't do that here. He hasn't forgotten the overall premise that began this train of thought. We are the salt of the earth and the light of the world. Both our misguided grasp for sinless perfection and our one shot at true perfection affect unbelievers because of the mindsets that accompany either quest. We think an admission of sin harms our witness, but Jesus knows the admission is better than the alternatives: hypocrisy and a peculiar form of self-deceit that leads to judging others.

Today, we are actually taught an opposite lesson. We comprehend the part of the lesson that deals with sin but we totally miss the part that addresses pride and how it hurts our witness.

In fact, because we've learned that the point of this lesson is *how even certain thoughts can be sin*, we often impart to others an even greater sense of our newly self-realized superiority. After all, wouldn't this new realization make us more sensitive to sin than the Pharisees? This is our traditional take-away. We exceed the righteousness of the Pharisees because we realize that thoughts and attitudes can be sin while the Pharisees were focused on external acts.

This "realization" that thoughts can be sinful is (as many of our pastors like to remind us) a *new higher standard* we are held to as Christians. Not only are we responsible for our actions, we are now also responsible for our thoughts. Once we grasp this higher standard, we think our righteousness will surely exceed that of the Pharisees. Instead, it leads us to become even bigger Pharisees than the Pharisees. Our interpretation leads us to exceed them in the wrong way. In the same way the Pharisees could pray, "Thank you God that I am not like other sinners," we think we can now pray, "Thank you Lord that I am not like the Pharisees. You have taught me your new higher standard."

There is no new, higher standard. It is a figment of our imaginations. Scripturally, we have always been responsible for our thoughts as well as our actions. God gave examples in the Old Testament of the importance of thoughts and attitudes. The Ten Commandments deal with thoughts specifically when God says *you shall not covet*. Coveting is thought or attitude. The standard isn't new, it has always been in place and it has always been too high for us.

Jesus' point is not that we should eliminate sinful thoughts, but that we should eliminate a sense of pride in our progress. Remember, pride is the opposite of love. Our sense of coming closer to this new "higher standard" can silently negate our living witness.

The mission here is to correct the misperceptions we have about ourselves so we don't inadvertently communicate negative non-verbal attitudes. Jesus' words in verses 21 and 22 are the first examples in his argument.

> *"You have heard that it was said to the people long ago,*
> *'Do not murder, and anyone who murders will be subject to judgment.'*
> *But I tell you that anyone who is angry with his brother will be subject to judgment.*(Matt 5:21a)

Jesus doesn't mean an angry argument, he'll deal with that next. Here he means the anger we hold inside, even if we don't express it. Jesus challenges us to look more deeply into the law by moving us from the extreme external expression of murder to the extreme internal expressions of emotions and attitudes. Attitudes are and always have been inherent in the law.

None of us can say we've never been angry. The problem is that we often aren't troubled by our anger. We think we have a right to be angry. We have a term for it—righteous anger. In our minds, it doesn't even matter whether people hurt us intentionally or not. We can build as strong of a case in our minds against thoughtless acts as we can against deliberate ones. What happens in our minds is exactly the starting point for this section on sin.

Jesus means: *"Don't think you are doing well because you haven't murdered anyone. You are still walking around with bitterness in your heart. Do you think people around you can't sense it? This very attitude will destroy your witness. If you claim you are forgiven, but won't forgive others, it makes them think, "If this is what it means to follow Jesus, I want nothing to do with it."*

Jesus wants something special from us. As usual, that something special is love. The love comes from recognizing our sinfulness along with the gratitude of knowing we've been forgiven. Don't forget that Jesus explained in Luke 7:47 that he who (realizes that he) has been forgiven much, loves much.

> *Again, anyone who says to his brother, 'Raca,' is answerable to the Sanhedrin.* (Matt 5:21b)

Now we move to the external. *Raca* was a term of derision in much the same way we might call someone an idiot or moron. It does not carry the sense of being morally deficient as much as it connotes someone being stupid. Raca was like a swear word to the Jews of that day. It is also a comment directed toward a *brother*, a fellow Jew. Jesus reminds his hearers that this expression was already considered serious enough to be subject to judgment, in this case by the Sanhedrin.

The Jews divided the world into Jews and Gentiles. We use the same concept when we divide the world into Christians and unbelievers. Leave it to our loving Savior to divide us instead into brothers and neighbors. His kingdom focus is evident in his descriptions.

When we exhibit angry or disdainful sentiments towards a brother or sister, we are answerable to our church leadership (the modern correlative of the Sanhedrin). Now Jesus broadens the plain by telling us that when we denounce *any person* we are answerable to *him*.

> *But anyone who says, 'You fool!' will be in danger of the fire of hell.* (Matt 5:21c)

Since the person *says* something aloud rather than thinking it, our new, higher standard theory begins to unravel. Speaking is an action. Jesus' teaching centers on the word "fool."

While *raca* called someone's mental capacity into question, a *fool* could be intelligent but was morally misguided. To call someone a fool was an offense in Jesus' mind, but it wasn't answerable to the Sanhedrin because Jews thought of Gentiles as inherently amoral—fools. We think in much the same way today. Aren't unbelievers the people we are most likely to think of as morally deficient? We wonder how they can be so smart and still not "get it," the *fools*! When we complain about the foolish, wicked world we live in, we're somehow flirting with the fires of Hell.

Jesus forces us to explore our attitudes of anger and contempt by showing us how squarely they fall into self-righteous opinions of superiority. Saying "*raca*" to someone or calling someone a fool are perfect examples of this. In either case, we have determined that we hold a position superior enough to make such judgments. Saying "*raca*" (calling them an idiot) suggests our greater intelligence. We wouldn't call Einstein an idiot because we know he was smarter than we are. Calling someone a "fool" is much the same thing. To do so implies we are in a position to determine another's degree of foolishness.

> *"Therefore, if you are offering your gift at the altar*
> *and there remember that your brother has something against you,*
> *leave your gift there in front of the altar.*
> *First go and be reconciled to your brother; then come and offer your gift.*
> (Matt 5:23–24)

Therefore ties verses 23 and 24 to the previous passage. When we worship we come humbly before the Creator of the Universe. Jesus wonders about the depth of humility and its effect on worship in a person who has just called someone else a fool or a moron. Have you ever had a boss who was fawning and polite in the presence of his boss but a tyrant when his boss wasn't around? That's the principle here.

What must God think when he hears what some of us have said to each other in the halls before service? The people who can give unsolicited "godly" advice are probably the same people who can effortlessly slip into worship mode, satisfied that they have done their part. But what about the recipient of that slight? They now have *something against* the advice-giver. Can they worship joyfully?

Jesus puts reconciliation above even worship here. It is an astounding thought but it probably shouldn't be. He thinks so highly of reconciliation that he is willing (just to make his redundant point) to invert the greatest commandments.

Now Jesus is going to tell us we need to sacrifice ourselves monetarily and even with an enemy. This will again show us how these ideas don't just apply to our relationships with other believers. It is the end of a logic progression: fellow believer (*raca*), the world (fool), and now, enemies (legal adversaries). We must treat them all well.

This next vignette is a break in the narrative flow *(you have heard it said . . . but I say to you)* meant to highlight our self-deception by its rhetorical difference. We aren't right just because we think we are.

> *"Settle matters quickly with your adversary who is taking you to court.*
> *Do it while you are still with him on the way, or he may hand you over to the judge,*
> *and the judge may hand you over to the officer, and you may be thrown into prison.*
> *I tell you the truth, you will not get out until you have paid the last penny.*
> (Matt 5:25–26)

These verses show our propensity for pride and self-deception. We may think we're in the right but an impartial judge might not agree. Pride distorts our view of reality, but Jesus tells us *the truth*. The truth is that sometimes *we* are in the wrong, and we will have to pay what we truly owe.

Now back to the main narrative. Jesus' next example is not as serious as murder.

> "You have heard that it was said, 'Do not commit adultery.'
> But I tell you that anyone who looks at a woman lustfully
> has already committed adultery with her in his heart.
> If your right eye causes you to sin, gouge it out and throw it away.
> It is better for you to lose one part of your body
> than for your whole body to be thrown into hell.
> And if your right hand causes you to sin, cut it off and throw it away.
> It is better for you to lose one part of your body
> than for your whole body to go into hell. (Matt 5:27–30)

Jesus shows here just how terrible sin truly is. Lust is probably the original victimless crime. It is not rape and it is not even seduction. Lust lives within the heart. Nobody gets hurt, right? Jesus disagrees. If we *look* with lust . . . pluck out the right eye. If our right hand causes us to sin (and most of us are right-handed) that's the hand he says to cut off. Sin is that serious.

On the other hand, Jesus isn't really advising amputation. The eye doesn't cause us to sin and neither does the hand. That's why Jesus says *if* they cause you to sin. He knows they don't. Our lustful impulses come from within, from the part of the mind we call the heart. Jesus is telling us how harmful sin is and how grievous it is to the Father, even when we think it is relatively harmless.

Lust in any manifestation is not a victimless crime. We are the first victims. It makes us malcontent. It raises our expectations to the level of our fantasies and that harms our relationships. Polling of Christians acknowledges that we are just as likely to view pornography as non-Christians are. We are also slightly more likely to get divorced. That's right, *more* likely.

Jesus is working his way down *our* perceived scale of sins. Starting with the worst sin and moving to the lesser. Lust isn't as bad as hurting somebody. Or is it?

> "It has been said,
> 'Anyone who divorces his wife must give her a certificate of divorce.'
> But I tell you that anyone who divorces his wife,
> except for marital unfaithfulness,
> causes her to become an adulteress,
> and anyone who marries the divorced woman commits adultery. (Matt 5:31–32)

Is Jesus suggesting that the lust of the previous verses could lead to divorce? Is he telling us that our victimless crime can have many victims? I believe he is. One of my original premises was that Jesus' thoughts within the sermon are linked. Here we reap a benefit of that premise. Instead of treating lust and divorce as separate subjects, as we most often do, we can see that the one can lead to the other.

Now that we're aware of the gravity of lust, I want to back up and look at Jesus' solution. He doesn't truly want us to pluck out, cut off, or even guillotine. *It's a joke!* Jesus is taking a poke at our pride and our methods; the futility of thinking we can make any progress on our own. I can only imagine Jesus offering this advice with a twinkle in his eye and a slight smile on his lips. We need to see this as a joke because it helps us to understand that Jesus is being loving and gentle. Without the joke, we might extrapolate anger in his tone. Without the joke we need to seriously consider amputation.

We can tell Jesus was joking because of his whimsical conclusion: we can avoid the fires of Hell by cutting off or plucking out. If this is true, we don't need his help except perhaps as an anesthesiologist. He's making fun of our prideful mindset, not offering an alternative to the cross.

Jesus may have been joking, but he wants us to realize how bad sin is and how bad we are at refraining from sin. That's why he reminds us that lust can lead to divorce. He knows we lust much more often than we commit adultery and we get angry with others even if we've never seriously considered murder. He wants us to acknowledge that we are still sinful and more than occasionally.

Jesus realizes better than we do how chronically sinful we actually are. He gives us these examples to help us understand this because, in his eyes, the only thing worse than sin would be *sinning while thinking we're actually doing fairly well.*

The next few verses (once I understood why they were there) were the ones that caused me to rethink the whole passage. They present a surprising twist that modifies Jesus' whole thought progression. It startled me to realize the following verses contain no sin. Up until now, it has been sin, sin, sin. Murder, anger, superiority, specious lawsuits, adultery, lust, and . . . *keeping an oath?*

> "Again, you have heard that it was said to the people long ago,
> 'Do not break your oath, but keep the oaths you have made to the Lord.'
> But I tell you, Do not swear at all: either by heaven, for it is God's throne;
> or by the earth, for it is his footstool;
> or by Jerusalem, for it is the city of the Great King.
> And do not swear by your head,
> for you cannot make even one hair white or black.
> Simply let your 'Yes' be 'Yes,' and your 'No,' 'No';
> anything beyond this comes from the evil one. (Matt 5:33–37)

This example of oaths is the key to the whole passage. It should send shock waves all the way back to *do not murder*; no, all the way back to *exceed the righteousness of the Pharisees*. Jesus has tricked us, and to good effect. He has pandered to our expectations that more righteousness = less sin. But keeping an oath wasn't a sin. The Hebrew Bible specifically instructs us to keep any oath we make to the Lord. Yet it is exactly this that Jesus rejects.

It should begin to dawn on us, or perhaps slap us in the face, to understand that Jesus was never truly speaking of sin. In a masterful gambit, he was setting us up to knock us off our high horses. He used examples of sin, but his real subject has been pride. We should see that now as we consider his teaching on oaths.

As Jesus has moved down in degree of seriousness with each sin example, he moved up in degree of pride. Murder is more serious than adultery, but we feel more remorse for anger than we do for a lustful look. To keep an oath isn't a sin at all, but pride-wise? Whoa!

All along, Jesus has been setting us up to get us to this passage. He wants us to reexamine our underlying mindset. We can't swear *by things* because we didn't make *any thing*. God made it all. We can't even swear by some part of ourselves because we can't control ourselves very well either. We can't even control the color of our hair (Grecian Formula for Men and Lady Clairol notwithstanding).

Actually, hair dye is a particularly useful metaphor. It is a temporary fix, and a prideful attempt to change the way the world sees us. That's the best we can manage when we think clean living is a proper witness. We can "dye our hair" but before long, the world will see our roots. The roots are our pride in our progress. If love is God's tool, pride is the Devil's. That's why Jesus said anything more than yes or no *comes from the evil one*.

Jesus opened this subject with our righteousness needing to exceed the righteousness of the Pharisees. The Pharisees had clean living down cold. If they were Christians we would think well of their Christian walk. If not showing their sinful nature publicly was a light unto the world, Israel during Jesus' lifetime would have been the land of the midnight sun.

Now, with oaths, he directs us back to that sin behind all the other sins he has mentioned, pride. The Pharisees had two shortcomings, two places we need to exceed them in righteousness. The first was their understanding of sin. A major sin of the Pharisees was *thinking* they were better. They acted better. They taught us to be better. Yet they weren't poor in spirit. They couldn't acknowledge that they were as sinful as other people were.

They didn't murder but they became angry. They called other people fools because they were more learned in the law. They didn't commit adultery but they lusted after women in their hearts. They thought their private sin had no consequences and so they became blinded to their sinful natures. They were unable to see themselves as God saw them.

When they swore, they swore by all that was good and right. They swore by heaven and they swore by Jerusalem, but they didn't even have the right to swear by the color of the hair on their heads.

When Jesus expands on this mindset later, in one of the defining parables of the whole gospel, he describes a Pharisee this way: *The Pharisee stood up and prayed about himself: 'God, I thank you that I am not like other men—robbers, evildoers, adulterers –or even like this tax collector'* (Luke 18:11).

In a way the Pharisee had a right to pray like this. He wasn't bragging about being better in his own right, he was *thanking God* that he was better. He was giving glory for God's help. We're guilty of the same mindset today. We admit with one part of our brain, that we have no righteousness of our own. But with the rest of our brain, we thank God that we are better. Jesus means for us to know that we're not necessarily better. The whole passage is meant to teach us to stop thinking we are better and to realize we are still more sinful than we know.

The praying Pharisee did things others didn't. He tithed. He fasted twice a week. So while in a way he was right, in a bigger way he was so wrong. He was following the law but he wasn't living for the kingdom. He even did more than the law required when fasting twice a week. The Jews of that day were only required to fast on the Day of Atonement, *Yom Kippur*. This Pharisee would look at Christians today the way *we* look at the unsaved world around us—as ethical weaklings who can't even understand the rules, let alone live them out.

Actually, it is how the Pharisees looked at Jesus. They were zealous for what the Bible said and Jesus seemed to disregard it in so many ways. This teaching on oaths is an example. The Old Testament teaches exactly what Jesus said it did, that we must keep an oath we have made to the Lord. The Lord abrogated the Old Testament command because they had perverted the process. Instead of making a humble promise, they swore by Jerusalem, or the throne of the King.

We're all prideful, believer and unbeliever alike. Pride is tied to our mortality. While we walk this earth, we want to feel some special significance. Swearing by Jerusalem was a way of identifying with Jerusalem. It transferred some of the glory of God's city to themselves. They were special, in part, because God had chosen them and God had placed them in his chosen city.

Pride is what makes atheists believe Christians are foolish and weak. And for this same reason, Christians look down their noses at atheists. Pride is always the first sin to appear and the last sin to leave, and I doubt that it ever really does leave.

How do I know pride was the problem? From the way the praying Pharisee was described by the Holy Spirit. *To some who were confident of their own righteousness and looked down on everybody else, Jesus told this parable:* (Luke 18:9).

Are we confident of our own righteousness? Are we sure we sin less... and less horrendously? Sometimes I'm pretty sure that's true of myself. Yet even if it is true, it misses the point. The mistake is in making the comparison in the first place, and then hanging my hat on the difference.

We can tell if someone is confident in this way if we hear them complaining about the depravity in the surrounding world. It is incongruous. Would we listen to a killer complain about the murder rate? Do burglars lament stories of other home invasions? How then can a sinner complain about the sin of others? It is only because of pride that we can look down on anybody else.

We say, "Oh, the world is so wicked." That's wrong. That's the conclusion of the praying Pharisee. Our only complaint should be "Oh, the world doesn't know Jesus." Anything else smacks of pride and confidence in our own righteousness.

Jesus' goal in this section of the sermon wasn't to redefine our rules but to redefine the way we think about ourselves. Jesus wasn't telling us that he gave us the rules in Exodus but now he is upping the ante with a new, higher standard. He's telling us that we can't cover *any* of the bets.

We shouldn't think we are doing well just because we haven't taken someone's life. Rather we have to "fess up" to the fact we are still sinners even if we only get angry with others or think them more foolish than we are. We shouldn't point with pride to the fact that we haven't slept with someone outside of marriage because we need to acknowledge that we have lusted and fantasized.

Our ultimate fantasy is our own righteousness. If we have pride enough to think we can stand on a promise promised to the blameless, we are still too sinful to be blameless. The world may believe they are justified when they swear to something based on their own good name but we should know better. Humility should drive us to let our yes be yes and our no be no. Humility is us thinking rightly about us. An honest look inside will reveal we haven't earned the right to swear by anything.

So what is the antidote? We have this sin we can't quite beat and pride that's even worse. Do we work on them until we die? Of course! But there is something more; an additional step. An antidote doesn't flush poison from the system, it neutralizes it. We can't get rid of sin and pride but we have an antidote; an opposite that neutralizes.

You know what I'm going to say. I would hesitate to keep sounding the same note on my own, but Jesus is the one who keeps talking about it. Love is the antidote. Pride is thinking of ourselves first and love is thinking of others first. The opposite of sin in this sermon isn't right living; it is mercy. Using mercy to combat pride is a subset of our contention that the opposite of pride is love.

We are building to the first great crescendo in Jesus' sermon. He is about to show us how to be perfect. It has nothing to do with sin; it has everything to do with love and mercy. Jesus has consistently come back to this theme. He implied it in the Beatitudes and has just demonstrated the need for a better solution by speaking of sin and pride. Now he will further broaden his point.

> *"You have heard that it was said, 'Eye for eye, and tooth for tooth.'*
> *But I tell you, Do not resist an evil person.*
> *If someone strikes you on the right cheek, turn to him the other also.*
> *And if someone wants to sue you and take your tunic,*
> *let him have your cloak as well.*
> *If someone forces you to go one mile, go with him two miles.*
> *Give to the one who asks you,*
> *and do not turn away from the one who wants to borrow from you.* (Matt 5:38–42)

We can tell Jesus hasn't changed subjects because he begins with the same phrase, *you have heard that it was said*. Taking an eye for an eye was an important principle when it was first given. It limited retribution by the government, making the punishment fit the crime. The king couldn't have the cook beheaded because a prince broke his tooth on overdone barbeque. But this set of instructions isn't to a government, it is to individuals. A government can't give up a cloak or turn the other cheek.

As individuals, it is prideful in Jesus' estimation to believe we can exact retribution. It implies we have not only the right, but also the ability to make such a determination. Remember Lamech's boast that he killed a man for merely injuring him? Pride.

When we're injured, we plot revenge in our minds. We think of what we should have said, and of what we will say the next time we see the offender. The best definition of an enemy I have heard is that *our enemy is the person we lie awake at night thinking about*. We're built to seek justice but we crave vengeance.

Instead Jesus ask us to surrender our rights and grant more than is required. He is remarkably consistent. Don't strike back, show mercy; turn the other cheek. Do this and your adversary will see your good deeds and praise your Father in heaven. Jesus expects us to do the unexpected. Show mercy when none is due. Your Father is doing the very same with you. This is how we show Jesus to the world.

Jesus knows we can't show the world his sinlessness. We are incapable. Instead he gives us this more achievable alternative—to show mercy, unexpected mercy. This type of mercy is different from what the world understands as mercy because it is actually an *admission of our own sin*. We are most grateful and most merciful when we are in full understanding of the fact that we have been forgiven so much. Those who have been forgiven much, love much. If we remember how much we've been forgiven, we can empathize with others who need mercy.

And now we learn how to be perfect. Actually we are commanded to be perfect, it is not an option.

> *"You have heard that it was said, 'Love your neighbor and hate your enemy.'*
> *But I tell you: Love your enemies and pray for those who persecute you,*
> *that you may be sons of your Father in heaven.*
> *He causes his sun to rise on the evil and the good,*
> *and sends rain on the righteous and the unrighteous.*
> *If you love those who love you, what reward will you get?*
> *Are not even the tax collectors doing that?*
> *And if you greet only your brothers, what are you doing more than others?*
> *Do not even pagans do that?*
> *Be perfect, therefore, as your heavenly Father is perfect.* (Matt 5:43–48)

This is the culmination of the section that begins with Jesus telling us we are blessed if we are persecuted. Jesus tells us here to pray for those who persecute us and to do it to be like our Father. My pastor teaches that when we see "therefore" in a passage, we have to look at the preceding verses to see what it is *there for*. So when Jesus says *be perfect,* therefore, *as your Father in heaven is perfect* he is referring to the acts of our Father that he has just mentioned:

Our Father sends the sunshine even for evil people.
Our Father sends the nourishing rain even to the unrighteous.
Our Father loves his enemies.

These are some of the ways in which our Father is perfect. The same mindset is attainable by us. It allows us to be perfect in ways our heavenly Father is perfect. We can send proverbial sunshine and rain.

God loves and takes care of evil people, so who are we to judge them? If he nurtures the unrighteous, how can we in good conscience sit back and complain about their unrighteousness? Not only must we show his mercy and his love, we must do it in unexpected ways so (repeat after me) they may see our good deeds and praise our Father in heaven!

When something happens that causes me to have an enemy, when someone insults me or cheats me or hurts me in any of a thousand different ways, I don't want to love them. I want to hurt them back. I replay the offending incident in my mind, building my justification and magnifying the offense. I want vengeance but think of it as justice. Yet, a strange thing happens if I pray for them. Prayer stops the negative spiral. It re-humanizes my enemy. Not immediately, of course, praying for them is just the beginning of the process of healing. I have to heal from the incident before I can love my enemy and prayer for them hastens the healing process. Once I begin to heal, I can realize that I have done terrible things too, things not so different from the thing that hurt me. That was Jesus' point in the early part of this chapter, we sin almost reflexively and there's not a lot we can do about it. When we sin, we hurt people. Since I am forgiven, *true justice* would be that I forgive. God loves me without reservation and doesn't think it is too hard for me to do the same.

The Pharisee's fell short in two areas. They thought they could demonstrate God's righteousness, and they refused to filter the rules through love. The first is more understandable for we're taught clean living as a witness and feel pride when we think we've accomplished it to any degree. The second is crucial however, for it's the only real witness we're capable of achieving.

We must exceed the world's expectations. We must be merciful and loving when others wouldn't. It's the only way to show God to a world not used to seeing God in us. Love and mercy is the righteousness that exceeds that of the Pharisees, and our only chance for perfection.

The sermon is all about showing God's positive attributes instead of hiding our negative ones. Our responsibility for a proper kingdom witness should be clear. Jesus calls for us to be perfect, as our heavenly Father is perfect. He knows it is not beyond our capabilities because he commands us to do it.

11

Our Hidden Father

At first glance, Matthew 6:1 would seem to contradict what we've learned so far. Jesus taught us to be light before men so they may see our *good deeds and praise our Father in heaven.* Now Jesus will teach us *not* to let others see what we do.

There is no discrepancy. The key is in the middle line of the verse below. We can't do our deeds *to be seen*. Motive counts. Jesus will use variations of *to be seen* throughout this section to accentuate his point.

> *Be careful not to do your 'acts of righteousness' before men,*
> *to be seen by them.*
> *If you do, you will have no reward from your Father in heaven.*(Matt 6:1)

As Jesus makes this slight turn to discuss motive, his subject is still righteousness; we are still learning how to exceed the Pharisees. If righteousness is believing in the goodness and greatness of God and his plan, the antithesis is living to be seen by others. The first brings glory to God, the second calls attention to us.

'Acts of righteousness' is in quotation marks to convey Jesus' sarcasm. The word *acts* is not in the Greek. The first part of the verse should read *be careful not to do righteousness before men*. The NIV translators convey tone by adding *acts, your,* and the quote marks. All of the other translations I looked at had trouble conveying Jesus' gentle mockery. Some versions opt for something like *do not practice your righteousness,* while others employ the more concrete idea of *giving alms.*

Giving alms is the specific act Jesus addresses in this section. In the following verses (2, 3 and 4), if he were speaking Greek, Jesus was actually saying *giving mercy*. The Hebrew word for giving alms has its root in the word for mercy. We now have the context for Jesus' subject matter. *Giving mercy* conveyed the idea of performing a kindness because we empathize. The NIV translates it differently each time to hold our interest, but it is important to understand that Jesus stays on topic through the first four verses.

> "So when you give to the needy, do not announce it with trumpets,
> as the hypocrites do in the synagogues and on the streets,
> to be honored by men.
> I tell you the truth, they have received their reward in full.
> But when you give to the needy,
> do not let your left hand know what your right hand is doing,
> so that your giving may be in secret.
> Then your Father, who sees what is done in secret, will reward you. (Matt 6:2–4)

We can tell Jesus' sarcasm is gentle because of his trumpet joke. It is amusing to think of our good deeds as being announced with such fanfare. Jesus loved to poke fun at our silliness. Most of his jokes focus on our self-righteousness. We can't increase it with trumpets and we can't increase it by plucking out an eye or two.

I don't require trumpets, but I secretly desire some degree of recognition for my unprovoked kindnesses. When I do something as slight as letting someone get in front of me in traffic, I look to see whether they give a little wave of gratitude. Recognition isn't part of my original motivation. I don't let the other driver in just to experience the acknowledgment. However, after I've let them in, I look for appreciation. A wave of recognition gives me pleasure. If I'm not careful the desire for thanks can become my motivation.

The desire for credit was exactly what prompted Jesus' warning. It's a matter of who gets the glory. Trumpets cause others to focus on us rather than on God. We must focus on God if we would have others focus on him, but it's hard because we are self-centered. That's why, in verse 3, our left hand can't even know what our right hand is doing. Good thing we didn't cut off that right hand a few minutes ago, after Matthew 5:30!

If we look closely (and more reasonably than I just did) at these examples we can see there is no contradiction in Jesus' thought process. He's always reasonable and he understands the human heart. He anticipates our thoughts and feelings—like the one that I confessed a moment ago. Jesus knows how easy it is for us to corrupt kingdom living.

We can tell Jesus' concern is motive because of his common sense illustration. He has no problem with our acts of righteousness, except when we do them to be seen. The crippled and the blind waited in places in which they were most likely to elicit donations, primarily on the path to the Temple or synagogues. People coming to worship were more likely to give alms. In this context, there is no earthly way to give alms without the recipient knowing about it.

How could I give a lame man alms without the lame man seeing it? Perhaps if I became proficient in slight-of-hand. While I was materializing a dove for sacrifice from behind the lame man's ear, I could slip a denarius into his palm because his attention was diverted.

I don't think Jesus is advising us to become street magicians. Besides, a magician's left hand always knows what his right hand is doing. Jesus understands that at least one man is going to see your alms giving. That man is also the one most likely to give praise to your Father in heaven for the gift.

God's whole point is that the motive counts. Don't do it to make brownie points with God or man. Don't do it to raise your self-esteem. Do it to help, out of empathy. Do it because God has given you the means to do so.

> *"And when you pray,*
> *do not be like the hypocrites,*
> *for they love to pray standing in the synagogues and on the street corners*
> *to be seen by men.*
> *I tell you the truth, they have received their reward in full.*
> *But when you pray,*
> *go into your room, close the door and pray to your Father, who is unseen.*
> *Then your Father, who sees what is done in secret, will reward you.*
> *And when you pray, do not keep on babbling like pagans,*
> *for they think they will be heard because of their many words.*
> *Do not be like them, for your Father knows what you need before you ask him.* (Matt 6:5–8)

I had never considered that our Father would *reward* us when we pray in secret. Perhaps secret prayer is its own reward. Prayer is after all, an audience with the Creator of the universe.

Have you ever thought that if someone prays to be seen they are actually almost denying the presence of God? They are focused on a different audience. Ignoring God while pretending to pray to him must be a special form of blasphemy. Have you ever heard a quarreling couple throw verbal jabs at each other while pretending to talk to their children. They aren't really talking to their children; there is nothing of the parent/child relationship being communicated in those barbs. Praying to be seen denies either the existence of God or his most exalted position.

I have a strange thought for us to mull over. I'm not telling you this is true but it might be. I'm not positive that I believe it myself. Then again, I'm not very good at kingdom thinking yet. Here it is:

If we are not to pray on street corners, in other words in public places, then why should we lament the loss of prayer in school? Jesus told us to pray in our room *in secret*. If we would like our children to have the opportunity to pray in school, we merely need to train them to pray in school, in secret. When my son was young, this specific instruction never crossed my mind.

I know this idea flies in the face of the narrative behind our worldview. I mean the narrative that says society's ills partly stem from the Supreme Court decision to ban prayer in school. Yet, if Jesus is right (*if* Jesus is right, how absurd of me to use the qualifier) we lament the wrong loss. If he tells us to pray in secret and we instead mourn the lost opportunity to pray publicly, we not only disregard his instruction, we oppose it.

This proclivity of ours, to think we know better than Jesus, feels the same as our waywardness in regard to meekness. In both cases we approach challenges from a worldly viewpoint rather than Christ's.

Think again of the people he was addressing. Jesus lived in a society that tended to applaud public prayer. Although the real power emanated from Rome, within the confines of Judea, theocracy dominated. They had instituted laws based on the Hebrew Bible, and the Law was augmented by peer pressure toward the prevailing social mores and culture. This is the idealized goal of many Christians in America today. The Jews were not only allowed to pray aloud, it was encouraged. And the schools were for religious training, so of course they prayed in school.

Yet Jesus attacked the very thing they thought of (and we think of) as good: praying in public. He specifically advises us to pray privately instead. How do we comfortably squirm from his position to one in which we lament the loss of public prayer in our schools?

If we passed a constitutional amendment to allow prayer in schools once again, think of how it would be executed. I can think of two ways that would be the most likely, and they are the two Jesus counsels against in this passage.

Either the teacher might be a believer and offer aloud a heartfelt prayer specific to his or her class, or else prayer might be led by an unbelieving teacher who would recite some agreed upon rote prayer daily.

Either option would tend to deteriorate into exactly the situation Jesus speaks against. The specific, heartfelt prayer of a devout teacher in many cases might become, "Please help Mary to do her homework more faithfully and help little Johnny not to disrupt the class with his silly jokes." Prayer could become communication with the students rather than the Father.

The other option, rote prayer repeated daily, is exactly babbling *on like the pagans*, the other thing that Jesus warns against. Our worldview intimates that America isn't the same because we've dishonored God by outlawing public prayer. We think God blessed us more when everybody prayed in school but Jesus says our Father rewards us when we pray in secret.

If lack of prayer in schools hasn't caused the progressive breakdown of order in our society, what has? It might be us. We may be living outside the kingdom, motivated by the wrong things.

We watch too much TV, work too hard to acquire comfort and status, and place too great an emphasis on recreation and pleasure. Instead we should be training our children in the ways of God. Deuteronomy 6:7 tells us, *you shall teach them* (the Laws) *diligently to your sons and shall talk of them when you sit in your house and when you walk by the way and when you lie down and when you rise up* (NASB).

The responsibility to model kingdom living and teach our children about God belongs to us, not the school. Why would we expect a secular institution to act as our proxy? We're *believers* and we aren't doing a proper job of it. Should we require that all teachers in our public school be believers? Jesus, speaking in the midst of a society in which biblical values were trumpeted at every level, says it won't help.

We have ceded many responsibilities to our educational system, but parents must instill wisdom and morals, not our government. Schools can't teach our children our ethics unless every teacher shares our exact beliefs. The condemnation falls squarely on us! Once we've abdicated our responsibilities, we blame those in charge when they inexorably fail. Perhaps it's time we stopped thinking of prayer as an agent of social change and start remembering it is a secret communication with our hidden Father.

Societies change one heart at a time and most often in the face of adversity. Israel showed a predilection to return to God's teachings after periods of decline and none was more striking or enduring than the one they experienced after they returned from the Babylonian exile. No matter who ruled the country from then until the time of Christ (and perhaps *because* they didn't have total self-rule), they were more zealous for God's word than at any other period in their history. A peculiarity of human nature dictates a more complete return to God only when power is diminished. There are examples of this throughout the Old Testament. We rely on God when we can't rely on ourselves. But even if our country turns to God in greater numbers, it will still be our individual responsibility to teach our children. And one of the best things we can teach them is how to pray, as Jesus advises, in secret.

True communication with our Father is always an acknowledgment of our relationship with him, always an acceptance of our relative position and always an admission of his power. Even if we are only saying, "God, help us!"

Enough of my thoughts about prayer, let's see what Jesus had to say about it:

> *This, then, is how you should pray:*
> *'Our Father in heaven, hallowed be your name,*
> *your kingdom come,*
> *your will be done*
> *on earth as it is in heaven.*
> *Give us today our daily bread.*
> *Forgive us our debts, as we also have forgiven our debtors.*
> *And lead us not into temptation,*
> *but deliver us from the evil one.'* (Matt 6:9–13)

Many excellent books have been written about the Lord's Prayer. You've either read one or you have had a digested version fed to you from the pulpit. I can't add anything so I won't. I will however call your attention to one very important commentary on the Lord's Prayer. The commentator is Jesus.

After Jesus teaches us how to pray, he expands on only one topic within the prayer itself. This is the part of the prayer he thinks is either most important or most likely to be misunderstood. His commentary begins the moment he finishes the prayer.

> *For if you forgive men when they sin against you,*
> *your heavenly Father will also forgive you.*
> *But if you do not forgive men their sins,*
> *your Father will not forgive your sins.* (Matt 6:14–15)

Again Jesus accentuates the element of turnabout or Christian karma. (In that we will be judged, shown mercy, or forgiven in direct relation to the measure we exhibit these qualities to others.) Can there even be such a thing as Christian karma? I saw a bumper sticker once that said, "My karma ran over your dogma." I love that saying. Maybe it contains a kernel of truth. Jesus returns to this turnabout principle repeatedly. We should give it special consideration.

For if you forgive men when they sin against you, your heavenly Father will also forgive you. But if you do not forgive men their sins, your Father will not forgive your sins. Serious stuff.

With verse 16, Jesus returns to "when you." He has done "when you" give alms and "when you" pray, but then he stopped for a couple of minutes to instruct us how to pray. Now he returns to the bullet point presentation. This is more evidence of how organized his mind is and how focused he is on the words he chooses. Whether Jesus has rehearsed these words in his mind many times while preparing for ministry or it is his divinity peeking through, there is nothing haphazard in his discourse. All he is lacking is Power Point© and rousing music. It is a speech for the ages.

> *"When you fast, do not look somber as the hypocrites do,*
> *for they disfigure their faces to show men they are fasting.*
> *I tell you the truth, they have received their reward in full.*
> *But when you fast, put oil on your head and wash your face,*
> *so that it will not be obvious to men that you are fasting,*
> *but only to your Father, who is unseen;*
> *and your Father, who sees what is done in secret, will reward you.* (Matt 6:16–18)

Have you noticed the pattern Jesus has developed? All of the "when you" examples are things we think of as religious acts by individual believers: giving to the poor, praying, and fasting. Jesus wants us to keep our religious actions secret. If we keep the most prominent parts of our faith secret, what remains of our witness?

Jesus' instructions seem counterintuitive but they show a deep understanding of human nature. He is consistent. He is opposed to what we believe to be our Christian witness because he is concerned about our *effective* witness.

Earlier, we looked at the idea that actions speak louder than words. People discount our words because our words communicate our agenda. Words are tools of persuasion and we all know it, so we all view them with suspicion. The same principle holds for overtly religious acts. Unbelievers view them with suspicion for the same reasons; they can be tools of persuasion and they communicate agenda. We've looked at the inferred message of careless, overt witness. (I used to be like you, but Jesus saved me. Now I'm better than I used to be.) Now let's continue to look at these overt acts through the eyes of an unbeliever.

We want people to make a decision for Christ. No, let me restate the concept in more accurate terms. We want to *force* people to make a decision, either for or against Jesus. Their list of things to do probably doesn't include thinking about their eternal fate, but we aren't mindful of their list. We have our own list, and disrupting their list is on ours.

And then we say the most inane things. We tell them Jesus turned our world upside down and then ask them if they would like their world turned upside down. How do we think people will respond?

If the unbeliever is not in the midst of crisis, they tend to be repulsed by such a drastic suggestion. They are offended that we infer their present life is so bad that it would be good for them to change everything. No wonder people become angry.

We exacerbate the problem if we imply they must decide *right now*. I think we get this from the book of Hebrews, and specifically 4:7, *Therefore God again set a certain day, calling it Today, when a long time later he spoke through David, as was said before: "Today, if you hear his voice, do not harden your hearts."* This is a call to obedience for us, not for us to give to unbelievers. Hearts that have not yet been softened cannot be hardened.

Immediacy is a high-pressure sales tactic. When I am told that I need to decide right now, because the "deal" won't be available in the future, I become doubly suspicious and resistant. It's human nature.

Religious acts, even though they are actions, are akin to verbal witness. People read persuasion and agenda into religious acts just as surely as they do with verbal witness. Humans don't want to be persuaded; we prefer to persuade ourselves. Jesus recognized the complexities of the human psyche. That's why he counsels against overt religious acts. The sermon is about our living witness, but it is more about the living and less about the witness.

So, if we never tell people we are Christians, how can they know Jesus is the reason we do what we do? They can't. We *must* declare our status as Christians. The declaration is assumed in doing *good deeds so others can praise our Father in Heaven*. Others can't know which god to praise unless we tell them. There's nothing wrong, and everything right, with telling people whom we worship. The problems begin when we try to persuade them to do likewise. The persuasion must be done by our everyday actions.

Jesus alludes to working in secret seven times in this section of the sermon. He also reassures us three times, that our *Father, who sees what is done in secret, will reward you*. This is slightly different than his admonitions not to do our works of righteousness before men, to be seen by them. The latter relates to witnessing while the former addresses faith. Working in secret is faith manifested as relationship. God is invisible and that's why it is desirable for us to fast, pray, and give without being obvious. Our relationship to God becomes closer when we similarly work together in secret.

God has a good reason for working in secret. If he were obvious to all, faith would be worthless. God places a high value on faith. By remaining undetectable God sacrifices much greater adulation, honor, and praise, and he does it for the sake of our very souls. He gives up the greater worship he so richly deserves, worship that would be immediate, heartfelt, and continuous if he were an apparent God, and he gives it up out of love for us. Such worship is his due but he defers it to allow us faith.

God also takes the blame for evil. We ask how a good and all-powerful God can allow bad things to happen to good people. He does it because faith is almost as precious as love. If nothing bad ever happened to good people, or to Christians, or to children, we would have empirical proof of the existence of a good God. If we had proof, faith would be unavailable. Without faith, it is impossible to please God.

Allowing us faith is a primary way God shows his love. Faith is the only way to the unending bliss of heaven. Our ceaseless state is important to him. God remains hidden, deferring his glory and taking the blame, to grace us with saving faith.

We can draw closer to him if we mimic him, if we do things in secret for his pleasure. Secret worship not only strengthens our relationship with him, as we both do the same type of acts for the same reasons, it also shows our priorities. Can we forgo the immediate gratification of men for the delayed and lasting gratification of communion with God in heaven? That is God's motivation. So . . .

> *"Do not store up for yourselves treasures on earth,*
> *where moth and rust destroy, and where thieves break in and steal.*
> *But store up for yourselves treasures in heaven,*
> *where moth and rust do not destroy, and where thieves do not break in and steal.*
> *For where your treasure is, there your heart will be also.* (Matt 6:20–21)

These verses begin the conclusion of the main section of the sermon. The earthly accumulation of heavenly treasures is what makes the kingdom of heaven the kingdom of heaven. Heaven is Heaven whether humans inhabit it or not, but the kingdom of heaven is heavenly reality being dragged down to earth.

Jesus is saying faith is the sure path. If we believe there are treasures in heaven we can resolve to operate in secret here on earth. If we believe good deeds are a light to bring others to faith, denying ourselves becomes more bearable.

These concluding remarks show us how to live without agenda, or rather, how to live by God's agenda. We don't need to worry about the persuasion inherent in our actions, only whether they are righteous. God will take care of the rest. It is his job to draw the unbeliever. We can trust him to do his part if we do what he calls us to do.

Our main job is to live an attractive life instead of a repulsive one. Jesus is in the process of defining what is attractive and what is repulsive and, not surprisingly, he uses the world's definitions. Why wouldn't he? The world is the intended audience.

"The eye is the lamp of the body.
If your eyes are good, your whole body will be full of light.
But if your eyes are bad, your whole body will be full of darkness.
If then the light within you is darkness, how great is that darkness! (Matt 6:22–23)

If we are to be the light of the world, it will be because our bodies are full of light. Our bodies will be full of light because our eyes are good. This teaching is about more than a sparkle in our eyes, it's about what we do with what we have.

To have a *good eye* is and was a Jewish idiom. To have a *bad eye* is, not surprisingly, an opposite idiom. A good eye is one that has a generous attitude toward others. These were idioms a thousand years before Jesus spoke them. The Psalms and proverbs have examples of the same expressions.

We help people because God has given us the means to do so. God has put them in our path, and God asks us to help them. That's the good eye. The bad eye looks upon them with suspicion. Instead of helping them, we congratulate ourselves that we haven't fallen into the same bad situation.

If your eyes are good can also be translated *if your eyes are single*. Our eyes are single when we are looking at one thing: God's desires. We can focus on him or we can focus on ourselves compared to others. In all the bad examples Jesus warns against, we are focusing on others for our own glory rather than on God:

To be seen before men
To be honored by men
To be seen by men
To show men

When my son was young, we would play a secondary game while we played catch. I would look at my wife, but throw the ball to him, to try to surprise him. While it was great fun, I wasn't as accurate in my aim as when I looked directly at him while throwing. We will never be accurate in our understanding of God if we remain focused on ourselves or on the effect we have on others.

This concept brings to mind the paradoxes the Jews loved so much (so do I!). Jesus was fond of them as well. Sayings like, *If anyone wants to be first, he must be the very last, and the servant of all* (Mark 9:35). The paradox in chapter 6 is if you do something to be seen by men, God will also see it and he will not be pleased. If you do something to be seen only by God, men will see it and they will give God praise.

Finally, *if your eyes are good* can also be translated if your eyes are *clear*. When our eyes are clear, they give light to the whole body and that enhances our wordless witness. We become proper lights for the world.

Likewise, the words we translate as *But if your eyes are bad*, could also be translated "if your eyes are diseased" or "if your eyes are blind." The word means diseased or blind in the physical sense and evil or wrong in the spiritual. Jesus implies we have a tendency to look at things cross-eyed or with a double focus. He confirms that with his next example.

> *"No one can serve two masters.*
> *Either he will hate the one and love the other,*
> *Or he will be devoted to the one and despise the other.*
> *You cannot serve both God and Money.*(Matt 6:24)

The word translated here as money is really mammon or *mamon* in the Aramaic, and nobody really knows for sure what it means. Most likely it comes from the Hebrew word for riches, especially as in hidden riches because the Hebrew root word means buried or concealed.

God must be our treasure. Our hidden, concealed God will be shown to men by the way in which we use the earthly wealth he has allowed into our hands. Those of us who end up being faithful with these earthly treasures will be entrusted with much more. Jesus is simply telling us that as inhabitants of his earthly kingdom of heaven we must stay heaven-minded. To deny ourselves in this present incarnation with Heaven in mind is faith, and faith is the prerequisite for kingdom living.

> *"Therefore I tell you, do not worry about your life,*
> *what you will eat or drink;*
> *or about your body, what you will wear.*
> *Is not life more important than food,*
> *and the body more important than clothes?*
> *Look at the birds of the air;*
> *they do not sow or reap or store away in barns,*
> *and yet your heavenly Father feeds them.*
> *Are you not much more valuable than they?*
> *Who of you by worrying can add a single hour to his life?* (Matt 6:25–27)

You already know I dislike it when the translators are so gawdly they take Jesus' little jokes out of the Bible. The practice diminishes the acceptability of our own little jokes now and then. If Jesus didn't joke, how can I? The translators of the NIV are supposed to *translate* but in this instance they are purposely mistranslating.

In verse 27 he really said . . . *can add a single cubit to his life*. A cubit is not a measurement of time, like an hour. It should not be translated *single hour*. A cubit is a measurement of length. Jesus is really saying, "which of you by worrying can add a foot and a half to his life." The joke accentuates the absurdity of worrying. We can't add an hour anymore than we can add foot and a half. For heaven's sake, leave the joke in there! My pastor likes to start a sermon or illustrate an important point with a good joke. Jesus began the tradition.

> *"And why do you worry about clothes?*
> *See how the lilies of the field grow. They do not labor or spin.*
> *Yet I tell you that not even Solomon in all his splendor*
> *was dressed like one of these.*
> *If that is how God clothes the grass of the field,*
> *which is here today and tomorrow is thrown into the fire,*
> *will he not much more clothe you, O you of little faith?* (Matt 6:28–30)

Being salt and light, means focusing on different things than the pagans. Who could ever make this argument better than Jesus just did? Solomon was the richest guy in the world, and the wisest. Perhaps his wisdom also included a sense of fashion, but he still wasn't as well dressed as a lily in a field. Solomon was truly never clothed with the singularity of design, the color coordination, the combination of shapes and textures, the aroma, or conceptual flourishes that adorn just one Easter lily!

> *So do not worry, saying,*
> *'What shall we eat?' or 'What shall we drink?' or 'What shall we wear?'*
> *For the pagans run after all these things,*
> *and your heavenly Father knows that you need them.*
> *But seek first his kingdom and his righteousness,*
> *and all these things will be given to you as well.*
> *Therefore do not worry about tomorrow,*
> *for tomorrow will worry about itself.*
> *Each day has enough trouble of its own.* (Matt 6:31–34)

Jesus doesn't mean looking at the menu is bad. He made the incredible array of foodstuffs we use as ingredients in the foods and drinks we choose. He doesn't say don't choose. We are not required to live on locusts and honey. We are only advised to not *worry* about what we shall eat or drink.

God has provided us with so many different kinds of foods with so many different pleasing tastes. He only asks that we not become excessively caught up in the pleasure. He wants us to keep our focus in the right place. The right place for us to focus, according to Jesus, is on pleasing the Father by staying heaven minded and by treating everybody in a radically different way than they have ever been treated before.

We have to love everybody to show them the Father's perfect way of loving. We have to show mercy to remind them of his mercy. We need to look without judgment because God so fiercely desires to see Jesus' work in the light of everyone's eyes. We have to hunger and thirst after Jesus' kingdom by doing these things. We have to remain faithful because that is how the world can see the God who hides himself.

Faith is so precious and at the same time so lowly. It is the lowest common denominator and available to the very least of us. Faith is accessible to the child, to the mentally damaged, to the emotionally abused, to the physically impaired. We will all take a pass/fail test with one question. It is an open book exam and we are the open books. The answer is available to all. The Answer is Jesus.

Everyone takes the test. God provides the answer and he provides it through you and me. Let someone copy over your shoulder. Let them look at your answer. Let them look where you are looking but make sure you're looking in the right place. Focus.

The eyes are the light of the soul. We only need to focus.

12

Judgment

I USED TO THINK Matthew 7 was the only sharp change in subject in the whole sermon. Jesus spent the end of chapter six teaching us how and why we should live by faith, and now he abruptly begins to teach about judgment. My error shows our natural predilections. We haven't changed subjects, we've moved to comparison by contrast. The heavenly-minded activities that end Matthew 6 are illustrations of the good eye. Judgment is part of the bad eye.

Matthew 7 is Jesus' opus about judgment in all its forms. It is a point-by-point treatise on why we should not judge, how to think about judgment, how to respond to others concerning their future judgment, the one instance in which we *must* judge and finally, the reason we must think about judgment in this way. Let's look at it now.

> *Do not judge, or you too will be judged.*
> *For in the same way you judge others, you will be judged,*
> *and with the measure you use, it will be measured to you.* (Matt 7:1–2)

There it is—the verse that gave me so much trouble. I'm glad that trouble can be a good thing in God's economy.

The Bible speaks so often against peer judgment because the desire for justice is so deeply ingrained. We were built to be just; and not even the devil has been able to purge this inclination from our being. Instead, he perverts it at its weakest point. He tempts us to usurp as he usurps, and to judge what we have not been given leave to judge.

Do not judge is a horizontal rule that keeps the Vertical in mind. It is much deeper than the Golden Rule. It is a Platinum Rule that means to do unto others as we wish *God* to do unto us. We are to be merciful so that we can be shown mercy. Jesus is talking about showing the love of the Father to those who should be our enemies, as he shows his love to us, the people who used to be his enemies.

I looked up the word *judge* in the Hebrew. The first thing that struck me is that Judge is one of God's names, which means it is one of God's duties, one of his responsibilities. As early as Genesis 18, Abraham calls him the Judge of all the world. Judges 11:27 makes this same point when it says, *'Let the LORD, the* Judge, *judge between the Israelites and the Ammonites.'* The take away from these verses should be to not judge because God is the Judge; for us to judge would be to usurp his exalted position. That's the pinnacle of pride—to think we can do what he does. The idea is implicit in Matthew 7:1 and 2. Don't judge others or the *real* Judge will judge you for it.

A surprising aspect of the Hebrew word for *judge* is that it is actually a primitive root that means, of all things, *to establish* or *set up*. This is foundational to the idea of judgment. Only our Father has the right to judge because he is the one who established the universe and set up the laws of life.

When God created the world, he intended us to live in a certain manner. Now he gauges our actions and reactions to see how close we come to fulfilling his wishes. Fulfilling God's wishes calls to mind our revised definition of righteousness. Problems arise because we can't fully understand his vision but usurp his authority anyway.

To make sure we understand how very important this is, Jesus introduces his views on judgment at the start of Chapter 7 by promising us consequences for our disobedience, just as he has other times when he talked about forgiveness, mercy, or judging. God will show us mercy if we are merciful. God will forgive us in the same way we forgive others. And now, we will be judged in the manner we judge others. Instead of judgment, we need to react in mercy because we require mercy. Oh, how we need that mercy! To judge others is a sign that we take mercy for granted.

The eternal (not to mention theological) implications of these two verses are staggering. We teach that Jesus died so his blood might cover our sins. Can judging possibly negate his efforts on our behalf? I want to think, no. I want my assurance to be unconditional. But there has to be some sense in which these verses are true. Jesus doesn't lie. There must be something additional, some consequence we have not yet discovered.

Look at the second half of the companion verse, 6:15. *But if you do not forgive men their sins, your Father will not forgive your sins.* I want my sins forgiven. This is important. We had better take heed. Forgiveness needs to be a top priority.

I would be remiss if we didn't pause here and at least look at an unorthodox and unpalatable possibility. What if my Father does not forgive my sin as he promises not to in 6:15. Can I take them to heaven with me? Will some people in heaven still be saddled with their sins because they have judged others? That kind of heaven sounds an awful lot like earth. I could be wrong, but I don't think people with unforgiven sins are going to make it to heaven. Yet 6:15 says *Your Father will not forgive your sins*. It isn't as if God has no choice in the matter. He is the Lord.

He is also unchanging. His words to Moses on Mount Sinai apply even today. *I will have mercy on whom I will have mercy, and I will have compassion on whom I will have compassion* (Exod 33:19b). He made the rules and if we interpret them incorrectly, he is not bound by our misinterpretation. We can try to put him in a box and say he must do this or he must do that, but he does as he pleases. He will have mercy on whom he will have mercy. Get it? If not, he repeats it in a different way. He will have compassion on whom he will have compassion.

Look at the theoretical big picture from God's point of view. If we sin, we go to hell. Isn't that what we're taught? Yet he devised a get-out-of-hell-free card before we ever put ourselves in this untenable position. Jesus, in his loving sacrifice as ordained from before the foundations of the earth, ransomed us. No matter what we've done, no matter how wicked we have been; our Father graciously overlooks it because of the blood of Jesus. But this is only true if we are saved, if Jesus is the Lord of our life. I have heard it called the Eternal Life Insurance Policy.

We should at least contemplate the possibility that this Insurance Policy has an exclusionary clause; judge others and the policy is voided. Our earthly insurance policies often contain exclusionary clauses, hidden in the fine print. If they didn't, people contemplating suicide could postpone it for a week or two to get extra life insurance to take care of their families. An extra million dollars of life insurance would make committing suicide the equivalent of winning a very grim lottery. The fine print is both to discourage a hopeless act and to keep everyone's premiums that much lower.

There is no fine print in the Sermon. The principle of like retribution is boldly proclaimed to us repeatedly. If you judge, you will be judged. Your sins won't be forgiven. It may be that Jesus is plainly giving us fair warning.

One earth shaking circumstance, Jesus' atoning sacrifice, circumvents the eternal rule of reaping what we sow and gets us into heaven. Another earth shaking circumstance, judging others, reinstates the rule and gets us tossed out.

When I wrote that I would be remiss if I didn't discuss this possibility, it is because this is one very legitimate way to interpret the texts. In fact, it is the most semantically precise interpretation. I will not have anyone's eternal blood on my hands because I refused to point it out. I don't personally believe that people who are saved and judge are on their way to hell, but I don't have all the answers. The man who has all the answers says something like it though, so whether it ends up being the correct interpretation or not, we had better err on the side of caution and stop judging anyone other than ourselves.

The reason I don't personally believe this is a correct understanding has more to do with what I believe the essence of God to be rather than a parsing of the text. When he says he will have *mercy on whom* he *will have mercy*, I read his tone as loving rather than threatening. The verses in Exodus that follow this proclamation contain an element of temporary judgment as well as lasting mercy, judgment to the third and fourth generation and mercy to the thousandth. Perhaps the judgment Jesus warns of will also be temporary.

I understand that God must judge, and he judges in part because he loves us. He will not easily allow us to hurt others, because he loves them too.

God's love is the part of God's essence I best understand. He invented love because he is love. When I tend to think I will get into heaven even though I have judged, it is only because I am relying on God's character, as I understand it. This reliance on the Father we *know* is a biblical tradition. Moses obeyed God before he received the Pentateuch. Abraham trusted God even though he had no scripture to guide him. He relied on his own understanding of God. The same can be said of all the Patriarchs.

Because God has decreed everlasting life through Jesus Christ, love is greater than judgment. When I add these all up, because I understand the love of God in this way, I don't think he is going to send me to hell for judging others. I hope I'm right.

It has been suggested to me that there is another way for God to judge us in the manner we judge others without negating Jesus' great sacrifice. He can judge us now rather than in the afterlife. He can chastise us here on earth using the same standards we apply to others. Rather than some minor sin having small earthly consequences, perhaps we reap more dearly than would seem appropriate. We may have a rougher time in this life because we are judgmental.

Let's say we waste a little time at work on tasks unrelated to our job, such as paying our bills or planning dinner. We can justify it in our minds because at least we aren't goofing off all day long like a certain co-worker. According to this alternative theory, they may get the promotion we thought should be ours, as a judgment for our judging them. Or God's more severe judgments might appear random. The edict might not be related to the judging offense. We might undeservedly lose a job even though we don't judge other coworkers too harshly, to strip us of some of the pride inherent in our judgment in other circumstances. This could be effective. I've seen the pride of "saintly" men eroded by circumstance.

Effective or not, I don't think this is Jesus' intent either. Temporal judgment for judging others probably takes place, but I think it would be only as a method of molding us into better people here on earth, one of the chastisements God performs because he loves us, not the fulfillment of an eternal principle concerning judgment.

There is one more way to interpret this verse, and I think it may be the most consistent with the rest of Scripture. Or maybe I just hope it is the most consistent, given that first alternative.

Do you remember that verse from Second Corinthians we looked at, about Jesus judging us all? *For we must all appear before the judgment seat of Christ, that each one may receive what is due him for the things done while in the body, whether good or bad* (5:10). What if this is the juncture at which we won't be forgiven? If we're all to be judged at the *bema seat*, this is most likely the place where we will be judged for judging.

We can tie this verse to another of Paul's that speaks of us being judged for judging. *So when you, a mere man, pass judgment on them and yet do the same things, do you think you will escape God's judgment?* (Rom 2:3). This verse says we won't *escape* that judgment. If we string it to one more passage from Paul through the idea of *escape*, we can have a glimmer of hope. We won't escape judgment, but we will escape everlasting judgment, barely.

> *For no one can lay any foundation other than the one already laid,*
> *which is* Jesus Christ.
> *If any man builds on this foundation using gold, silver, costly stones,*
> *wood, hay or straw, his work will be shown for what it is,*
> *because* the Day *will bring it to light.*
> *It will be revealed with fire,*
> *and the fire will test the quality of each man's work.*
> *If what he has built survives, he will receive his reward.*
> *If it is burned up,* he will suffer loss;
> *he himself will be saved,*
> *but only* as one escaping through the flames (1 Cor 3:11–15).

This seems to synch with the Second Corinthians passage. The *things done while in the body* corresponds to laying the *foundation*. *Good* matches up with *gold, silver,* or *costly stones*. *Bad* would be the same as *wood, hay or straw*.

This is one of the passages from which the Roman Catholic Church has built the doctrine of purgatory. We don't need to go that far, but can you see where the principle might be applicable? The foundation Paul speaks of is Jesus Christ's work. His work is his atoning sacrifice to save us from judgment. Some of the other materials we can build a foundation on are good works or comparative holiness. The *Day* is, of course, *our* Judgment Day, the day that each of us will *receive what is due him for the things done while in the body, whether good or bad.*

If all three passages are truly theologically connected, the Father will not summarily forgive our sins. When we come before the *bema seat* of Christ, rather than being forgiven, we who judge *will be saved, but only as one escaping through the flames.*

Escaping through the flames to get to heaven seems like a terrifying journey, a vivid description of some concept I don't want to experience. While escaping any situation that involves flames, our fate would seem uncertain. That's not what I want to experience at heaven's gates. I want to be welcomed.

These are the three scenarios I envision when Jesus speaks of our sin not being forgiven by our Father: hell, earthly retribution to escape hell, and heavenly retribution to escape hell. None of them are desirable. Whatever the time or method of the judgment promised to us if we judge, Jesus thinks it so important that he promises to predicate his judgment on us relative to how well we execute this command. I believe he feels this way because of the potential eternal consequences our judging can have on others. We could in effect, turn people away from the Gospel of Jesus.

I know the previous paragraph quarrels with classic Predestination but there may very well be a sense in which it is true. The calls to spread the Gospel are too numerous for them to be unimportant. We are learning what Jesus believes is the best method for spreading the word. The *why* becomes secondary in light of the command.

Let us at least admit that our judging could build walls Jesus doesn't want erected. Communicating with a loved one is easier face to face than over a wall. We know Jesus is concerned for those still lost. We know he desires that none should be lost. We know he would prefer not to judge harshly. And now we know he promises to judge us more harshly if we judge others in such a manner. He wants to leave us no option except not to judge. This concept of not judging is alien to us. We can barely comprehend it. We want to reject it. We want to believe it can't be right. The command against judging is general and led to our theoretical musings, but Jesus quickly brings us the practical and situational.

> *Why do you look at the speck of sawdust in your brother's eye*
> *and pay no attention to the plank in your own eye?*
> *How can you say to your brother, 'Let me take the speck out of your eye,'*
> *when all the time there is a plank in your own eye?*
> *You hypocrite, first take the plank out of your own eye,*
> *and then you will see clearly to remove the speck from your brother's eye.*
> (Matt 7:3–5)

Here again Jesus uses humor to enhance the message. This must be his fifth or sixth little joke so far. It is absurd to think of a plank sticking out of my eye. What a word picture! It is just as absurd to think I could worry about my brother's sin while in that precarious condition. Should I speak to him about some sin in his life, or should I beg him to drive me to the emergency room?

If I had an unwieldy object like a plank protruding from far above my center of gravity, and it wasn't eternal-life threatening, it would at least certainly throw me off balance. A plank in my eye would also keep me at a distance from others lest I bump them and lodge the plank more firmly. That is the quality of our judgment, when God doesn't ordain it. We are distant and out-of-balance.

Indeed, since the plank is a euphemism for sin, *can* we remove it? Can we get rid of our own sin or did Jesus have to die to accomplish what we could not? In our continuous internal dialogue, we try to justify our actions. We all attempt to think sin is not sin, but the nagging realization of it lies below the surface.

In unbelievers, the magnitude of their sin may be unrealized but the unspoken awareness of it lurks just beneath their particular version of internal dialogue. They differ from us only in their method of self-justification. They try to counterbalance their sin by works. When unbelievers say they've tried to live a good life, this is exactly what they mean.

When an unbeliever rationalizes, searching his deeds for the good, much lies unexplored just behind the thought. The first is the admission that not every act and thought was actually good. They may not call sin *sin* but they know the difference between good and bad. That means they also believe in a cosmic balance beam of judgment where these relative acts are weighed.

Who could weigh them other than a judge? Who could that judge be other than the Judge? And so, finally, although they may not admit it consciously, most people believe in sin, ultimate justice, and God. The only difference between believers and those who we consider unbelievers is the defense strategy employed.

Our present method of verbal witness dictates that first we get the lost souls to see they are sinners and then convince them that they will be judged. This step is often unnecessary. Almost everyone is slightly closer to salvation than we think.

An unbeliever's quarrel is not with judgment; it is with the judge. They understand better than we do that judgment is not our place. They think we should take the plank out of our own eye before we try to perform any type of lumber-jacking surgical procedures on them. They know we are just as incapable of removing our planks as they are. They know they can't remove their own sin so they try works. They know they have lusted in their hearts but they have also held the door open for that woman who was using a cane. Where we plead Jesus Christ, they plead common decency.

Sometimes in our reliance on Jesus, we disregard common decency. Yet common decency is akin to mercy and loving-kindness. In our pursuit of godliness we have taken for granted the attribute of God that affects us the most. Once we admit we can't remove our own plank, we can admit we are incapable of removing anybody's speck or splinter. The admission should lead to mercy.

This very subject came up during last week's Bible study. A classmate reminded us to confess our sin very thoroughly before we remove the speck from our brother's eye. He understands that Jesus removes our sin. He meant to point out that we must confess our sin because First John 1:9 says God is faithful to forgive our sin when we confess it to him. This brother figured once he was free of sin based on John's instruction he was ready to deal with the sin of another person. I think that by the pride of believing himself to be sinless at the moment of confession, he was reinserting the plank. If we could remain poor in spirit, we wouldn't allow ourselves the pride of sinlessness, or even relative sinlessness.

My friend's statement was only half-correct theologically because it was only half-correct logically. Is it logical to acknowledge we are incapable of removing our own sin and then believe we are somehow capable of removing the sin of a brother? Jesus knew full well that he was destined to die an agonizing death to finally deal with our sin. He isn't promoting a method by which we can deal with the sin of another person. Jesus is saying it is absurd to think we can.

The next verses are the ones where the commentaries seem to think Jesus moves away from the subject of judgment. They have it partially right, thinking he is speaking of witnessing, then prayer and finally salvation. He is, but he is exploring them all in the context of judgment. He never leaves the twin subjects of judging and our living witness. He speaks now of application and strategy.

> *Do not give dogs what is sacred*
> *do not throw your pearls to pigs.*
> *If you do, they may trample them under their feet,*
> *and then turn and tear you to pieces.* (Matt 7:6)

Dogs are pictures of unbelievers, and pigs are pictures of what is unclean. However, Jesus isn't reinforcing a point through double images, he is linking two strategies by contrast and teaching that neither one will work. To his Jewish listeners pigs were always regarded as unclean. Deuteronomy told them so. And here is Jesus himself on the subject of dogs in Matthew 15:24–27:

> *He answered, "I was sent only to the lost sheep of Israel."*
> *The woman came and knelt before him. "Lord, help me!" she said.*
> *He replied, "It is not right to take the children's bread and toss it to their dogs."*
> *"Yes, Lord," she said, "but even the dogs eat the crumbs that fall from their masters' table."*

When Jesus called the Samaritan woman a dog, he was either being playful or purposely provocative. She is not one of God's Chosen, Israel. She is the picture of an unbeliever. Dogs and pigs are the unclean unbelievers. If *pigs* and *dogs* are the world, and *pearls* and *what is sacred* refer to the things of God, could Jesus be telling us not to witness?

The commentators think so and they are almost right, but for the wrong reasons. They think he is telling us *to judge in advance* as to whether we should witness or not. This is 20 seconds into his speech after he says *"do not judge."* Yet many commentaries agree. They say Jesus is saying to decide in advance whether or not to witness. Judge the character of a person to ascertain whether the hearer might be a worthwhile project. As if we are supposed to decide whether we witness or not! I thought we were to be led by the Spirit.

To bolster their argument, the commentators point to a specific instance when Jesus did not witness. Jesus did not witness to Herod. They say he didn't witness to Herod because he judged what kind of person Herod was and decided not to do the whole dogs/sacred and swine/pearls thing. But couldn't there be a different reason he didn't witness to Herod? Could it be as Isaiah 53:7 says in the midst of the Suffering Servant prophecy?

> *He was oppressed and afflicted, yet he did not open his mouth;*
> *he was led like a lamb to the slaughter,*
> *and as a sheep before her shearers is silent,*
> *so he did not open his mouth.*

Jesus probably chose not to witness to fulfill the prophecy. Yet the commentators have decided he *judged in advance* that Herod was not going to get into the kingdom. That's more than a stretch; it's preposterous, especially if we are trying to apply one of Jesus' divine attributes of knowing the thoughts and fate of another to ourselves. We are not omniscient.

Jesus witnessed to all sorts of people that subsequently chose not to follow him. Some possibilities of Jesus giving unfruitful witness (I say possibilities because we have no idea whether or not these people eventually came to faith) are the wealthy young ruler, the scribes, the Pharisees, and the disciples who turned from following him during the "I am" speech. He wasn't judging people in advance; he was spreading the gospel to everyone he could. He must have thought they had a choice.

What Jesus communicates to us is how not to witness. The *dogs* reference explains there is a wrong manner of witness and the *pigs* illustration shows there is a wrong time.

Jesus knows no one comes to the Father unless the Father draws him. He also knows how dearly we would like to see our loved ones saved. At some junctures in the lives of our loved ones, these factors may be diametrically opposed to one another. God in his wisdom knows the proper time and place. He is an expert on the human psyche and an expert at drawing us. Jesus doesn't want us to get in the way.

Do not give dogs what is sacred. What is sacred? Sacred means that which is set apart for holy purposes. God's word is sacred, but he surely doesn't mean we should never quote Scripture to an unbeliever. What does God mean? God means us. We are *what is sacred*. We've been set apart for God's holy purposes.

When Jesus says *don't give dogs what is sacred*, he means that we should not act like pagans. For their sake don't judge them; but for heaven's sake don't act like them either. This is the dual strategy that allows us to remain among them while we are yet set apart, as we live out our witness. To stay close enough to affect them as salt and light we must not judge. That means we can't expect them to conform to our standards, but neither should we conform to theirs.

We can't, for example, condemn them for laughing at a dirty joke but neither can we laugh at that same joke. (Unless it is *really* funny, not too dirty and we can't help it.) The trick is that we shouldn't laugh but we also shouldn't communicate condemnation for their laughter.

We Christians can be strange people sometimes. So often we try and impose our standards on a lost world, yet we get really angry about the times they impose their standards on us. Most of the time they just want their standards to be their standards, and it doesn't bother them if we choose to follow or not. They are only trying to live their own unsaved lives in their own unsaved way. That tends to bother us immensely. Yet isn't that exactly what we did before we were saved? So don't judge them, and don't give up that which sets you apart for Christ. Don't give to dogs that which is sacred.

Next he tells us not to *cast our pearls before swine* and explains why. Far from flitting from subject to unrelated subject, Jesus is moving much faster and truer than we can easily grasp. In this analogy, pearls *are* God's Plan, his Word and our witness. The swine/pearls analogy is in such close proximity to the dogs/sacred example, within the same sentence, that it is no wonder we have linked them. We've missed Jesus' intent that they are grouped not to link them, but to contrast them. He clarifies the second half of the illustration in Matthew 13:45 and 46. Scripture, as usual, explains Scripture.

> *Again, the kingdom of heaven is like a merchant looking for fine pearls.*
> *When he found* one *of great value,*
> *he went away and sold everything he had and bought it.*

Our salvation through the gospel message, our *entry* into the kingdom of heaven, is that one great pearl. Jesus doesn't warn us against casting that *one great pearl* before swine, he uses the plural, *pearls*. Multiple Gospel messages. He means we shouldn't badger our loved ones repeatedly with our spoken witness. An unprompted witness can build a wall as high as traditional judgment.

How can we influence those we love if they avoid us? If we witness repeatedly to them, they may begin to avoid us. Worse yet, they may come to resent us. They may resent us so much that they sever the relationship we previously enjoyed. The message of salvation we hold so dear can become an abomination in their minds. It can become the words that caused them to lose a relationship with someone they truly loved—you. Our verbal witness can become that thing that turned you into a "crazy person." So, by all means, give them the gospel, but if they reject it, *do not throw your* pearls *to pigs. If you do, they may* trample them *under their feet, and then turn and tear* you *to pieces*.

We don't want them to trample the gospel under their feet and we don't want to provoke them to turn and tear us to pieces, even if it is only verbally. We are all familiar with the reactions the world can have to the Gospel and the name of Jesus. It is only natural that they react this way if the Father does not draw them. These reactions are prevalent because we are tearing up the seedbed while it is still being prepared for sowing.

After we give the gospel to our loved ones, if they reject it, our mission must change to silent witness mode. We learned earlier that if we are not salt and light, our witness is worthless and deserves to be trampled by men. Now we see that repeated witness is a form of judgment and may also be trampled. Both Testaments say *blessed are the feet of the messenger that brings the gospel of peace.* Not the mouth of the messenger, but the messenger's feet; actions not words. Likewise, if the unbeliever rejects the gospel of peace, it is with their feet, by trampling.

So what if we witness to those we love and they reject the message? If we are not to verbally witness repeatedly, are we to just accept their eternal damnation? Are we to simply give up? God forbid. Jesus has another strategy. He gives us strong hope in this strategy and so they should be words of great comfort. He says to pray:

> *Ask and it will be given to you;*
> *seek and you will find;*
> *knock and the door will be opened to you.*
> *For everyone who asks receives;*
> *he who seeks finds;*
> *and to him who knocks, the door will be opened* (Matt 7:7–8).

The verbs Jesus used to describe prayer are progressively more aggressive. Seeking is more proactive than merely asking. Seeking is active pursuit. Knocking is a stronger action still. These increasingly stronger verbs are not a more vehement witness to those we love; they are more desperate petitions to God.

So if we witness to no great effect, we shouldn't keep witnessing. Instead we should start praying. If your loved one still isn't saved, pray harder and more often. Seek God's favor for him or her. If your prayers are of no avail, pray harder still. Fervent prayer avails much. James tells us so and Jesus agrees. He says *the door* will *be opened.* Once he has opened the door we can again witness to that loved one, if the Spirit calls us to the task. We also may pray and have the door opened, but not know our prayer has been answered. The door may be opened for somebody else to walk through. Our job may be to only plant the seed. Someone else may be sent to reap the harvest.

We want to do more than only pray. We affirm that we believe in the power of prayer, but in the back of our minds, we wonder if prayer is forceful enough. We have all heard stories of people who prayed daily for the salvation of a loved one but had that loved one die without accepting Christ. We all fear that this will be the fate of those we love.

Jesus advocates more than daily prayer. Daily prayer may not be as effective as fervent prayer. Remember how the verbs Jesus employed got progressively stronger? We may need to set aside time to go to the Lord with only this request if our regular prayer regimen isn't getting results. Or we may need to combine our fervent prayer with fasting. We may need to utilize a progressively more intense spiritual effort.

We shouldn't feel like we are trying to manipulate God through these methods. Prayer for another is not selfish. Jesus is the one who suggests we become more aggressive by steps. By doing as he asks, we are being loving, desperate, reliant and obedient. We are working together with our Father as we go to him in secret. We will be rewarded.

Our worry isn't manipulation; it is taking undue responsibility. We don't have the final decision in the salvation of another. The outcome is not based on our piety or faithfulness. We only have to pray. We must also keep in mind that we may not be able to discover when our prayers have been answered. God may have answered our prayer by drawing our loved ones in ways we won't know, because our loved ones either won't tell us about it (for fear of reopening the subject with us) or because they didn't recognize it for what it was. Spiritual things can be difficult to discern for those who aren't spiritual. Just because they didn't recognize the call doesn't mean the Holy Spirit wasn't involved. An important lesson for us to learn is that Jesus gives his promise and so we should be confident that he will keep that promise. A great tool for the Holy Spirit must be to call attention to our kingdom witness. This is a witness we can give repeatedly without conflict, without danger of being trampled.

To confirm that prayer is the continuing strategy, Jesus amplifies on the subject. He tells us by way of reassurance:

> *Which of you, if his son asks for bread, will give him a stone?*
> *Or if he asks for a fish, will give him a snake?*
> *If you, then, though you are evil, know how to give good gifts to your children,*
> *how much more will your Father in heaven give good gifts to those who ask him!* (Matt 7:9–11)

Many people have taught that the seeking, asking and knocking is for unbelievers to do. Jesus isn't talking to unbelievers in this sermon. He is instructing believers in the methods of kingdom living. The advice is for us. However, he *is* talking about salvation. He counsels us to ask, seek, and knock for our loved ones' salvation.

We are the children of our Father. This is about us asking for something and the Father answering by granting a good gift. What is the *good gift*? The Holy Spirit! Why would we ask for the Holy Spirit if we already have the Holy Spirit? Jesus isn't talking about being filled by the Spirit. He isn't veering from the subject at hand. He means we are to seek for the Spirit for our loved ones who don't yet know him.

I'm getting ahead of myself here. I said that by *good gifts* Jesus means the Holy Spirit, but I didn't explain how I reached that conclusion. In Luke's corollary to the sermon, he explains what Matthew leaves out. Luke explains the good gift that Jesus speaks of here: the opportunity for salvation. The words *good gifts* in Matthew are replaced by Luke with the words *the Holy Spirit*. All the other words in the two verses are identical.

> *If you then, though you are evil, know how to give good gifts to your children,*
> *how much more will your Father in heaven give the Holy Spirit*
> *to those who ask him!* (Luke 11:13)
>
> *If you, then, though you are evil, know how to give good gifts to your children,*
> *how much more will your Father in heaven give good gifts*
> *to those who ask him!* (Matt 7:13)

We don't need to ask for this good gift for ourselves. The Spirit has chosen to dwell within us. We know this because we are his children. Do we need to ask for what we already have? No, but we need to ask for the Holy Spirit to be given to those who don't yet have him. And if we, who are evil, know how to give good gifts, how much more will our Father in heaven know to give the Holy Spirit to those for whom we ask? *We* need to pray so *they* might be saved.

These are the steps of our most effective witness. Jesus knew before anybody that actions speak louder than words. We emphasize verbal witness, but it is a small piece of the whole formula. The only verbal step isn't even listed, it is implied. Loving kindness and lack of judgment are the common thread, the guardrail that keeps us on the proper path. Keeping poor in spirit should order our steps. Here's the progression as Jesus sees it.

We aren't to give dogs what is sacred. This means we aren't to ingratiate ourselves by unbecoming behavior. Bad behavior isn't what Paul meant when he said he would be all things to all people. Others won't notice our change of heart except through a change in our behavior.

1. Freely admit that the changes within you are due to Jesus. Don't talk about how bad you were before. Your loved ones already know *just* what you used to be like. Don't talk about how much better you are now. No one wants to hear it, and you may not be that much better yet. If we were as good as we thought we were, Paul wouldn't need to chide us to judge ourselves soberly or to not think more highly of ourselves than we should. Never forget you are a work in progress. Not forgetting helps you to stay poor in spirit.

2. Don't continue to witness verbally when your loved ones shut the door to your witness. You don't want them to build up a resistance to the message. You don't want them to trample the message or turn on you.
3. Pray. Prayer can do what we cannot.
4. Pray more fervently (Jas 5:16). And don't forget that effectiveness is not tied to how good you may think you are while in preparation to pray. After all, *Elias was a man subject to like passions as we are, and he prayed earnestly that it might not rain: and it rained not on the earth by the space of three years and six months* (Jas 5:17 KJV).
5. Keep praying, energetically.

Only the Holy Spirit can open a closed door. Knock that the door will be opened. Set aside a special time in which prayer for your loved one is your only petition. Maybe fast and pray. *Remember this: Whoever turns a sinner from the error of his way will save him from death and cover over a multitude of sins* (Jas 5:20). Do you know what else will cover over a multitude of sins? Of course you do. *Above all, love each other deeply, because love covers over a multitude of sins* (1 Pet 4:8).

> *So in everything, do to others what you would have them do to you,*
> *for this sums up the Law and the Prophets.* (Matt 7:12)

Jesus returns full circle with *do unto others*, because it is the inverse of 7:2. *For in the same way you judge others, you will be judged*. When Jesus says, "*So in everything*" the word *everything* refers to Matthew 7:1 to 7:11. *Everything* is an affirmation that the whole passage from, *do not* judge onward, is informed by a single theme. The use of the word *others* at both the beginning and end of the passage act as guides to keep us focused on the subject of judgment.

So in everything, do to others not only sums up the Law and the Prophets, it is a summary of all we've learned in Matthew 7. Treat others in the manner you would have God treat you. Don't work on their sin because you can't fix yours. Don't badger others with chronic verbal witness unless you would invite them to persistently try to change your mind about life's most important decision. Don't pray for others unless you would like them to pray for you. (I just threw that last one in to see if you're still paying attention.)

Obeying God and not judging others sums up the Law and the Prophets but it also fulfills the greatest commandments:

> *This* (loving God) *is the first and greatest commandment.*
> *And the second is like it: 'Love your neighbor as yourself.'*

All the Law and the Prophets hang on these two commandments." (Matt 22:38–40)

This is the Law and the Prophets, the greatest commandments and the Golden Rule, summed up and fulfilled in kingdom living. Who are we to do otherwise?

13

Two Roads

"Enter through the narrow gate.
For wide is the gate and broad is the road that leads to destruction,
and many enter through it.
But small is the gate and narrow the road that leads to life,
and only a few find it. (Matt 7:13–14)

THESE VERSES HAVE BEEN as misunderstood as any we've looked at thus far. We think they teach that only a few will be saved. I can see why, if we pull the verses out of context and consider them on their own. It plainly says most people will travel a road to their ultimate destruction. Only a few find the path less taken, eternal life.

If this is the meaning, we're left to ponder some tough questions. Did the Godhead conspire to construct a plan that practically guarantees the vast majority of humanity would suffer everlasting torment? Did Jesus want to make a small impact? Did he hope to suffer for the relative few?

I've been to a thoughtful atheist website where our answers to these questions are the author's main objections to Christianity. She can't understand the God of John Calvin, who devised a narrow path to heaven and chose only a few to travel it, and then built a grand boulevard to hell for the vast majority.

We know the Bible says God loves us. He zealously pursues us. John 3:16 says God loved *the world* so much that he sent his son. Pondering the gravity of God's sacrifice should lead us to realize that our standard interpretation of verses 13 and 14 must be incorrect. A recap of how we got to verse 13 should bring some perspective.

In the passage just prior to this, Jesus gave us a strategy for those who have rejected the gospel. He counseled prayer. He then explained that our Father wants the same thing we want: salvation for our loved ones. Jesus wasn't setting us up just to crush our hope. He doesn't mean, *"Pray for your loved ones, but hey, don't feel bad if they don't accept me as Lord because only a few will be saved anyway."* The interconnectedness of Jesus' thoughts saves us from such a misinterpretation. His real point is far more hopeful than we have understood through such a shallow reading.

Let me ask you a question. How did you get on to the narrow path? Did you stumble across it in you comparative religion class? Were you able to deduce the Passion from the grandeur of nature? Did you first meet Jesus in a dream?

Now let me answer for you. "No. Someone told me about Jesus, and then..."

I know that's your answer because that's the way almost everyone gets on the narrow path. We need to be led there by someone else. Jesus isn't giving us the arithmetic of predestination, he's asking us to grab someone's hand and gently lead them to the narrow path.

I'll bet you're thinking, "The guy who has been arguing against verbal witness just admitted we all find the narrow gate through verbal witness!" Not really. I have insisted we declare our status, so people can glorify our Father in Heaven. I've only advocated against forcing a choice for Jesus or against him. I think he'd agree with me, because that's his point in verses 13 and 14, and they are the culmination of a long argument for a living, rather than a verbal witness.

Before we can walk through the steps of the argument, we have to understand what Jesus means in the narrow gate analogy. I call it that because Jesus begins and ends with references to the narrow gate. The key is the first line. *Enter through the narrow gate.* As believers, we don't have to worry about the size of the gate. We've already passed through it. Yet this is an instruction to *us*. Why would Jesus direct us back to the narrow gate? Does he want us to go out the way we came in? No, he asks us to enter, not exit.

The Greek verb tense used for *enter* means the word can be viewed as something we begun doing at a certain point in the past and now should continue doing. We could paraphrase it as *"You have entered through the narrow gate, now keep on entering through it."* If the narrow gate leads to salvation, why must we continue to enter? To lead others by our example.

What should that example be? Well, let's take another look. Jesus began with us doing good deeds so others could praise our Father in Heaven. We start with our status because no one would know whom to praise unless they know we are Christians.

By way of contrast, he began to describe the broad road. The broad road is clean living. The pagans think so, and we seem to think so as well. Jesus shocked us with the idea that we have no chance of attracting the world with our relative sinlessness. We can beat some sin but not all sin, and the hardest sin to beat is pride. When we try to witness by our lessening sin or our claim to lessening sin, we are shoving others to the very center of broad road. The quantification of sin is the formula they already live by.

Then Jesus suggested that even if we can't be perfect, we can still show *one* of our Father's good qualities. We can love, even our enemies. Loving is easiest when we first step on to the narrow road because it is one of the earliest fruits of the Spirit (along with joy and peace). When I got saved, I don't think I felt ill will toward anybody. I had to be taught the world was my enemy. I learned to be suspicious of people who didn't think like "we" do; progressives and liberal theologians, those on welfare and those that would weaken the family. Yet Jesus said I had to love them as the Father loves them. I need to love them unreservedly and I need to respect their opinions.

After that, he told us not to act religious. We weren't to give alms, pray, or fast in order to be seen. We have to do them secretly. When we act religiously, we emphasize actions. The broad road is filled with people who are pinning their hopes on their actions. The Pharisees were great at pointing people back to the broad road. That's why Jesus said they make converts twice the children of hell that they were (Matt 23:15).

At this point in the sermon, Jesus explains more about the narrow road of faith and love. He does it through parallels. There are two roads and there are two eyes. The good eye looks to the narrow gate, Jesus. The bad eye is the way we naturally look at life. Likewise, there are two masters. One is the travel agent for the broad road and the other is Jesus.

It takes faith to have a good eye, a generous eye, when we might not have very much to share. Paul probably said it best: *the only thing that counts is faith expressing itself through love* (Gal 5:6b).

Finally Jesus tackles the biggest roadblock on the entrance to the narrow road. Judgment. Judgment is exactly what everyone expects at the end of the broad road, so it is particularly pernicious. Who knows how many people have wandered close to the entrance to the narrow road only to be steered away by the judgment of people who should know better, people that believe they have escaped being judged themselves?

The broad road/narrow road analogy reminds us to stay the course. The broad road is the law and the narrow road is grace. The narrow road is illogical by the world's standards. It can't be deduced so very few find it. If we tread the wrong path to the wrong gate, we lead others to their destruction. However, if we continue entering through the narrow gate (the Grace

Gate) we lead others to salvation. Is this not a major purpose of kingdom living—to point the Way?

If the narrow road is the good road, why did God make the broad road so broad? The broad road is also a wonderful expression of God's love. He has ordained that we all walk it. Jesus says *many* enter through the wide gate, but he doesn't say many travel down the broad road. That's because we *all* travel it. Yet we don't all enter the wide gate that leads to destruction. He wants us to leave that path for the superior one before we enter through the wide gate. The wide gate has to be at the end of the broad road or the broad road would have no purpose, and the broad road has a wonderful purpose.

The purpose of the broad road is to keep us on our best possible behavior. We sometimes say when someone is living rightly, that they are walking "the straight and narrow." How ironic! Actually, that person is walking "the straight and broad." And God wants us all to walk the broad road because it makes the world a better place. Our best possible behavior makes life bearable for everyone else, but it directs people away from the Grace gate.

Every Beatitude has been echoed elsewhere in the Sermon except for one: *Blessed are those who mourn, for they will be comforted*. When we studied this verse (way back in the fourth chapter) we noted the ameliorative properties impending death has on our behavior while we are still alive. Everyone's hope that *something* lies beyond the grave makes life's brevity purposeful. Whatever we think that *something* is, we think it will happen after a judgment. Fear of that potential judgment makes our earthly life more bearable for others. The journey down the broad road is a gift from God that we daily give to each other.

The broad road is an antidote to our antediluvian predisposition. *Every inclination of the thoughts of his* (humankind's) *hearts was* only *evil all the time* (Gen 6:5). Via the flood and the ensuing reduction of natural lifespan, God eradicated the word "only" from Genesis 6:5. (You can read where God essentially repeats Genesis 6:5 without the word *only*, in Genesis 8:21.) And that is the purpose of the broad road.

Before I was saved, my thoughts were primarily evil and always selfish, but they weren't always evil. In the back of my pagan mind, I knew I wasn't going to live forever. I believed God would someday weigh my life on the balance of his Justice. So I tried to do good, to make up for some of the evil I did. I did so out of selfish motives, but at least I didn't do evil continually. My thoughts weren't *only* evil all the time.

Every religion plays the tune of final judgment, whether it means eternal torment or returning as a turd beetle. This expectation of judgment is the broad road; the one that makes us hope our good deeds will outweigh our bad. We don't need to *find* this broad road any more than we need to be taught to breathe.

If we begin a verbal witness the way we should, with Jesus' love and triumph over sin and death, we are handing over the map to eternal life. If we then talk about how much less we sin; we may be snatching it back. Emphasizing anything other than Jesus as the path (the Way) confuses the hearer. They already have a natural affinity for, and a comprehensive experience with, the broad road. If we say we were great sinners before but lesser sinners now that we follow Jesus, what is the predominant subject? What do people hear us emphasizing? Sin. Sin and lessening sin. What keeps people from choosing Jesus if it isn't their sinful nature and the prospect of *less* sin?

Sin is fun, at least initially. Sin is exciting, if only in our minds, because we are products of our fallen world. Our thoughts are evil most of the time. So if we talk about how we used to sin a lot (like them) but now we sin less, where's the inducement to convert? They hear, "Come and follow Jesus, you'll have less fun and excitement!"

It's a wonder that anyone responds to a message like this. The only way it can be effective is if the hearer is in the midst of so much trouble that trading away the fun and excitement of sin suddenly seems like a more attractive alternative. Unfortunately, or perhaps fortunately, life on earth provides us with an abundance of troubles, so a witness emphasizing sin can be occasionally effective. In fact, it is effective just often enough to reinforce the validity of witnessing in the mode of highlighting our before and after behaviors.

But this method can also lead to a false witness by keeping our hearers bound to the broad road. Living better isn't what gets us to heaven. Faith in Christ Jesus gets us to heaven. Jesus is the narrow path that leads to life. Jesus is the Way to the narrow gate, the Grace Gate. The gate is narrow because it is one Jesus wide.

Judging is never full of grace. Judgment shines our light in the wrong direction, on our actions rather than on our God. Judging confirms the unbeliever's expectation that sin is the problem and so they've got to stop sinning. Judgment says, "you are doing it wrong." Jesus says, "Trust in me." Judging is the Devil's trap and sometimes we seem all too willing to assist him.

Instead of verbal witness, we can use the method Jesus prefers, the wordless witness of kingdom living. We can, as Jesus advises in these verses, continue to walk the narrow path to the small gate. We can keep entering in the same way we did initially. Others, once the Spirit draws them, can then follow us. A few may *find it* but most need a map. And better yet, almost anyone can follow a Christian down the narrow path if we take him by the spiritual hand.

Thus, God's vision is actually very different from ours. His first priority (and finest work) is saving us. The plan for Christ to provide a way has been in place since before Adam and Eve rebelled. God desires that none be lost. It doesn't make sense that he would build a wide road leading to destruction and a narrow, hard-to-find gate that limits who can get in. Yet, that has been our perspective. We have been content with a surface reading and shallow explanation. We don't understand Jesus' road/gate analogy in relation to God's saving grace.

And so these two verses, rendered so disheartening by a surface reading, are actually verses of God's great hope for us all, and a warning to the believer that we must walk the only road that counts: *faith expressing itself through love*, the true straight and narrow.

14

By Their Fruit

Watch out for false prophets.
They come to you in sheep's clothing, but inwardly they are ferocious wolves.
By their fruit you will recognize them.
Do people pick grapes from thornbushes, or figs from thistles
Likewise every good tree bears good fruit,
but a bad tree bears bad fruit.
A good tree cannot bear bad fruit, and a bad tree cannot bear good fruit.
Every tree that does not bear good fruit is cut down and thrown into the fire.
Thus, by their fruit you will recognize them.
Not everyone who says to me, 'Lord, Lord,' will enter the kingdom of heaven,
but only he who does the will of my Father who is in heaven.
Many will say to me on that day,
'Lord, Lord, did we not prophesy in your name,
and in your name drive out demons and perform many miracles?'
Then I will tell them plainly,
'I never knew you.
Away from me, you evildoers!' (Matt 7:15–23)

IN THE LAST CHAPTER, Jesus explained that judgment points people to the broad road. Now with these verses Jesus tells us about the *one* exception to *do not judge*. We must judge our prophets. False prophets can lead people away from the narrow road as surely as judgment can. Jesus remains focused on the overarching importance of the narrow road.

We must first judge our prophets to determine whether they are true or false prophets. The NIV says we are to watch out for the false ones. The King James says we are to beware. We have to beware because false prophets will prophesy falsely. If the primary function of a prophet is to proclaim the truth of Scripture, the false prophet will twist that truth. False prophets start with the Word of God but end in some unholy place. They derive deceitful meanings and applications.

Jesus could have used some other title to describe them—false leaders, false teachers, or false pastors—but he doesn't. He uses *false prophets* because it is all encompassing. Jesus calls us to judge our pastors and teachers, our televangelists and radio hosts.

> *Watch out for false prophets.*
> *They come to you in sheep's clothing,*
> *but inwardly they are ferocious wolves.* (Matt 7:15)

What an apt description! False prophets look like us. They wear sheep's clothing. Yet they don't feed on the word of God as sheep do. When Jesus talks about ferocious wolves in sheep's clothing, he means leaders who we think are called to lead us but seek to mislead us. They seem godly in their way (hence the sheep's clothing) but they work to turn us to *their* will instead of to the will of our Father. They may even believe their will and God's will are the same. These "prophets" are the most dangerous.

How then do we differentiate? How are we to recognize false leaders? Jesus carefully directs us to a precise definition. As he does in so many other places within the sermon, he starts with a logic problem to chip away at our preconceptions. Then he provides illustrations to bring us to the intended conclusion. Jesus starts with *By their fruit you will recognize them*.

What is the fruit of a pastor? We might think it is whether a pastor lives an exemplary life. They're supposed to, aren't they? Paul deals with the qualifications of a leader in his pastoral letters and emphasizes proper behavior. We've talked in this book about how leaders are held to a higher standard. Also, we've been taught that *fruit* means the consequences of our behavior. If we add together all these cherished concepts, we would think *by their fruit* means by their lifestyle.

Actually, *by their fruit* has nothing to do with whether or not our leaders live an exemplary life. Jesus wants to be certain we don't equate bad fruit with sin, or good fruit with good deeds or the lack of sin. He presents it logically to ensure there is no misunderstanding.

> *Likewise every good tree bears good fruit, but a bad tree bears bad fruit.*
> *A good tree cannot bear bad fruit,*

and a bad tree cannot bear good fruit. (Matt 7:17–18)

If a *good tree* is a Christian leader and sin is *bad fruit*, Jesus would be saying that no Christian leader can sin. Read the clause again, that's exactly what he would have to mean because *A good tree* cannot *bear bad fruit*. Logically then, a Christian *cannot* sin. However, we know from our own lives that the idea of not sinning again after our conversion is silly. The Epistles are filled with admonitions against sin, and those letters were written to believers. The admonitions wouldn't be needed if we weren't still prone to sin. So good (or bad) fruit must mean something other than whether or not we sin.

Even though *fruit* is a common theme in both Testaments and considered a consequence of our behavior, only once is fruit absolutely defined. Apostle Paul in his letter to the Galatians (5:22, 23) defines the fruit of the Spirit, and all the attributes are good: *But the fruit of the Spirit is love, joy, peace, patience, kindness, goodness, faithfulness, gentleness, and self-control.*

For years I thought Paul listed them in an order of importance. I thought: love, joy and peace were given first to accentuate them. Self-control was listed last because the last item on a list is also memorable. That was my brain's shorthand memory of a verse I hadn't memorized: *love, joy, peace . . . and self-control.* I tended to forget the ones in the middle.

Now I think they are listed in the order we are likely to attain them. Don't we experience *love, joy* and *peace* immediately upon being saved? *Patience* (according to passages like the one that starts the book of James) tends to come later, through the trials we experience as believers. *Patience* should lead to *kindness*, and if we can be patiently kind to others, we show the essence of *goodness*. Unwavering *faithfulness* comes later in the process. That is why God promises that even when we are faithless, he remains faithful. *Gentleness* is a necessary prelude to true *self-control*.

True self-control is probably an outgrowth of all the other components attained together through the Perfecter of our faith. Self-control without the other fruits of the Spirit is likely a false self-control, leading to either legalism or self-righteousness. Either fork in the narrow path misleads by directing people to the wide road that leads to destruction. If a leader is zealous for self-control without the necessary intermediate steps of patience, kindness, goodness, faithfulness, and gentleness, he is short-circuiting the Spirit's progressive program. A false self-control can very well be the misguided goal of a false prophet.

The fruit of the false prophet contrasts with proper spiritual fruit. Let's look at a few of its facets. The first fruit of the Spirit is love. If the pastor doesn't love God, he's not a believer. The number of pastors and ministers who don't believe in God is astonishing. According to surveys of pastors themselves, in some denominations the figure is over ten percent. That means an incredible number of people are going to church and *not* being pointed toward Jesus.

How can a pastor not believe in God, let alone not love God, without his congregation knowing it? He could be very intelligent and very deceitful. We would call such a man "slick." Slickness can hide a multitude of sins besides unbelief. Think of the pastors that have fallen and had their fall reported in the media. One was a national voice against homosexuality that dallied with gay prostitutes. Another consorted with female prostitutes. A third had a mistress but was brought down by greed. They were all men of extraordinary talents and for a time, they deceived us. We all practice this same deceit (or conceit) to some extent. We dress nicely and say the right things when we go to church. If we believe we are successful in our slight subterfuge, why couldn't a pastor be equally adept?

If we practice deceit, wouldn't judging our leaders for the same thing be hypocrisy? We know Jesus abhors hypocrisy. The answer has to be yes, and that is why a pastor's sin is *not* a consideration in Jesus' exposition. The judgment we are required to exercise here pertains to *the real fruit of a leader*. If fruit doesn't mean sin, what does it mean and how can we recognize it?

The real fruit of a leader is the collective heart of his followers; the *fruit of the Spirit* as exhibited by the flock. It takes a long time for a tree to bear fruit. For many fruit trees, it takes as long as four or five years. In one parable, the owner of an orchard commands that an unfruitful tree be cut down, but the servant argues that he will exercise special care if the owner will allow it one more year to show evidence of fruit.

We may need a long time to discern whether a pastor is a wolf or a shepherd if we seek to search his heart. Yet his congregation has already been in place for just such a length of time. We can look to them for clues because the congregation is the fruit of a pastor.

God calls a true pastor, but we are also called. The difference in our calling and a pastor's is not one of degree; it is one of responsibility. Our responsibility (*beware of false prophets*) is to follow the right leader. Otherwise we might have to acquire the fruit of the Spirit from among thistles and thorn bushes.

> *Do people pick grapes from thornbushes, or figs from thistles?* (Matt 7:16)

Here Jesus gives us the criteria for judging our leaders more surely. The key is the word *people*. Watch the people, not the prophet. How does the congregation as a whole exhibit the fruit of the Spirit? The *people* are the pastor's fruit.

Grapes and figs are good fruit. They are tasty and nutritious. They have antioxidant properties. It is difficult for people to pick fruit or to have fruit in their lives if they are following the wrong leader. Thorn bushes and thistle patches are sharp and sticky places. They can keep us from reaching the good fruit. A wolf in sheep's clothing will corner us in the thistle instead of leading us into the orchard. The wide path is replete with patches of thorns and thistle.

On the other hand, our Shepherd, the greatest and truest Prophet, makes us lie down in green pastures. He leads us to still waters and restores our soul. These are the resting places along that narrow path that we must continually tread. Jesus tosses off these metaphors as if they were afterthoughts, yet when we take the time to meditate on them, we can recognize their depth.

In the end it will be easy to discern the heart of our leaders.

> *Every tree that does not bear good fruit is cut down and thrown into the fire.* (Matt 7:19)

A pastor may be a great humanitarian, a doer of the social gospel. He may fight for the rights of the oppressed. He may lead a thousand television viewers to salvation. He might heal or lead a mega church with twenty thousand members. But unless he follows God, he is a ferocious wolf. He is a predator. He sounds like his father, Satan, in First Peter 5:8: *Your adversary the devil, as a roaring lion, walketh about, seeking whom he may devour.* (KJV) Peter calls us to be sober, to be vigilant. Jesus calls us to beware. If we are to be wary, we are not to wait until the final act, the cutting down and the throwing into the fire. We are to be on our guard from the start.

> *Thus, by their fruit you will recognize them.* (Matt 7:20)

There it is again, *by their fruit*. Jesus wants to make sure we know he is talking about the fruit of a leader, not the fruit of a Christian. Thus, the *Thus*. The admonition to judge the fruit brackets the instruction on false leaders.

I have wondered how a false teacher can lead someone to Christ. Saving a soul seems like good fruit. But then I remember it is the Holy Spirit that saves us. The false prophets can still lead us astray afterward. A believer pointing to the wrong path can mislead the lost within his sphere of influence. A leader pointing to the wrong path can mislead a multitude.

Healing someone, leading them to Christ, or performing other miracles seems like the very best fruit, but these acts are not the fruit Jesus speaks of. He drives that home next.

> *Not everyone who says to me, 'Lord, Lord,' will enter the kingdom of heaven,*
> *but only he who does the will of my Father who is in heaven.*
> *Many will say to me on that day, 'Lord, Lord, did we not prophesy in your name,*
> *and in your name drive out demons and perform many miracles?'*
> *Then I will tell them plainly, 'I never knew you. Away from me, you evildoers!'* (Matt 7:21–23)

False prophets will refer to the name of the *Lord* repeatedly as they mislead. They may use it in their ministry more often than we do. Jesus quotes the false prophets twice, and both times they address him as *Lord, Lord*. Yet theirs is a different Lord than ours. Our Lord will say he never knew them. Their evildoing is in directing their followers to the broad road.

Their sins don't disqualify them; they can't. Likewise, great works can't qualify them; they also can't. A false prophet can still prophesy in Jesus' name, but he will prophesy falsely. Regardless of their earthly accomplishments, Jesus will tell them *away from me, you evildoers!*

So what chance do we have to avoid coming under the leadership of a false prophet? What do we look for when observing the flock? Love for God and love for our neighbors: that sums up the law and the prophets. The love the flock exhibits should be unconditional and unreserved like the love of Jesus, not the tough love of judgment. Tough love, when it is needed, is between the leader and individual followers in specific instances.

We can especially discern the false leader if we use Jesus' criterion in verse 19, *only he who does the will of my Father in heaven*. What is the will of my Father? Duh. What can we say Jesus is teaching us if not how to live and think in the kingdom? We are to work to fulfill the plan God envisions. This is the will of our Father. Jesus said he could *only* do the will of his Father and we can surmise that the Holy Spirit works under the same beautiful restriction. The will of the Father produces the fruit of the Spirit. Are our pastors seeking to do the Father's will, or are they seeking to do their own will? Do they encourage or do they manipulate? Do they exhort or do they extort?

Our Father doesn't force us to toe the line. He gives us choices. He wants our love returned to him freely. He teaches, prods, and chastens and then waits patiently for us to return like the prodigal. When we return he embraces us with open arms. If the Father's will doesn't include manipulation and forced conduct, than neither should a pastor's will. Jesus doesn't force us to conform to an outward code of conduct. He teaches us to filter the rules through love.

As evidenced by his words in verse 21 through 23 about great acts performed by those who don't know him, actions are not what it's all about.

Don't look for a church that impacts the world so much as a church that exhibits the fruit of the Spirit. If the people show such fruit and then also impact their community, so much the better, God is at work there.

Beware also of the pastor that uses peer pressure from within the church body to keep members on the straight and narrow. According to the book *Churches That Abuse*, this is always the first step and first sign that a congregation is on its way to hell on earth. If conduct is the heart of the Body, the Body has no heart. Churches that abuse always make their members believe they are an elite. The membership pursues purity of conduct with a paramilitary zeal. The Pharisees had conduct down cold but Jesus says, unless our righteousness exceeds that of the Pharisees we will not see the kingdom of heaven.

If a pastor's fruit is its visible representation amongst his people then we have to look at the congregation for evidence of the fruit of the Spirit. Is the predominant feeling in the church one of love, joy, and peace, or is it an atmosphere of judgment and legalism? The spirit of the flock is the fruit of the pastor.

The Holy Spirit does not sit on our shoulder, waiting to berate. He is not the Hammer of our soul. He is the still, small voice. He convicts of sin but he rarely prompts others to convict us of sin. He dwells within other believers in the same way he dwells within us. He works from the inside with others just as he works from inside of us. If these are the ways of God, then this is the will of God. We must only follow leaders as they follow the will of God. We need to remind ourselves that we are in the midst of Jesus' teaching on judgment.

These are the questions we must ask: does our pastor (servant/leader) try to bend people to his will or does he gently mold them to the will of the Father? Is he a harsh taskmaster like the devil or is his yoke easy? Does he emphasize conduct like the Pharisees or love and mercy like Jesus? Judge your leader's actions and his teachings, looking for the mark of the Pharisee, but be aware that the flock is his fruit. In this only are we called to judge.

We all love our pastor. We wouldn't attend the church we do if we didn't love him. Yet we must look for serious, consistent error. We must beware of legalism and look for love. Over time, the people of the church will show the pastor's heart. The Body as a whole is the telltale heart. Such a body led by such a pastor will not produce an abundance of the fruit of love, joy, peace . . . on its own amidst thorn bushes and thistles. We may still bear good fruit, but much less of it.

On the other hand, don't look for the perfect body. Oscar Wilde once said he wouldn't join any club that would allow him as a member. Don't go overboard. I know my pastor to be a good steward. I know whose will he is attempting to follow. I know whom he seeks.

We need to take a small detour here. I would like to emphasize that you will *not* know your brother, your sister, or your unsaved friend by their fruit. *"By their fruit you shall know them"* is a wrong teaching unless used in the context of our leaders. Luke also quotes *by their fruit* in the context of leadership. He says a false leader is like the blind leading the blind. Jesus gives us this test for our leaders because it is important we be under proper leadership.

So when a brother or sister quotes this phrase as a standard by which we gauge another member of the flock, show them the proper context. Tell them they are using it in a different way than Jesus intended. Tell them Jesus was very careful to make sure we don't use it to judge anyone individually. Show them that He makes it clear that fruit isn't sin or the lack thereof. The fruit he speaks of is the overall attitude and heart of the church. God will himself judge individuals by their fruit, but all teaching on judging shows it is God's prerogative, not ours, unless he specifically assigns the task to us as parents or in other leadership roles.

Then mention that fruit is tied, not to sin, but to the fruit of the Spirit from Galatians 5. You can point out that the fruit reference pertains to leaders or false prophets and is exhibited by the flock as a whole. Show them how Jesus makes this stunningly clear in this passage. *Don't* mention that they are exhibiting exactly the opposite of the good fruit Jesus tells us to look for in the Body, just keep it in mind for your own future conduct.

But by all means, for heaven's sake and for yours, judge your leaders. Beware of false prophets. This earthly life is too short to follow the wrong leader.

The very first responsibility of the Christian is to love God. The primary way we show our love to him is through obedience (John 14:15). If the second responsibility is to love others, the third must be to be in the right local body. The love and encouragement we receive in the right place can help sustain us, but the judgment and discouragement we receive in the wrong place can be devastating. At certain times in our lives, thorn bushes and thistles are more than an annoyance; they can totally block the way.

There is a saying: "The Army of the Lord is the only one that shoots its own wounded." That doesn't have to be the case. When you sin, when you fall, (if it becomes known) how will you be treated? Who will throw the first stone? If we are stoned and the stoning is not fatal, it will drive us away. If we are driven from the Body, how can we be restored? The very Body that would worry about the sin of another rather than its own sin would be guilty of causing us to forsake the assembly we so desperately need. *Let us not give up meeting together, as some are in the habit of doing,* but let us encourage one another (Heb 10:25).

If we are not encouraging each other, if we are not feeling encouraged, the habit of meeting with other believers will be broken. Jesus is preaching encouragement through lack of condemnation. Paul writes at the start of Romans 8, *There is now, therefore, no condemnation for those who are in Christ.* If there is no condemnation for those in Christ, presumably from Christ Himself, then there should be no condemnation from those who are in Christ's body. There would be no condemnation if we all only worried about our own relationship with God. The plank in our own eye should preclude anything else. Paul says in Romans 2:1, *You, therefore, have no excuse, you who pass judgment on someone else, for at whatever point you judge the other, you are condemning yourself.* That sounds a lot like Jesus. Jesus says, *'for in the same way you judge others, you will be judged.*

Jesus is the Rock. Jesus is the Cornerstone of the foundation. Jesus is the Word of God become flesh. Upon his words we must build the firm foundation of our churches. If our churches were to follow his teachings in this sermon and if his chosen leaders sought to do his will, the Body could withstand anything.

In the great storms of life, especially the storms we create ourselves, we need support. We can count on Jesus' support as we work toward restoration, but we can't really see it except in hindsight. So we need this Body on earth to minister in a concrete way. We need to show his love and mercy as his proxy. We need to be Jesus *to each other* as well as to a lost world. This will give us a strength and unity through love that we have never achieved doctrinally. The earthly church needs to be three things: a house of love, a house of prayer, and a house of worship. Jesus shows us in the sermon that this is the proper order. This is God's blueprint for wisdom and strength.

The strong house on the rock is not the church or a church. The house on the rock is only the church that puts the principles of kingdom living into practice, the church that hears all these words of Jesus we have studied and puts them into practice.

> *Therefore everyone who hears* these words *of mine and puts them into practice*
> *is like a wise man who built his house on the rock.*
> *The rain came down, the streams rose, and the winds blew and beat against that house;*
> *yet it did not fall, because it had its foundation on the rock.*
> *But everyone who hears* these words *of mine and* does not put them into practice

*is like a foolish man who built his house on sand.
The rain came down, the streams rose, and the winds blew and beat against that house,
and it fell with a great crash.* (Matt 7:24–27)

Both men in Jesus' story desired to build a house for the Lord. They both *heard* his words because they were both believers. Yet only one built it on a foundation of love and the principles Jesus teaches in the sermon. Let's make the house of the Lord one that will withstand anything. We've seen enough great crashes. All the properly built houses together will make up the kingdom of heaven on earth that Jesus envisions for us.

We start by not judging. We welcome all those who are—or would be—our brothers and sisters. We are to share what we have, who we are, and Who we know. Let's work to stay strong as individuals by not sinning, as much as that is possible. Let's serve each other by showing hospitality. Let's shout to the Lord and make a joyful noise as we worship. We need to be united in worship and united in loving encouragement. Let us beware of wolves in sheep's clothing that seek to pervert these activities. Let's build our house on the Rock, the Rock who has taught us about love, mercy, kindness, and peace.

*When Jesus had finished saying these things,
the crowds were amazed at his teaching,
because he taught as one who had authority,
and not as their teachers of the law.* (Matt 7:28–29)

15

Re: Rebuke

Now that we've finished our deconstruction of the sermon, I'd like to revisit my original conundrum. When it first became clear to me that *do not judge* meant do not judge, so many passages to the contrary came to mind that I knew I was missing something. The Bible is full of examples of judgment. We can't read long without running across them. A thousand years before Jesus' birth we have: *better a wise man's rebuke than hidden love*. And after Christ's resurrection: *expel the wicked man from among you*.

It would have been unwieldy to consider possible contradictions as we walked through the Sermon. It would also have been confusing for me to deal with them in that context. And you, God bless you, have already had to put up with too many digressions on my part. But now we need to look at these contrary examples. Judgment is so deeply ingrained within us that I'm afraid we will negate Jesus' teaching unless we can show it in harmony with these other passages.

I considered them (all that I could find) in those early days of illumination, before I began writing. They were important in determining the final shape of what I have argued Jesus wants us to know. Actually, I had done a lot of the preliminary work previously, without knowing it would relate. When my church was in danger of splitting, in 1998 or 1999, I wrote an open letter to the elders. The letter contained my thoughts on Paul's letters to the Corinthians, which we will cover in the next chapter.

A few years later, I did a word study on rebuke. I can't even remember why. But I do remember that the word study brought me to that initial idea of verticality. I remember bringing it to a Bible study, thinking I was in for a fight. My Pastor graciously gave me a few minutes to present my idea.

When I finished, he wholeheartedly agreed, and we moved on to a different subject. So as we start to look at the biblical examples that seem counter to *do not judge*, rebuke seems like a good place to start.

No doubt it is biblical and no doubt it is necessary, but here's the thing about rebuke: it is not your responsibility. There are over sixty uses of the word in the Bible, and with a single, debatable exception, (we'll come to that one last) it was never done in a peer-to-peer relationship. This is the predominant biblical example. It is never our job to rebuke a brother, sister, or neighbor. Rebuke is always vertical. Rebuke implies that special responsibility we've talked about, and a hierarchical relationship. A Pastor can rebuke a churchgoer. A teacher can rebuke a student. A parent can rebuke a child. Oh, and God can rebuke anyone he pleases. He retains the ultimate in verticality.

Because God ties the role to the responsibility, the opposite is also true. The lesser can rebuke the greater. A follower can rebuke a leader when that leader is clearly wrong. That's why Jesus tells us to judge our leaders: to beware of false prophets. Rebuke is always vertical and always based on God's ordained relationships. That's how it works in the Bible.

I don't mean that every verse will show verticality. Some are position-neutral. Just as the Bible instructs us how to be good servants or masters rather than condemning slavery outright, many of the verses teach us how to receive rebuke rather than condemning it. These verses focus on relationship rather than insurrection or conflict. Slavery and rebuke will be a part of our reality as long as we are fallen.

Because the concept of rebuke is so important, we will consider every pertinent mention, instance by instance. Before we do, I would like to look at some verses about dealing with others that *don't actually* use the word rebuke. They provide a counterbalance. To consider verses that seem to argue for an approach different than rebuke will help us accentuate the cognitive dissonance. If some verses speak of rebuke and others speak against it, we can come to see the need to uncover the special circumstances when rebuke might be appropriate. First, let's listen to Jesus answer Pharisees who were counseling rebuke:

> *On hearing this, Jesus said,*
> *"It is not the healthy who need a doctor, but the sick.*
> *But go and learn what this means:*
> *'I desire mercy, not sacrifice.'* (Matt 9:12–13)
>
> *If you had known what these words mean,*
> *'I desire mercy, not sacrifice,'*
> *you would not have condemned the innocent.* (Matt 12:7)

I desire mercy, not sacrifice. Do we know what these words mean? Both quotes are from Matthew, so it isn't the same situation being quoted in different gospels. Jesus taught it more than once.

The sick people in the first teaching are sinners. That's obvious. What is not obvious is that in the second quote, the *innocent* are also sinners. They are disciples of Jesus that had broken the Sabbath by plucking grain as they walked through a field. Jesus compared them to another group of "innocent" sinners: David's men that had broken the Temple Law by eating consecrated bread. I've described them as sinners because that's how they would have looked to us had we been observing them. They broke the Law. However, that's not how Jesus saw them. He saw both his disciples and David's men as innocent.

This is one reason we need to show mercy. We can interpret Scripture correctly, call sin sin, and still be wrong. The outward act can't reveal as much to us as the heart reveals to God. In light of this observation, is it any wonder Jesus desires mercy instead of sacrifice?

The sacrifice Jesus doesn't desire as much as mercy is the Temple sacrifice. The Hebrew Bible insisted that the ordained sacrifices took away the sin of the Jews. We understand that they are no longer necessary because they are redundant and less splendid than Jesus' supremely merciful sacrifice. With his work on the cross and after, Jesus changed the arc of justice. His sacrifice was once for all and so he redirects our attention to mercy.

He contrasts sacrifice with mercy because mercy so often requires a sacrifice of self. Mercy is part of taking up our cross daily. Mercy is how we show Jesus to others. He has completed the sacrifice of atonement so there is nothing left for us but mercy.

Well, I've done it again. I promised to fit Jesus' ideas with the rest of the Bible, but then I went right back to quoting Jesus. I tend to fixate on him and I hope it's not a fault. Let's look at what the rest of the New Testament has to say.

Here are a few thoughts from Paul about judgment. We think of Paul as the Apostle who most often counsels us to judge others, but we have instances of him counseling exactly the opposite. The first implies rebuke and also clarifies innocence

> *My conscience is clear, but that does not make me innocent.*
> *It is the Lord who judges me.*
> *Therefore* judge nothing *before the appointed time;*
> *wait till the Lord comes* (1 Cor 4:4 and 5).

Oops, I was wrong! We can judge. We only have to wait until Jesus returns.

Here's another verse that shows our twin responsibilities. We must obey (keep our own conscience clear) while not judging others.

> *The other man's conscience, I mean, not yours.*
> *For why should my freedom* be judged *by another's conscience?* (1 Cor 11:29)

These citations of Paul are important because they show him to be in agreement with Jesus. We tend to accentuate a couple of instances in which he *seems* to offer advice that runs counter. By offering the contrary advice as a clarification of Jesus' real intent, we allow ourselves a rationalization for judging when we shouldn't.

In his letter to Colossi, Paul seems to infer that we can be holy without the burden of keeping our brethren (and sistern) on the straight and narrow.

> *Therefore, as God's chosen people, holy and dearly loved,*
> *clothe yourselves with compassion, kindness, humility, gentleness and patience.*
> *Bear with each other and forgive whatever grievances you may have against one another.*
> *Forgive as the Lord forgave you.*
> *And over all these virtues put on love,*
> *which binds them all together in perfect unity* (Col 3:12–14).

The last sentence hints that love, not doctrinal uniformity, is the source of unity. And this isn't the only time Paul links unity to love. These qualities (forgiveness, mercy, encouragement, love, and not judging) are a consistent biblical theme. How do we reconcile them with rebuke? Responsibility is the key. We only rebuke those God has given us the responsibility to help mold.

Now let's look at each instance of rebuke in the Bible. We'll omit the times when God rebukes; we all agree he has that right. For the sake of brevity I will also leave out the times we are told *not* to rebuke. They aren't in dispute. Let's look at the rest. Here goes, in biblicalogical order. Pay attention to the relative position of the participants:

His sons, however, did not listen to their father's rebuke, for it was the Lord's will to put them to death. (1 Sam 2:25) Father to son, right? Vertical.

Oh, I forgot about David and Solomon. In the Psalms, Proverbs, and Ecclesiastes, these *rulers* often state that it is good to *accept* a rebuke. This supports my hypothesis. Again, it is vertical, follower to leader. We'll explore the solid reasons for this shortly. These three books also state variations on the theme of how a wise man accepts a rebuke gladly. Deciding to accept a rebuke well is valid advice and keeps resentment from festering in the Body over an ill-advised rebuke. Counseling us to accept a rebuke is far different from counseling us *to* rebuke. The former acknowledges our sinful propensities and gives us a strategy to deal with them peacefully, the latter is sin we must work to eliminate.

The wise man's alternative would be to *rebuke* the *rebuker* for *rebuking* him. That wouldn't get anybody anywhere. That's how incidents become feuds and feuds become wars. Accepting a rebuke is a far cry from rebuking. Here are David and Solomon, leaders and kings, writing about a king's rebuke or accepting rebuke from a follower:

> *Let a righteous man strike me—it is a kindness;*
> *let him rebuke me—it is oil on my head.*
> *My head will not refuse it.*
> *Yet my prayer is ever against the deeds of evildoers* (Ps 141:5)

The advice is to accept a rebuke graciously. These verses are not a license to rebuke any more than they are a license to strike another, even if we are righteous. Actually, especially if we are righteous.

> *If you had responded to my rebuke,*
> *I would have poured out my heart to you*
> *and made my thoughts known to you* (Prov 1:23).

Most of the proverbs are traditionally attributed to King Solomon. What's more, they are ostensibly a father's advice to his son. The king also offers advice to other leaders. He tells them the qualities to look for in the wise men they should seek out as advisers:

> *Do not rebuke a mocker or he will hate you;*
> *rebuke a wise man and he will love you* (Proverbs 9:8).

> *A wise son heeds his father's instruction,*
> *but a mocker does not listen to rebuke* (Prov 13:1).

> *He who listens to a life-giving rebuke will be at home among the wise* (Prov 15:31).

> *A rebuke impresses a man of discernment more than a hundred lashes a fool* (Prov 17:10).

> *Flog a mocker, and the simple will learn prudence;*
> *rebuke a discerning man, and he will gain knowledge* (Prov 19:25).

Those advisers, rather than being worthless yes-men, could then offer sage advice:
> *Like an earring of gold or an ornament of fine gold*
> *is a wise man's rebuke to a listening ear* (Prov 25:12).

Better is open rebuke than hidden love (Prov 27:5).

Do you think this distortion couldn't happen to Solomon or David? Do you think they couldn't be insulated by their power? Do you think no one feared them for their authority? After all, one was the wisest man alive and the other was a man after God's own heart.

Let me change your opinion.

Here are David's Famous Last Words. They are an instruction to Solomon. After all David had been through, after all he had accomplished, after all God had done for him and for Israel, here is what was on David's mind in the very last moments of his life:

> "And remember, you have with you Shimei son of Gera, the Benjamite from Bahurim,
> who called down bitter curses on me the day I went to Mahanaim.
> When he came down to meet me at the Jordan, I swore to him by the Lord:
> 'I will not put you to death by the sword.'
> But now, do not consider him innocent.
> You are a man of wisdom;
> you will know what to do to him.
> Bring his gray head down to the grave in blood."
> Then David rested with his fathers and was buried in the City of David (2 Kgs 8–10).

You are a man of wisdom. David and Solomon were both men of wisdom. Not because they were perfect, but because they knew leaders need rebuke. Yet here is David instructing Solomon to kill a man David had sworn not to kill. The instruction was literally the last thing on his mind. (Another set of David's last words have also been recorded in Scripture, but I think of them as more of a public utterance, his last words to the nation. This private exchange between father and son are more likely his last words before he died.)

If absolute power corrupts absolutely then relative power corrupts relatively. Leaders today in our churches may not have the power of life or death but they still wield an enormous relative power. They are the power at the top of an important social hierarchy. This means they still will be liable to feel a certain distortion from those who would seek to please them. Leaders will always find themselves in the midst of yes-men and subtle flatterers. Leaders need access to rebuke. From the opposite side of the power spectrum, followers need to be sure they are following the right leader. That is why Jesus told us to beware of false prophets in Matthew 7.

Now let's move on to the New Testament uses of the word *rebuke*.

So watch yourselves.
"If your brother sins, rebuke him,
and if he repents, forgive him (Luke 17:3).

If he sins against you seven times a day,
and seven times comes back to you and says, 'I repent,'
forgive him (Luke 17:4).

Luke 17:3 is tricky. Taken alone, it advocates rebuking for sin. However, the context is personal rather than general. We can see this more clearly in the next verse. Jesus narrows his advice to situations in which your brother sins against *you*. In Matthew 18, he also talked about how to handle it when another sins against us. In both instances Jesus means to advise us on the best course when we are personally harmed by an action. He never intends for us to harbor resentment for wrongs done *to* us by another believer. We might need to rebuke him, confront him, or gently restore him to finally effect reconciliation or stop the offense. Yet regardless of the means we use to end up getting our point across, it is clear from the verses that end the Sermon on the Mount that we should start our conversation gently. We find the same implied progression in Matthew 18.

Again, this rebuke is for wrongs done against us specifically, not for use when we are merely personally offended by the sins of another. When the second situation occurs, it is the pastor's role to decide whether the believer needs rebuke. It is the role of the pastor because he is the leader and rebuke must be vertical.

Some of the Pharisees in the crowd said to Jesus,
"Teacher, rebuke your disciples!" (Luke 19:39)

Hmmm, the Pharisees knew about rebuking!

The final uses of *rebuke* are contained in instructions given to Timothy and Titus. Both men aspired to the same position, pastor. These were directives given to a pastor outlining his duties and responsibilities. That's why scholars refer to them as the pastoral letters. They are superior to follower. Even then, Paul is careful that the rebuke generally needs to be gentle.

Do not rebuke an older man harshly,
but exhort him as if he were your father.
Treat younger men as brothers (1 Tim 5:1).

Preach the Word;
be prepared in season and out of season;
correct, rebuke and encourage –
with great patience and careful instruction (2 Tim 4:2).

> *This testimony is true.*
> *Therefore, rebuke them sharply,*
> *so that they will be sound in the faith* (Tit 1:13).

The sharp rebuke here is telling. The men to which Paul refers were *teaching* (one of those roles granted by God) the traditions of men and upsetting whole families. This might seem like a peer-to-peer rebuke, pastor to teacher, but it isn't. These "teachers" were not truly granted that authority by the Lord because they were teaching works rather than faith, and, Paul makes it clear that they were doing it for their own gain. The rebuke retains its verticality.

> *These, then, are the things you should teach.*
> *Encourage and rebuke with all authority.*
> *Do not let anyone despise you* (Titus 2:15).

Here is one last instance of peer-to-peer. The devil is not superior to the archangel. In theory, they are equals. It is noteworthy that Michael would not rebuke his peer, but left it to God.

> *But even the archangel Michael,*
> *when he was disputing with the devil about the body of Moses,*
> *did not dare to bring a slanderous accusation against him,*
> *but said, "The Lord rebuke you!"* (Jude 1:9).

We have covered seventeen uses of the word. We have left out forty-three additional times where the Lord rebukes. Not once have we discovered an example of a brother or sister rebuking a peer for some sin in their life. Not once have we found a believer rebuking another for doctrinal error. It is not our responsibility. It is the responsibility of our pastors and our teachers because God gives them this responsibility and holds them accountable in a special way. This is how God has established it. It keeps us from pandemonium. Remember, he knows our hearts. He has seen the chaos we can cause.

God uses the same principle in the secular world. He has ordained civil authority. Governments also have a special responsibility. When we see a drunk driver, we don't pull them over and make a citizen's arrest. We call the police. If we see kids in the park smoking pot, we don't handcuff them and haul them off to our basements to serve a thirty-day sentence, we call the police. If we catch our own kids smoking pot, we do deal with them in the way we see fit because they are our responsibility. That's how God has set things up.

Christians are good at understanding the civil boundaries of responsibility. The same principles should apply to the Body. Where did we get the idea that we are the spiritual police? We can get it from many different places but the root cause is pride. We think we are smart enough and wise enough to rebuke a brother, sister, or unbeliever. We believe they are not smart or wise enough to realize they are in error. If we think *we* are wise enough and *they* are not, our pride is working overtime. It stems from not being *poor in spirit*.

It also comes from a lack of reliance on God. We fret about evildoers instead of resting in the Lord. We rationalize that we must speak because they have quenched the Spirit. If they have quenched the Spirit, it is the responsibility of the pastor to gently instruct them or to rebuke them. We must be careful that our judgment does not cause the same effect we are trying to curb in another. Look at this quote from Ephesians. It intimates that it is easier for us to grieve the Spirit than we would think it to be to quench (or stifle) the Spirit.

> *Do not let any unwholesome talk come out of your mouths,*
> *but only what is helpful for building others up according to their needs,*
> *that it may benefit those who listen.*
> *And do not* grieve *the Holy Spirit of God,*
> *with whom you were sealed for the day of redemption.*
> *Get rid of all bitterness, rage and anger, brawling and slander,*
> *along with every form of malice.*
> *Be kind and compassionate to one another,*
> *forgiving each other,*
> *just as in Christ God forgave you* (Eph 4:29–32).

We all know we can *quench the Spirit* by habitually ignoring his gentle promptings. It is a process. But here we see that we can *grieve the Holy Spirit* with a single act, by malice toward others or not being kind, compassionate, and forgiving.

To not grieve and to not quench: these are our twin responsibilities. Obedience operates within and mercy flows outward. Lack of obedience quenches the Spirit and lack of compassion grieves the Spirit. This is the yin and yang of our Christian walk, if such an oxymoronic activity is even possible to contemplate. The Spirit wants us to speak *only what is helpful for building up others according to their needs*. Why? So *it may benefit those who listen*. If we rebuke a peer, they may hear us but they may not listen.

The ability to listen is a trait of effective leaders. It is especially strong in those displaying the servant leadership characteristics Jesus modeled. A good leader understands that we are called to fine-tune their leadership. It is our own fault if we follow a bad leader. We won't be able to blame them on the day we stand before God. We will be judged as individuals.

Rebuking a leader should always be a solemn task. Although there are instances in the Bible that show a follower can rebuke a leader, there are also passages that suggest rebuking a leader erroneously has serious consequences. The Nathan passage is an example of appropriate rebuke. *God* sent Nathan. That is a good biblical model. We should be sure we are rebuking our leaders only with God's blessing. If we think we have a matter serious enough to confront a leader, we should take it to the Lord and wait for him to release us to the task. Otherwise, we might fall into that other category of rebuking a leader, improper rebuke. I think of Aaron and Miriam speaking against Moses in Numbers 12. God gave Miriam a skin disease for a week as a warning to change her thinking.

This is an interesting story for its honesty and grasp of human nature. Aaron and Miriam believed they were prophets on the same level as Moses and so had the right to speak against him, peer-to-peer. The fact that Moses was their little brother may even have entered into it. God called the three of them together and disabused them of the notion. He told Miriam and Aaron they received prophesies as dreams in the night whereas he spoke to Moses face to face. Moses was the greater and his followers needed to exercise care before speaking against him. This example suggests we only upbraid our leaders when God clearly grants us leave to do so.

On the other hand, there are numerous examples of godly biblical men *not* rebuking leaders. Peter, Paul, and John all leave us no example of rebuke for the political leaders of their day. Caesar, Pilate, and Herod certainly had need of rebuke yet no rebuke came from these godly men. John the Baptist rebuked Herod and it ended up costing him his life. The apostles were beaten and jailed for witnessing, yet while in court, they did not rebuke the power structure that commanded the injustice. They only stated that they had no other choice but to follow the leading of the Spirit.

We've looked every pertinent use of rebuke in the Bible except for the very first. It is the only verse in the Bible that indicates it was proper to rebuke a peer. Here it is. *Do not hate your brother in your heart. Rebuke your neighbor frankly so you will not share in his guilt* (Leviticus 19:17).

This was a clear, strong message from God: if we don't rebuke our neighbor, we share in his guilt. I believe a single verse in the whole of the Bible can negate a teaching and this seems to be a great example of the exception disproving the rule. However, if we look at the command in context, we'll see we can disregard it because circumstances have changed, and the command was only valid in those special circumstances.

Some scholars think Leviticus was the first book given to Moses at Sinai. The Law was probably established before the history (Genesis and Exodus) as a matter of practicality. The people needed to know how to treat each other and what God expected of them. Leviticus was twenty-seven chapters of densely packed rules *spoken* to the people by Moses. No one could remember them all except for Moses, who would later write them down. In the time between the oral dissemination and the written code, the people still needed to follow the rules. Pastors today believe their congregations will retain only about fifteen percent of what they hear in a sermon. The rules given in Leviticus took considerably longer to speak than a sermon, and were much more complex.

Although no one could remember all the spoken commands, everyone could remember some of them. Each listener would naturally remember what seemed pertinent to his or her situation. I can imagine, as the rules were being given by Moses, a listener thinking, "I hope old Abe in the next tent heard *that one*. That's bugged me since the day he moved in." Don't we still think the same way when we hear a sermon today? This was how the teachings must have been spread at that early date. They were disseminated orally, neighbor to neighbor. If they knew a law and a neighbor did not, it would be incumbent upon them to teach their neighbor. In this early context, not rebuking *would* cause them to share the neighbor's guilt.

God gave many rules and penalties in this early period that Jesus would later repudiate. A man gathering wood on the Sabbath was killed for his sin. It was a spectacular mnemonic device. Better that one man die than the whole young nation lose their weekly rest. By the time Jesus taught, a whole set of secondary Sabbath rules had been established and the people knew them all well. Despite—or perhaps because of—their Levitical sophistication, they no longer stoned men for Sabbath infractions. Even this more lenient treatment irked Jesus. He taught us that it was fine to work in order to do good on the Sabbath.

Leviticus 19:17 basically means: You know this particular facet of the Law. If you see your neighbor living contrary to it, you've got to tell them about it. They might not know they are doing anything wrong. If you allow them to continue in their ignorance, you're guilty too. The loving thing to do would be to point out the infraction.

Later, after the rules were committed to parchment and the priesthood was established, the means to spread the knowledge given in Leviticus would have changed. Once the Lord set up the power hierarchy, the people could be taught in a different manner. Once verticality was introduced, the priests became responsible for training and rebuke, not the people.

Today, we've moved even further from the passage in Leviticus. Now we have another Teacher who is committed to the task. We have been relieved of the responsibility. As I've said many times, it is not our job. Just as we no longer kill those who work on the Sabbath or stone adulterers or quarantine those with acne, we no longer need to rebuke our neighbor frankly.

There is a clue a few verses later in Leviticus, given to temper the advice. It is a reminder not to judge and to love our neighbor. When Jesus quoted the greatest commandments, this is the verse where he got number two. *Do not seek revenge or bear a grudge against one of your people, but love your neighbor as yourself. I am the Lord.* (Lev 19:20) He is the Lord. It is his job.

And now we are not to rebuke. We must still be very careful to keep the commandments for our self. We must still work to keep ourselves pure. That is what God tells us in the first half of Leviticus 19:19. *Keep my decrees.* Yet the separation has been fulfilled with Jesus' birth. He has ordained that the wheat must remain among the tares. The kingdom of God is *among* us. We can wear a shirt that is a cotton/polyester blend. The rest of verse 19 no longer applies:

> *Do not plant your field with two kinds of seed.*
> *Do not wear clothing woven of two kinds of material.*

Separation was crucial to God's plan of calling a people to spread his word and his fame. He used Israel's culture as a learning tool for the rest of the world. Now that Jesus has accomplished this phase, we must live among the world as a means to a more effective witness. Let's not separate from others by implying that we are better than they are. Let's not attempt to remove the speck from their eye. Let's not build walls through rebuke. Let's love them and keep them close. That is the method of gently restoring them. *Brothers, if someone is caught in a sin, you who are spiritual should restore him gently.* (Gal 6:1) Let's be spiritual.

When Paul speaks of a man that is spiritual, it is a man that observed less of the rules or traditions, not the man who is observed sinning less. We need restoration rather than rebuke. My Pastor says he can see someone sliding back into sin. When they're on fire for the Lord, they sit near the front of the Sanctuary during service. Once sin becomes chronic, they begin to sit farther back. Soon they are sitting in the last rows. Then they begin to miss a week here and there. And then they are gone.

How can we gently restore these people before they leave? How about making them feel love and mercy coming from the body? That would be the house built on a rock. The path leading to that house is one of gentle restoration.

16

Rebuking Rebuking

THERE ARE OTHER REASONS we say it's okay to judge. These reasons stem from traditions based on our common wisdom. Because they are our ideas rather than scripture based, I'll argue against them with ideas rather than scripture.

We all make judgments every day.

Of course we do. Do you remember our discussion in chapter one? We differentiated between the type of judgment needed for successful living and the type of judgment Jesus speaks against. Since this difference is the heart of Jesus' teaching, it bears repeating. The judgment that Jesus says will get us judged is executed from an assumed position of superiority or authority that has not been granted to us by God. Words can have more than one meaning. So let's think more precisely.

The difference between judging and good judgment is small but significant. If I think someone might be a gossip, it is right that I not judge. I should not confront them in the hope that they might be reformed. On the other hand, I need be extra careful in what I tell them. Otherwise, I might hurt myself or have a hand in hurting other people. Being careful (just in case) is using good judgment. If I knew another person had a bent toward thievery, I wouldn't leave my wallet lying in the open. Using good judgment is a form of love and yet it is not tough love. Loving them regardless of their faults is all the responsibility I am given.

If I feel the gossip may be harmful to the Body the very most I can do is tell my concerns to a pastor. As the leader of the flock, it is his job to decide a course of action or inaction. The very best I can do is bring it to God. Not for his sake (God already knows if they gossip), but for mine.

I know people who gossip. It is a deeply ingrained trait. Gossip affects the way they think about almost everyone. However, confrontation might drive them from the church. Or worse, it might begin a feud. Gossip is not better or worse than many of the sins that so easily beset us; it is just more apparent. Other than not giving gossips anything to gossip about, I shouldn't treat them any differently than any other brother or sister. That's the difference between judging and using judgment. Let's work hard to not confuse the meanings.

How about *if we didn't practice judgment and discernment, error would be rampant in the body*?

Error is already rampant in the body. It always has been and always will be. Look at the error we uncovered regarding the biblical principle of rebuke. Or the error of thinking *by their fruit you shall know them* should be applied to a peer rather than to a leader, or thinking *fruit* speaks of sin rather than love, joy and peace. Given the fact that we are human, there will always be error within the body.

When we worry about rampant error, I wonder if we are really more concerned about non-uniformity. Toeing the party line is not a bad thing as long as we all believe the right thing. This book does not toe the line and neither did Jesus.

Finally, I've saved the most difficult passage for last. There is an extreme and extremely clear example of *judging* given by Paul in his first letter to the Corinthians. This example may have been in the back of your mind for at least this whole chapter and perhaps for the whole book. Paul upbraids the members of the Corinthian church for *not judging* a man for his very wicked actions. Because the pericope (famous passage) is so very germane and important to our discussion, we are going to look at it in depth.

Here's First Corinthian 5, the whole chapter. I've included the whole chapter because it is all about rebuke. We could view it as another example of vertical rebuke (Paul writing to the leaders of the church about rebuking a wayward follower) except for one dominant word, *you*. In this passage it is most often singular, which means (in context) that Paul was addressing the body as a whole rather than only giving advice to its leaders. I'm not even certain the Corinthian church had a strict leadership structure. The many emphases, as always, can only be mine:

> *It is actually reported that there is sexual immorality among you,*
> *and of a kind that does not occur even among pagans: A man has his father's wife.*
> *And you are proud!*
> *Shouldn't you rather have been filled with grief*

and have put out of your fellowship the man who did this?
Even though I am not physically present, I am with you in spirit.
And I have already passed judgment on the one who did this,
just as if I were present.
When you are assembled in the name of our Lord Jesus
and I am with you in spirit,
and the power of our Lord Jesus is present,
hand this man over to Satan,
so that the sinful nature may be destroyed
and his spirit saved on the day of the Lord.
Your boasting is not good.
Don't you know that a little yeast works through the whole batch of dough?
Get rid of the old yeast that you may be a new batch without yeast –
as you really are.
For Christ, our Passover lamb, has been sacrificed.
Therefore let us keep the Festival,
not with the old yeast, the yeast of malice and wickedness,
but with bread without yeast, the bread of sincerity and truth.
I have written you in my letter not to associate with sexually immoral people –
not at all meaning the people of this world who are immoral,
or the greedy and swindlers, or idolaters.
In that case you would have to leave this world.
But now I am writing you that you must not associate with anyone who calls himself a brother but is sexually immoral or greedy, an idolater or a slanderer, a drunkard or a swindler.
With such a man do not even eat.
What business is it of mine to judge those outside the church?
Are you not to judge those inside?
God will judge those outside.
"Expel the wicked man from among you." (1 Cor 5:1–13)

Well, there it is. Paul is plainly telling them to judge this man. *Are you not to judge those inside?* He tells the Corinthians to hand this man over to Satan. It is interesting that Paul writes that handing him over to Satan will save his spirit while destroying his flesh (translated *sinful nature* in this passage). Ah, so *that's* Satan's job, to destroy our sinful natures. Jesus taught, in regard to Satan, that a house divided against itself cannot stand. Wouldn't Satan destroying our ability to sin run counter to his purposes?

Paul writes, *you must not associate with anyone who calls himself a brother but is sexually immoral or greedy, an idolater or a slanderer, a drunkard or a swindler.* So it seems we are to judge! We can't even eat with those people. If the Father requires us to *love mercy* in Micah and Jesus tells us he desires mercy, it seems they would have to look to someone other than Paul for it. Didn't Paul tell them in the previous chapter to judge nothing, but wait until the Lord comes back? How can we even begin to reconcile these contradictory commands?

Before we attempt to do so, let's muddy the waters even more. Later, in Chapter 11 of the same letter, Paul takes some of the people to task for drunkenness and gluttony during, of all things, the Lord's Supper!

> *When you come together, it is not the Lord's Supper you eat,*
> *for as you eat, each of you goes ahead without waiting for anybody else.*
> *One remains hungry, another gets drunk.*
> *Don't you have homes to eat and drink in?*
> *Or do you despise the church of God and humiliate those who have nothing?*
> *What shall I say to you? Shall I praise you for this?*
> *Certainly not! . . .*
> *A man ought to examine himself before he eats of the bread and drinks of the cup.*
> *For anyone who eats and drinks without recognizing the body of the Lord eats and drinks judgment on himself.*
> *That is why many among you are weak and sick,*
> *and a number of you have fallen asleep.*
> *But if we judged ourselves, we would not come under judgment.*
> *When we are judged by the Lord, we are being disciplined*
> *so that we will not be condemned with the world.* (1 Cor 11:20–32)

This passage seems to present two perspectives, and neither is consistent with his earlier advice from chapter five. Getting drunk at the Lord's Supper is the reason why many of them are sick or weak and others have died as a judgment from the Lord. I understand it so far. Jesus has that right. Paul also commands in this section that we judge ourselves. As far as I am concerned, that is the heart of the Bible on the subject of judging; judge myself but not others.

But why doesn't *Paul* judge these people as he stated they should be judged in chapter five? *You must not associate with anyone who calls himself a brother but is . . . a drunkard.* Why doesn't he order the same ostracism here? In chapter five Paul says to not even eat with a person such as this. Yet in chapter eleven he not only *doesn't* counsel them *not* to eat with these people, he doesn't make the greater distinction of it being a more serious form of drunkenness because the meal they are eating is the Lord's Supper!

In chapter 11, there is no instruction for the church to judge them at all. They were to be judged by the Lord if they didn't judge themselves. However in chapter five, Paul said to expel the wicked man, *so* God would judge him. In chapter five, they were not to eat with a drunkard yet in chapter eleven many were drunk while eating, yet Paul put the onus on the drunkard to change, not on the sober to rebuke or ostracize.

Perhaps the advice was situational, but if so, Paul didn't define the situations. If we are unable to discern the appropriateness wouldn't we be best to default to Jesus' oft-repeated advice, *do not judge*?

Some cling to the concept of the situational appropriateness. They say the advice to expel the man in the first passage was due to the public nature (the openness) of his sin. *It is* actually reported *that there is sexual immorality among you*. This may be the case, but what about the other behaviors on his list such as being *greedy, an idolater or a slanderer, a drunkard or a swindler*? Some of these are not public sins, yet in Paul's mind they still warrant the same ostracism.

Swindlers wouldn't be effective if it were known they were swindlers. And who among us knows who is greedy at our church? We may know some that are wealthy, but finding evidence of greed would be more difficult. Large anonymous gifts are sometimes given at my church and I can only imagine that they are from some of the wealthier families. Greed may be evident in some but still it is not generally a public sin. The drunkenness and gluttony at the Lord's Supper was also *reported* according to chapter eleven, so they were certainly public sins, but there was no instruction to ostracize or expel.

If publicness was the criterion for deciding to expel a brother, wouldn't that support and enhance the same hypocrisy Jesus so vehemently opposed? He took the Pharisees to task for having different principles in public than in private. If public sins were singled out for punishment, we would advance the legalism of the Pharisees while learning to hide our sin better.

In my mind, the most striking example of error in chapter five is Paul's misuse of the metaphor of yeast. He appropriates Jesus' example of yeast and stands it on its head. Whenever Jesus spoke of yeast, it had a specific meaning. Yeast was the legalism, hypocrisy, and spirit of condemnation epitomized by the Pharisees that was in danger of working its way through the whole batch of dough. Paul instead writes of yeast as being wickedness and malice and counsels condemnation.

The Apostles were usually very true to Jesus' intent when using the words he used. Think of John's use of the word *light*. He mirrored both of the ways Jesus used the word. One was Jesus' singular contribution (*I am the Light of the world*) and the other was of the Christian's shining example (*you are the light of the world*). Paul used *salt* in exactly the same way Jesus used it. *Let your speech always be with grace, as though seasoned with salt, so that you will know how you should respond to each person.* (Col 4:6 NASB) The

Bible is uncanny in its consistency when it comes to the use of certain words to convey a concept, especially considering the number of writers involved. That is why word studies are valuable to us today. Yet here, Paul uses the metaphor of yeast in exactly the opposite way Jesus used it, and Jesus had used it his way more than once.

Suppose for a moment that Paul is wrong here with regard to his instructions in First Corinthians. I know this is akin to heresy, but what if Paul is telling us the opposite of what Jesus told us? What if the *not associating with...* and the *hand this man over to Satan* are anomalies, errors, by Paul? Is it possible that Paul could be instructing us to follow a false doctrine, one that collides violently with his other statements about not judging in deference to letting God judge? I believe we can make a strong biblical argument to that effect using Paul's own words.

I believe Paul also realized his error and repudiated his own instruction to the Corinthians. Perhaps he took time to reflect on his advice. Perhaps as the Spirit sanctified him, he learned to act with more maturity. Let me quote Paul in his *second* letter to the church at Corinth, from chapter two.

> *For I wrote you out of great distress and anguish of heart and with many tears,*
> *not to grieve you but to let you know the depth of my love for you.*
> *If anyone has caused grief,*
> *he has not so much grieved me as he has grieved all of you,*
> *to some extent—not to put it too severely.*
> *The punishment inflicted on him by the majority is sufficient for him.*
> *Now instead, you ought to forgive and comfort him,*
> *so that he will not be overwhelmed by excessive sorrow.*
> *I urge you, therefore, to reaffirm your love for him.*
> *The reason I wrote you was to see if you would stand the test*
> *and be obedient in everything.*
> *If you forgive anyone, I also forgive him.*
> *And what I have forgiven –*
> *if there was anything to forgive –*
> *I have forgiven in the sight of Christ for your sake,*
> *in order that Satan might not outwit us.*
> *For we are not unaware of his schemes.* (2 Cor 2:4–11)

In my mind, this passage clearly refers to what he wrote in chapter five of First Corinthians. He starts by saying *for I wrote you out of great distress*, so we know he is referencing a previous letter. Paul could mean a different letter, one lost to antiquity, but then we are left to grapple with the plenary inspiration behind verses four through eleven excerpted above. Would the Holy Spirit deem it necessary to reference a letter not preserved for us?

Could we instead conclude the Spirit intended to preserve a third letter but we failed to appreciate or canonize it? Either question answered in the affirmative would demean the mind and power of at least part of the Trinity. Besides, the parallels in vocabulary and subject matter are too striking for them to be referencing separate incidents.

In verse seven he makes it clear that it was the actions of a *man*. *You ought to forgive and comfort him, so that he will not be overwhelmed.* The only man Paul wrote about in First Corinthians is the man he told them to hand over to Satan. He must mean the same man. I said the *subjects* are parallel yet the advice is not. The advice given in Second Corinthians contradicts the first letter. That's why I say Paul is backtracking.

Paul tells them to forgive the man and reaffirm their love for him because the guy has suffered enough. Most likely the man repented, but we don't know for sure because it isn't spelled out. Maybe the father's wife dumped him. Maybe she died. Who knows?

It has occurred to me that perhaps someone at the Corinthian church rebuked Paul (follower to leader) for the advice in the first letter. *If there was anything to forgive* might be a verbal clue to that effect. Paul may have reacted to gossip in the first letter. *It is actually reported.* Rereading the excerpt from Second Corinthians in this light yields a consistency in tone and logic. We can't know for sure this side of heaven.

Whatever the reason, Paul tells them to forgive and readmit him to the body so he isn't overcome by excessive sorrow. Repentance on the man's part, if that is the reason for the change in Paul's advice in the second letter, isn't important enough for him to mention, but reconciliation is. Although it can be argued that these facts agree in both letters, the rest of the second letter clearly repudiates what Paul wrote in the first.

After the scolding he gives them in the first letter, he now says he wrote *not* to grieve them but to show his love for them. That could be perfectly acceptable. Perhaps Paul is introducing the concept of tough love.

But wait, that's not it at all. Paul continues to spin his previous advice. In verse six of *Second* Corinthians 2, he says it didn't really grieve him so much as it grieved them. *He has not so much grieved me as he has grieved all of you.* Yet in the *first* letter he took them to task *because they weren't grieved,* he was! *Shouldn't you rather have been filled with grief and have put out of your fellowship the man who did this?*

In verse eight, Paul again slants his previous advice. In the *first* letter he said, *and I have already passed judgment on the one who did this, just as if I were present.* Paul had already passed judgment.

Yet in the *second* letter Paul says judgment *wasn't* the reason for his counsel. He now says his reason was only to test their obedience when he wrote the first letter. *The reason I wrote you was to see if you would stand the test and be obedient in everything.* It was a trick all along! He was trifling with a man's life as an experiment in obedience!

We have the advantage of being able to compare the passages side-by-side. *If there was anything to forgive?* Paul truly must have had a short memory. Or maybe the man was innocent and Paul really had believed some gossipy slander as the truth. But then Paul would be a *slanderer* and the Corinthians would not be able to associate with him if he ever returned to Corinth. They would not even be able to eat with him.

What about the Satan references? In First Corinthians it was *hand him over so Satan could destroy* his flesh and in Second Corinthians it is *forgive him so Satan might not outwit us.* The *hand him over to Satan* advice contradicts some New Testament teachings. One of the roles of the church is to protect the believer *from* Satan. Is the church only for the protection of those living above a certain level of sin?

There are examples in both Testaments of God at a certain point giving men over to their sinful desires. Paul tells us this three times in the first chapter of Romans. When God no longer intervenes, it is an act of judgment. I can think of no more sorrowful situation on this earth then to have God give a man over to his own desires.

Although this may be how the Lord in his wisdom chooses to deal with the unbeliever, it is not *de facto* practice for the joint heir with Christ. The believer is chastened by God rather than abandoned. *Those whom I love, I reprove and discipline;* (Rev 3:19 NASB). In Hebrews 12, the writer likens it to the discipline of a father for his son. The man in First Corinthians is a believer. The biblical principle seems to be discipline for the believer and a giving over to evil desires for particularly incorrigible unbelievers.

Although Paul counseled handing him over to Satan as an act of judgment in First Corinthians, perhaps an older, wiser Paul is backpedaling because he has learned better. Maybe he was unaware of it when he wrote the first letter but now he is *not unaware of his* (Satan's) *schemes.*

I believe Paul understood the gravity of his foolish advice upon contemplation. This "correction" is the first subject he addresses in his second letter after the gracious general compliments with which he always began a letter to the churches. He wanted to correct the situation as quickly as possible. If I am right, then Paul was wrong in First Corinthians and we cannot cite it as proof that we should judge. If this conjecture on my part proves to be true, we are back to not judging again. Paul learned he was wrong by the time he wrote Second Corinthians and he worked hard to *almost* admit it.

I know the resistance you may have to disregarding a portion of Scripture. You are thinking, "If Paul was wrong, what about the inerrancy of Scripture? You, Mister Smarty Pants, are saying the Bible isn't true!"

On the contrary, I believe every word is God-breathed. I also believe both letters have come down to us just as God intended. Is it so far-fetched to think God purposely used a mistaken stance on the part of the apostle to correct a propensity for judgment on our part—or his?

We know God allowed us to see Peter's foibles concerning the Judaizers in Galatians 2 and then allowed us to see Paul set Peter straight. We can easily surmise that God wanted us to see the missteps of Peter to accentuate how easy it is to fall into a legalistic mindset.

Could it be that God allowed First Corinthians 5 to prove Paul is human and then had Paul write Second Corinthians 2 so we didn't misunderstand and think that God allows us to judge? Or perhaps God is making the point that it is all too easy to judge even though we shouldn't, the Holy Spirit's way of saying, "Look! Even Paul judged when he shouldn't!" The Lord is always honest. Both Testaments contain numerous examples of the faults of our biblical heroes. Why couldn't this also be true of Paul?

This directs us to a more sophisticated view of inerrancy. We point to Second Timothy 3:16 and 17 as proof of inerrancy, but it doesn't say everything in the Bible is true. That would be ludicrous. It says:

> *All Scripture is God-breathed and is useful for teaching,*
> *rebuking, correcting, and training in righteousness,*
> *so that the man of God may be thoroughly*
> *equipped for every good work.*

I don't see the word "true" in there. There are hundreds of verses in the Bible that aren't true. The first untrue verse is Genesis 3:4 *"You will not surely die,"* the serpent said to the woman. The verse is certainly God-breathed. How could Moses know what the serpent told Eve unless God showed it to him? Yet Eve did surely die. Genesis 3:4 is given without comment because God knows we are smart enough to figure it out on our own. Satan's reassurance was the first lie from the Father of Lies.

Genesis 3:4 is not true but it is *useful for teaching, rebuking, correcting and training in righteousness.* The verse *teaches* us not to listen to the serpent. It allows us a means of *rebuking* Satan, a superior being to us. (Get behind me Satan, you've deceived since the Garden and I will not believe your lies right now.) It also *trains* us *in righteousness*, because it teaches us about God's original plan for us.

But what about *correcting*? Correcting must be different from rebuking or teaching. If it were the same, Paul wouldn't have mentioned all four uses in the same sentence. Three, *teaching*, *correcting*, and *rebuking*, sound like methods of *training*, but all four must be different. We know what teaching means, and training speaks to practical application. We've learned about rebuke, but what about *correcting*? How is it different than the other three?

I think scripture *corrects* scripture in the same way we say scripture interprets scripture; the two ideas are essentially the same. Genesis 3 offers Satan's retort without comment but Jesus later tells us Satan is the father of lies and Revelation tells us he is the wily serpent of old.

Could Paul in Second Corinthians be *correcting* Paul in First Corinthians? I think that was Paul's intent. He revisits the issue and comes to an opposite conclusion. Yet he doesn't come right out and say he was wrong. This may lead some of you to think my reasoning is too tenuous.

Okay, let's go deeper. Scripture was inspired by the Holy Spirit but written by the hands of men. Men are flawed. Have you ever seen a man witness, hopefully filled with the Spirit, and yet see him say the wrong thing? How many sermons have we heard that were in error? Was the pastor not a man of God? Had he not composed the sermon after praying about his message? Had he not asked the Spirit to speak through him before delivering the message?

You may tell me that a man or a pastor is not the same as the Bible or a prophet but I would suggest they are different only by degrees. Prophets must be godly, giving God's message, but they are still imperfect. Only the Bible as a whole is perfect, and only when considered *in toto*. As godly as a prophet must be, a prophet is still a man and men are never perfect. Only God is perfect.

The overriding principle in play in any interactions between God and man is always the same:choice. We can ask God to fill us with his Spirit and he will; he is gracious. However, if we decide twenty seconds later to take up our own mantle again, God will allow that with equal aplomb. He is unperturbed by our vacillations and just because he doesn't control us like robots doesn't mean he isn't in control.

I can imagine this to be exactly the way the principle played out while Paul was dictating his first letter to the Corinthian church. Paul was cruising along in the spirit, communicating exactly what God wanted known, when suddenly Paul was overcome by his zeal for God's name when he thought about the situation we are looking at. God may have decided at this point to let Paul finish his diatribe so he could use it to make an important point about judgment, knowing he would later have Paul correct his error—as he did in Second Corinthians.

God knows what he is doing. He has given us remarkable minds to puzzle through all this. He has given us this unequaled, breathtaking Bible, and given us generations of the most devout men to unlock its puzzles. The Bible contains incredible clues; we only need to be faithful enough and discerning enough to understand them. One clue that all the verses in the Bible are not inerrant is Paul's own contrasting words in the Corinthian letters.

Then there is this from First Corinthians, chapter seven. *To the married I give this command (not I, but the Lord): A wife must not separate from her husband* (10). Two verses later, Paul is careful to differentiate. *To the rest I say this (I, not the Lord):* Many scholars think he is saying verse twelve is not necessarily inspired by the Holy Spirit, or he's not sure if it is or not, so he's warning us. What if it is not inspired? The verse is part of Scripture. Archbishop Ussher gave it a verse number. Second Timothy doesn't say *all Scripture is God-breathed except what I wrote in First Corinthians 7:12b*.

I happen to believe it was inspired. Yet it can't be inerrant. If the instruction (his advice to them) is inerrant, *(To the rest I say this:)* then the qualifier is wrong *(I, not the Lord)*. If the qualifier is correct, Second Timothy is in error (All *Scripture is God-breathed*). It is a simple rhetorical equation. If the instruction is inspired, the qualifier surely isn't, because if the instruction was inspired, the "*I, not the Lord*" part is superfluous; God had no reason to inspire it to be written. Unless, they are both inspired by God to suggest to us that there are other parts of Scripture that are God-breathed but incorrect. I know I'm being a bit tongue in cheek, but the point stands.

Other examples in the Bible that seem to be incorrect are verses that point to a works-based salvation. We can *seem* to have a number of conflicting verses, and yet when we sort them out we can usually see a second way of looking at one of the sets of verses. *All scripture* is useful for correction and what it sometimes is correcting is other scripture. This is of utmost importance! Remember, I don't think incorrect is necessarily bad. God straightens it all out in due course.

Look at the conflicting stories of Judas' death, and at who bought the field with his thirty pieces of silver. Luke was reporting what he believed to be fact based on his investigations, he admits as much at the beginning of his writings. Hermeneutic correction is done all the time. The verses that suggest works-based salvation are corrected by the verses that strongly validate faith alone. We need a slightly more sophisticated hermeneutic to show that the Gospel of Matthew corrects the historical explorations of Luke in Acts.

This next example is the one I promised earlier, the one that proves Scripture can be inspired by the Holy Spirit without being inerrant. Here goes, from Acts, Chapters 6 and 7:

> *They chose Stephen, a man full of faith and of the Holy Spirit;* (Acts 6:5)
>
> *Now Stephen, a man full of God's grace and power,*

> *did great wonders and miraculous signs among the people*(Acts 6:8)
>
> *These men began to argue with Stephen,*
> *but they could not stand up against his wisdom*
> *or the Spirit by whom he spoke* (Acts 6:9c, 6:10)
>
> *All who were sitting in the Sanhedrin looked intently at Stephen,*
> *and they saw that his face was like the face of an angel.* (Acts 6;15)

> *Then the high priest asked him, "Are these charges true?"*
> *To this he replied: "Brothers and fathers, listen to me!*
> *The God of glory appeared to our father Abraham*
> *while he was still in Mesopotamia,*
> *before he lived in Haran.*
> *'Leave your country and your people,' God said,*
> *'and go to the land I will show you.'*
> *"So he left the land of the Chaldeans and settled in Haran.*
> *After the death of his father,*
> *God sent him to this land where you are now living.*
> (Acts 7:1-4)

Stephen was a man of God's grace and power, and yet much of the above text is wrong. He was full of the Holy Spirit. He did wonders and miraculous signs. The Sanhedrin could not stand up to his wisdom *or the Spirit by whom he spoke*. And although he was all these things and spoke by the Spirit, he erred.

The Bible faithfully records this, but without comment. The Sanhedrin didn't even catch it although I would have thought that at least some of them would. I don't know why I caught it although I hope I was guided by the Holy Spirit to catch it. I am not bragging, except humbly on the Lord. (Now I'm starting to sound like Paul at his worst!)

Anyway, Stephen erred. He was speaking by the Spirit, giving his last speech on earth, (remember, he was the first martyr after Jesus' death) and he either misremembered or he misinterpreted Scripture. This man with a face shining like an angel, a prophet who in a few minutes would see Jesus or a vision of Jesus standing in heaven, inadvertently botched the details.

Let me show you the errors. First a minor debatable one:

> *The God of glory appeared to our father Abraham*
> *while he was still in Mesopotamia, before he lived in Haran.*
> *'Leave your country and your people,' God said,*
> *'and go to the land I will show you.*

God didn't tell *Abraham* to leave Mesopotamia and go to the Promised Land. God told Terah, Abraham's father to do that. From Genesis 11:31:

> *Terah took his son Abram, his grandson Lot son of Haran,*
> *and his daughter-in-law Sarai, the wife of his son Abram,*
> *and together they set out from Ur of the Chaldeans*
> *to go to Canaan.*
> *But when they came to Haran, they settled there.*

Now Genesis 12:1, spoken to Abram while he was in Haran, not Mesopotamia:

> *The LORD had said to Abram,*
> *"Leave your country, your people and your father's household*
> *and go to the land I will show you."*

So it's minor, but God didn't tell Abraham to leave Mesopotamia *before* he lived in Haran (as Stephen stated), he told him to leave *while* he lived in Haran.

The debatable part is that God may also have told Abram the same thing at the same time he told it to Terah: to leave Mesopotamia. This is unlikely because Terah knew the destination to be Canaan according to 11:31. But according to Hebrews 11:8, Abram didn't know the final destination when he left Haran. God didn't tell him to go to Canaan, he told Abram to *go to the land I will show you*. God told *Terah* to go to Canaan while he lived in Mesopotomia, but Terah must not have relayed the destination to Abram. It wouldn't be logical for God to become more mysterious with his instructions later by telling Abram to go to an unspecified land if he had already specifically told him to go to Canaan. The instruction was given to Abram in Haran, not in Mesopotamia as Stephen states.

Stephen could only know God also spoke to Abram in Mesopotamia (if that is the truth) by the leading of the Spirit, not by the text of Genesis. That's what makes this error slightly debatable. It's like Eve saying God told them not to *even touch* the fruit. God may have told Eve exactly that but the text doesn't confirm it. The text only says that God told *Adam* not to *eat* of the fruit. There were no stated restrictions on touching.

If God told Abram to leave his father's household before Terah moved to Haran, Abram didn't obey and the Bible doesn't comment. It seems more likely that the Lord told him to leave *while* he lived in Haran, as Genesis 12:1 states, and Stephen got it wrong.

The next error is not conjecture. Stephen, full of the Spirit in a way that few men ever have been, with his *face shining like an angel*, is clearly wrong.

Here it is, again from Acts 4. *After the death of his father, God sent him to this land where you are now living.*

Stephen is wrong here because Abraham didn't leave *after* the death of his father; he left *sixty years before* the death of his father. The text doesn't say so outright but it is clear from a piecing together of the verses from chapters 11 and 12 of Genesis.

> *After Terah had lived 70 years,*
> *he became the father of Abram, Nahor and Haran . . .* (Gen 11:26)
>
> *Terah lived 205 years, and he died in Haran. . .* (Gen 11:32)
>
> *So Abram left, as the LORD had told him;*
> *and Lot went with him.*
> *Abram was seventy-five years old when he set out from Haran.* (Gen 12:4)

So Terah was 70 when Abram (the eldest) was born. Abram was 75 when he left Haran, and that means Terah was 145 when Abram left. Yet Terah lived until he was 205.

70 + 75 = 145, Terah's age when Abram left.

205 − 145 = 60 years that Terah lived after Abram left Haran.

Stephen, full of the Spirit, says Abraham left Haran *after* the death of his father but Genesis says he left 60 years *before* the death of his father. Later, in verse 55, Luke reiterates that Stephen was full of the Holy Spirit. Being full of the Holy Spirit is no guarantee against making a human error and being inspired by the Spirit is no guarantee that an individual scripture is inerrant.

The inerrancy of Scripture was claimed by a paper called The Chicago Statement in 1978. The statement itself is detailed and nuanced, qualifying the use of the term inerrant in much the same manner we have advanced here, yet we have somehow come to use its general claim for inerrancy as a shorthand to say every verse of Scripture is correct. The Chicago Statement didn't claim inerrancy for individual Bible verses, only for the whole of the Bible. The Bible never claims inerrancy for itself. The Bible says it is God's word, and that alone is enough for me.

All Scripture is useful for *correction*. The verses that advance faith alone correct the verses that suggest salvation by keeping the Law. Genesis 11 and 12 correct Acts 7. Matthew 27 corrects Acts 1. Acts 6 and 7 corrects our teaching that every verse is inerrant. Acts 6 and 7 are useful for teaching and I hope we have all been properly rebuked and trained in righteousness concerning this important principle! Second Corinthians corrects First Corinthians and these writings are *all* God breathed.

Even after all of Paul's admonishments not to judge, he still fell into the trap of judgment. I think God is merely showing us how easy it is for us to fall into a pattern of judgment by allowing us to see Paul do it. Paul realized his error but couldn't quite bring himself to admit it, so he corrected it with a flimsy excuse like, "I was only testing you." At least he did correct his error. We need to learn from Paul. We need to use the verses of Second Corinthians chapter 2 to correct our predilections for judgment. Because if we can learn from this not to judge, just as Jesus taught us not to judge, we will be *thoroughly equipped for every good work*.

The conflict between the letters to the Corinthians is no accident; it is exactly as God has ordained it. We understand the principle of *do not judge* in the context of peers; it's just that we think it applies to some cases most of the time. Instead we need to realize it applies to all cases all of the time. God spends so much time teaching us not to judge that it must make up a healthy portion of his will for us. If Paul's advice in his second letter to the Corinthians *corrected* his previous errant advice, which, don't forget, also ran counter to the advice he gave later in the same first letter, then I can only think of two reasons the Spirit allowed us to see the errant advice.

He wanted to show that even an Apostle is susceptible to the ubiquitous sin of judgment, just as he exposed Peter's return to legalism or he thought the rest of the letter was important enough to preserve for us, and knew he could correct the improper advice later.

Either way, we have to disregard the 1 Corinthians 5 advice, or accept that it the only spot in the New Testament, and practically the only place in the Bible that tells us to judge our peers.

17

Honesty

Do you remember the Barna poll? Eighty-seven percent of non-Christians under the age of thirty believe Christians are judgmental. Eighty-five percent also think us hypocritical. The percentages are comparable because the traits are similar. They are reasons to mistrust.

What the world thinks of us matters. Changing the opinion of the unsaved is an unspoken goal of the Sermon on the Mount. Our motivation should be to please our Father. His motivation is to affect the world through us. We need to do good deeds so men may see them and praise our Father in heaven. But our reputation for being judgmental leads to wariness in the unbeliever. Hypocrisy is worse still, because hypocrisy breeds outright distrust.

Distrust is the most serious of interpersonal obstacles. Distrust means we know the other person is hiding *something*, but we can never be sure what. Some personal interactions could be genuine, but which ones?

The world doesn't distrust us because it believes we are liars. We usually aren't. They mistrust us because they believe we don't grasp basic realities. We fail to see our own sin clearly while speaking out against the sins of others. If we fail to see our own sin clearly, if our good judgment is so impaired as to lack self-awareness, our opinions are suspect because they lack wisdom. If, on the other hand, we clearly see our own sin and yet still speak against the sin of others, we are hypocrites advancing an agenda.

Either is troublesome when we remember that the theme of the sermon is our unspoken, continual witness. If we are to be Jesus to the world and the world mistrusts us, then why should they trust Jesus?

The cure for hypocrisy is simple. We must never sin again. That means all of us, starting right now. If none of us ever sins again, we will offer a wonderful witness to the world and they would have no reason to distrust us. We could emphasize our behavior and tell them that they could live a sinless life, too. They would only need to make Jesus the Lord of their lives and they would be perfect ever after. Are you up for it?

Jesus directed his criticism of hypocrisy toward the Pharisees. This was not a coincidence. Of all the factions within Israel, the Pharisees were the most zealous for God, but they didn't possess the proper mindset. He called them whitewashed tombs. We teach that *whitewashed tombs*, means the Pharisees were dead on the inside but "pretty" on the outside. That's not exactly right. A tomb isn't dead, it *contains* death. The Pharisees weren't dead on the inside and neither are we. Yet they contained death because their hypocrisy led others to believe that proper actions were the road to salvation. They beautified what they thought people could see by accentuating what they believed were righteous actions.

The Pharisees thought they were providing a proper example by hiding that which was wrong in their own lives. Therein lies the hypocrisy. Hypocrisy was an offense that vexed Jesus more than sin. We all sin, but Jesus doesn't believe we need to be hypocrites.

When we don't admit our sin, the tacit denial becomes an improper witness. Whitewashing is a roadblock on the path to heaven. Remember what Jesus said about the Pharisees: *Those who are well have no need of a physician, but those who are sick. I did not come to call [the] righteous, but sinners, to repentance.* (Mark 2:17 NKJV)

Jesus called the Pharisees *righteous* because they sought after God's way. Yet he also told us in the Sermon that we needed to exceed their righteousness if we wanted to see the kingdom. In this verse, Jesus implied that the Pharisees had only varying degrees of righteousness. The Pharisees were doing what they believed they were called to do (individually) to advance God's plan, but they were hindering others from doing the same. Jesus was concerned for the sick and the sinners. He railed against the Pharisees because their hypocrisy only served to convince the sick and the sinners of the hopelessness of their lives. The Pharisees blocked the path to salvation.

We don't attract unbelievers by our exemplary lifestyles. They don't long for a lack of sin. They love sin. Unbelievers may want heaven, but they worry that they have to stop sinning to get there. If we stop whitewashing our tombs, if we admit our sin more freely, they might realize that becoming sinless is not a prerequisite. If we are poor enough in spirit, we can admit we still sin. If we are not, we deceive ourselves and the world distrusts us because our witness isn't true. *If we claim to be without sin, we deceive ourselves and the truth is not in us* (1 John 1:8).

Our hypocrisy affects our brothers and sisters as well. Six times in the gospels, Jesus spoke out against the leaven of the Pharisees. In each case he warned his disciples (and us) to beware of it. Leaven is the yeast that spreads through and affects the whole loaf. The finished product is different depending on whether the bread is leavened or not. Jesus is the bread of life but wants us to be tortillas or crackers.

What was the leaven of the Pharisees? *He began to say to His disciples first of all, Beware of the leaven of the Pharisees,* which is hypocrisy (Luke 12:1 NKJV). If no one at church will admit sin, we will have a difficult time admitting our sin. If none of us admits sin, the world will know us as hypocrites. Leaven causes the dough to rise; it puffs us up.

When I first got saved, I went to a fairly militant church in that they censured public sin publicly. Continued sin resulted in being dropped from membership. I can see now how people reacted to these situations; they were careful to hide their sin.

In a culture of hidden sin everybody looks squeaky clean from the outside. The example drove me away from that church after a time. Not because I knew hypocrisy existed. I was too much of a baby Christian to suspect it. It drove me away because I knew my own heart.

I knew I wasn't good enough to belong to that body of believers. I was not squeaky clean. I knew if I got close enough to others in the body, they would discover my propensity to sin. I read my Bible. I prayed. But I couldn't stop sinning. After a few months of attendance, I began to understand that I could never belong. I agonized over my predilection to sin in contrast to everyone else's apparent goodness.

I remember, after reaching that conclusion, getting up on Sunday mornings and driving to church. I didn't go inside but I continued to drive there. At first, on most mornings I would sit in the parking lot and listen to Christian radio. I felt I couldn't go inside to worship because I wasn't good enough. I also couldn't stay home because that wouldn't have been a good witness to my wife. She thought I was going to church. How's that for hypocrisy?

Every Sunday some people would come late for service and I began to dislike ducking down if they walked past my car, so I stopped parking in the church parking lot. Instead I drove out to the woods to listen to Christian radio and pray. What should have been a joyous time in the life of a new believer became instead a period of agony and self-recrimination.

I'm not saying I was better because I didn't hide my sin from myself. I'm only saying that I knew I was still a sinner. My inner wickedness drove me away because I couldn't get close enough to other believers to guess that they may have possessed some of the same wickedness. Eventually I stopped even pretending to go. My marriage fell apart so there was no reason to continue the charade. I didn't attend any church regularly for over twenty years. I continued to listen to radio sermons. I continued to read the Bible.

I realize now that God had begun to shape me for this present task. I had to develop some of my own ideas, drawing only from the word of God. The Word wasn't filtered through peer pressure or well-constructed traditions. My half-year or so of actually attending that church had taught me the basics of the faith, but twenty years of independent study altered the doctrines I had learned. They were modified by the whole word of God.

When my son had his seventh birthday, I knew I had to get him to a church regularly. I attended various churches in the area for a few weeks at a time, looking for one that came closest to my modified beliefs. I didn't know I was looking for a church that exhibited good fruit. I only knew that I wanted to go to any church other than the one that held such bad memories for me.

Guess where I ended up? Yep, that same church. God does as he pleases. When I went back (at first it was to take my mom because her car had broken down) the church had a different pastor. He seemed to get it. I still didn't really want to be there but God had arranged the circumstances. I knew it was where God wanted me to be.

I couldn't become a member because of the stringent membership rules. (The original pastor still ran things from his larger suburban location.) I knew I needed to be baptized but I wasn't allowed, because I wasn't a member. I was kicked out of the choir after it became apparent that I wasn't going to become a member. I was counseled to leave—to join a church that would allow me to believe what I believed without having to sign a paper saying something to the contrary.

The church's rules actually *prohibited* me from obeying the ordinance of God to be baptized. To some people in the church it appeared that I was just being disobedient. I wanted to be baptized but I also wanted to be true to my understanding of the Word. I also believed I was in the right church in that I was where God wanted me to be. I wanted to join, I wanted to be baptized, but I couldn't. It was a conundrum. I remained obedient to God even though others viewed me as disobedient.

It all worked out in the end. The pastor of the location I attended was forced out by the senior pastor and started a new church. I was privileged to be on the rules committee for the new church's constitution. We tried to make the membership yoke easier, based on the pastor's recommendations.

The new church fosters a much greater degree of openness and a lower level of judgment.

I have grown closer to many of the people who left the old church when I left. And I see their sin. I see it clearly, even when they don't intend for me to notice. Perhaps I am a little wiser, but I think it has nothing to do with me. I think the new spirit of openness allowed those brothers and sisters to drop their guard to a greater degree. Had I seen their sin at the old church, I wouldn't have spent so many hours in the parking lot or the woods. I would have realized that I belonged. I could have had fellowship with those brothers and sisters and learned from them.

Now I look forward to church, it is a highlight of my week. I love our Bible study. I can look my brothers and sisters in the eye. I can look my pastor in the eye. Not because I sin less, but because we are all more honest.

My brothers and sisters are probably sick of me. I never miss an opportunity to tell them what a sinner I still am. I also try to remind them what sinners we all still are. I'm still not brave enough to confess what my particular sins may be, but I know now how important it is to tell every one who will listen that I am still a sinner. I not only tell people at church, I tell my family and friends the same thing. My wife, my son, my mom and dad; I tell them all. It's not like they don't already know. I find it important that they know that *I* know I'm a sinner. I still try not to sin. I work at it. I work at staying close to Jesus so he can work on me.

Another funny thing happened after I began to confess my propensity to sin. People who knew me well would disagree with me. . .sometimes. Sometimes they would laugh and agree with me, and then confess that they too are sinners. I know it is probably bad to laugh about sin but God is more interested in honesty than he is in hiding sin.

The subject of this story is hypocrisy. It kept me from fellowship and it kept me from contributing. I know hypocrisy wasn't totally the problem. I'm not attempting to shift blame from myself. My character flaws and my inherent sin kept me away as much as the hypocrisy. Nevertheless, hypocrisy played a significant role.

My pastor preaches against hypocrisy occasionally. How could he not; hypocrisy is prominent in the Gospels. We call the techniques for diminishing our propensity for hypocrisy by certain buzzwords depending on what is fashionable in our churches at the time. We use terms such as openness, honesty, transparency and sincerity. We've tried to call it accountability, but that's really only a lack of hypocrisy between two or three at a time. Right now, we're calling it authenticity. I like that.

Regardless of what we call it, honesty is never easy. We are altogether too human for it to be easy. We want to present ourselves in the best possible light. More than a habit, it is a lifestyle. It is part of the pride of life John warns against. *For all that [is] in the world—the lust of the flesh, the lust of the eyes, and the pride of life—is not of the Father but is of the world* (1 John 2:16 NKJV). John warns against it because it is a problem for Christians. Although many of us may still battle the lust of the flesh and others are prone to the lust of the eyes, we all fall prey to the pride of life.

Why do you think God showed us some of Abraham's faults? Or David's? Or Peter's? God is honest enough to show us the faults of almost everyone in the Bible. They probably tried to hide them, like we do, but God doesn't. We're not the only people who have seen those faults. Abimelek and Pharaoh both caught Abraham. Nathan said aloud what they had all been thinking. Paul confronted Peter and then tattled to us through Luke.

Wouldn't it be easier to drop the facade and stop trying to show the world our relative sinlessness? When Jesus rails against hypocrisy, he isn't expecting us to stop sinning so our actions match our words; he's telling us to stop faking it so our words will match our actions.

Just as we show Jesus' love by extraordinary acts of mercy, we also need to demonstrate his truth by extraordinary transparency. Because we are in Christ, we possess both his love and his truth. Mercy and honesty are major weapons in our silent witness. They unblock the narrow path that leads to salvation.

If a few of us standing authentically may be misunderstood, many of us doing so will change the church, and a changed church will change the world. A little self-sacrifice and humility is good for the soul. Honesty strengthens us individually and it can strengthen us corporately. God has always called us to be courageous. Fear not! Admitting our sin takes only a little more courage than verbal witness does, but it will have more far-reaching results.

I'm not brave. I mentioned that I confess I'm still a sinner every time I can gracefully work it into a conversation, yet I rarely admit individual or specific sins. I think this is okay, at least as a starting point. James tells us to confess our sin to each other but he doesn't mean our specific acts of sinning. *Sin* is singular in the Greek of James 5:16. *Therefore confess your sins to each other and pray for each other so that you may be healed. The prayer of a righteous man is powerful and effective.* We always translate it *sins*, but it should be *sin*. Confessing our sins means describing individual acts. Confessing our sin could be admitting we are sinners.

This instruction from James is about calling for the elders to pray over us when we are terribly ill. I wonder if keeping our sin hidden from others, even though we are confessing it to God, harms us in ways we don't realize. The passage states that we have to confess our sin *so that we may be healed.*

Did you notice the word *righteous* in the verse? The righteous man is powerful and effective but he is not sinless. He confesses his sin to others. That's what makes him righteous in this instance.

The next verse says that *Elijah was a man just like us* (James 5:17a) but his prayer was effective. This means Elijah was subject to the same temptations we are and sometimes succumbed. He possessed a certain level of transparency. We know he didn't hide his depression and he didn't hide his fearfulness. Immediately after his marvelous and mighty defeat of the prophets of Ba'al (certainly a high point in his life) he ran in fear from the death threat issued by Jezebel. He left the country and stayed gone. God is honest enough to tell us about it. God also loved Elijah enough to nurture him through it. Far from being angry with Elijah for his profound depression and lack of faith, God patiently strengthened him for the next task. He understood Elijah, and Elijah was a man just like us.

Honesty is important because it provides common ground between believers and unbelievers: we both sin. That truth should be a starting point in any dialogue about faith, but instead we criticize the openness of unbelievers and the shameless way in which they highlight their faults. In a way, our complaint is right. They aren't shamed by their sin. Adultery and premarital sex are almost as common and accepted in real life as they are in books and movies. Every new sitcom has a guy who likes porn. TV shows insinuate that Sundays are for golf or reading the paper. The point of TV commercials is covetousness.

We accuse the media of shamelessly influencing real life, and it does. Yet the media reflects reality. That is the major difference between believers and everyone else. Believers hide sin to change perceptions of reality while the world is more likely to show life as it is. The biblical narratives are closer to the world's ways than to ours. The Bible is always honest and unashamedly shows the sin (and sins) of our heroes.

I'm not praising the world at the expense of Christianity. The world is still more likely to exhibit dishonesty than we are. However, their motivations are different. The world is more prone to lie for gain or to avoid loss than they are to hide sin. The investment bank Goldman Sachs has had the motto "long term greedy" for seventy-five years. Goldman Sachs alumni hold influential positions at almost every major financial firm and within our government. The idea of long term greedy permeates upper echelon America. Have you ever heard the motto before? Of course not, the people who live by it keep it well hidden.

Christians generally hold to a higher standard. We understand long-term consequences. Even more than this, we want to bring honor to our Lord. I've often seen Christians lose opportunities through truthfulness when unbelievers would not. That's the difference between us. The world won't hide their sin and we will. We won't lie for gain and they will. These are generalizations but they approach the truth. We'll never get the world to change their methods (unless they are converted), but we must change ours. They won't be converted as often unless we increase our honesty.

The world has no motivation to change but we have the greatest motivation of all. Let's be courageous. Our Lord already knows we are sinners. Our brothers, our sisters, and the world need to hear it as well, because against all of our own worldly instincts, the Bible teaches honesty as a facet of truth.

Jesus provides us with two major themes in the Sermon on the Mount: we must show Love and we must show Truth. They both demand self-sacrifice. As counterintuitive as it seems to us, freely admitting that we remain sinners brings glory to God. Being honest about our struggles will better prepare seekers for the abundant life should they decide to take the plunge. Whether we fail or not has no bearing on our eternal fate because Jesus has overcome sin and death on our behalf. Do we need him any less now than we needed him before he saved us? Perish the thought!

18

Inheriting The Earth

KINGDOM LIVING AS TAUGHT by Jesus in the Sermon isn't as easy as our traditional Christian message. It requires deep and sustained commitment, because it offers little in the way of individual gain. The traditional Christian message echoes Jesus' promise of abundant life, but has redefined the abundance. We are promised better relationships. We're told we can have peace and become healthier, wealthier, and wiser if we follow God.

Kingdom living promises none of these things. It is other-focused and designed to point the unsaved to Christ. Jesus knows we've already received a benefit beyond measure when we became poor in spirit, and our gratitude should spur us to pass it along. Kingdom living offers persecution, settling for less, and presenting a second cheek after the first has been slapped. Rather than assuming we will be at peace with all men, it assumes we will have enemies for which we will need to pray.

Our inherent selfishness might persuade us to live out the standard Christian model, but selfishness is the antithesis of kingdom living. How do we get past that? Faith can help; it is our greatest gift and a formidable weapon. A love for Jesus is also crucial if we are to put his desires above our own. And he promises blessing. Jesus tells us eight times in the Beatitudes that we can be favored by God.

But there is one more thing.

Jesus provides us with one additional help within the Sermon, an unspoken premise; a vein that runs throughout like a rich deposit of precious gold. We could miss it if we don't think deeply and so let's think deeply one last time. There is a beauty underlying this sermon that is unsurpassed in all of human literature, because it goes beyond the simple beauty of the words Jesus spoke.

This beauty lies in the unvoiced reassurance that we still possess that spark of the divine image that God first breathed into Adam. Jesus assumes we still have the means, somewhere deep within, to accomplish what he asks of us. He has mined the human heart and found yet a trace of nobility along with our penchant for evil and our great deposits of selfishness and self-centeredness.

This recognition of selflessness, in the midst of his frank assessment of us, brings light to his words. The force of it sustains his vision. The nobility Jesus sees in us is necessary to implementation of the sermon and it is equally necessary for us to acknowledge it. Without it, his instructions are unfair. If we miss it, we diminish the sermon's grandeur.

There has always been and there will always be the soldier who does not hesitate to fall on the grenade. There is the mother that understands the privilege and purpose of sacrificing for years to mold her children, and the teacher who, beneath a veneer of complaint and cynicism, still believes in making a difference. It is the noble within, the yearning to leave things better than we found them to which Jesus calls us.

Jesus has seen this tendency operate within us for thousands of years. He knows it is there and wants us to realize it and then to cultivate it. This view of us is what makes his message sublime. Jesus' opinion of us is why we're moved when we read it. The Creator of the Universe thinks we are capable of more than we think we are, and still believes we are worth his sacrifice.

One of my favorite movies speaks to that noble spark of the divine that resides within. The film preaches the Sermon in twentieth century terms. The movie is Frank Capra's *It's a Wonderful Life*. The premise of the story is that we are all here to influence humanity for the better in whatever manner God puts before us. The main character, George Bailey, does this and does it well, but he doesn't do it without complaint or rebellion. He wanted something different for his life. He had his own plan. George wanted to go to college, see the world, and then build great things; to leave his mark. It was a good plan but it wasn't a righteous plan because it wasn't part of God's plan.

In this fantasy, an angel shows George the impact his reluctant but faithful life has had on those around him. In reality, we all carry the same responsibility but we don't usually get to see the results of our actions. Yet we are still asked to live faithfully, with purpose and intentionality.

Faith needs to be a constant and continual decision because George Bailey's evil nemesis, Mr. Potter, also lurks within us all. He is selfish and bitter and devoid of faith. We can be Mr. Potter or we can be George Bailey. It's a daily decision.

Some of us may even strive to be Mary Bailey, George's wife. She embodied the nobility Jesus sees in us. She fulfilled her responsibilities gracefully and without her husband's penchant for complaint, because she had a joyful acceptance of her purpose in the Kingdom. Perhaps she's only an ideal, I don't know. But I do know that Jesus wouldn't call us to a life we weren't capable of living.

The Old Testament, so often a point of reference in the Sermon, is replete with God's efforts to draw out the best in us. He hopes and he cajoles, even when all evidence seems to point to the contrary. The Sermon picks up on these threads and weaves them together into one grand design for the future.

The New Testament gives one great example of sustained kingdom living by the earliest Christians in Jerusalem. It starts at Acts 2:1 with Pentecost, and continues through chapter 4. However, the selfishness and subterfuge of Ananias and Sapphira disrupted the perfect progression. I used to wonder why their penalty was so severe, death for a lie, but the context provides the reason. They had stopped the ideal advancing kingdom dead in its tracks. God hasn't changed his mind or his methods, we are still faced with the same choices today.

The early church outside of Jerusalem certainly didn't live out the kingdom perfectly either, but they understood its principles and did their best, and they grew exponentially. The early Christians' capacity for martyrdom and a life less sure was a potent witness that is missing in the western church today.

We haven't fallen from there to here in one fell swoop. We haven't made any conscious decisions to destroy the vitality and commitment that made the early church so effective. We have however, fallen victim to circumstances that we generally think of as favorable. If those earliest Christians could have peered into the future, they would have thought our circumstances beneficial as well.

I'm sure the early Christians were encouraged when Constantine proclaimed the legitimacy of the Christian religion and stopped the persecutions. Yet it had been their commitment in the face of persecution that provided gravitas to their living witness. Christians rejoiced in their new freedom to spread the Gospel, but this very freedom may have slowed the rate of conversions to Christ's Way.

If a lack of real persecution is the trouble with Christians today, Jesus offers a prescriptive remedy with kingdom living. His brand of persecution is not dependent on the philosophies of the pagans among which we live because the persecution is meant to be self-imposed. The small deprivations by which we are called to advance the kingdom may not carry the gravitas of possible martyrdom, but they will be noticed.

Kingdom living should create its own brand of adversity, and it is this adversity to which King Jesus calls us. Kingdom living is not only choosing to take up our cross daily; it is joyfully fashioning our cross with vitality and imagination.

Now that we understand the Sermon a little better, can we find ways to live it out? Jesus thinks we can, but he advises that it might not look the way we envision it. It is, after all, his vision and his plan, not ours. We can think to ourselves, "We will do this" or "We will give up that and send what we save to the poor," but I think very little of kingdom living will be premeditated. George Bailey would agree.

Kingdom living is an awareness we carry with us, situation by situation, like our mindfulness of Jesus. Opportunities will arise in which kingdom choices can be made. To not choose for the kingdom will usually be the easier choice, and probably not a sin. To not choose for the kingdom will also be a wrong choice. We have always had reasons to choose selfishly and the world continues to invent more.

Jesus sums up his entire sermon with a final point: *Therefore everyone who hears these words of mine and puts them into practice is like a wise man who built his house on the rock* (Matt 7:24).

This is the house we are to build; the one that will not fall because its foundation is the rock. I count two things we have to do in this verse: we have to hear the words of the Sermon and we have to put them into practice. The church as a whole does well with the parts of the sermon it has understood. But since we've understood only partially, we have gotten partial results. Trouble has come to our house on the rock because of the parts we haven't understood. The Devil has understood better than we have, and has used our lack of understanding against us. It doesn't have to be that way anymore. Now we understand the Sermon better. That's the hearing part.

Now all we have to do is put the concepts into practice. Jesus has given us a full and consistent teaching. He knows what we can accomplish. Let's recognize the importance of our calling. Let's supplant our old ways of thinking. Kingdom living is more than tactics or important areas in which we need to improve; it is one of the most important concepts in the Bible. *Kingdom Living is the primary way in which the world will ever see Jesus.*

Kingdom living is not an experiment. An experiment starts with a hypothesis and then attempts to prove or disprove it. Jesus doesn't hypothesize, Jesus knows. We can be confident that the results will be good, if unexpected.

The early church came close to this ideal and we saw how much it accomplished. Now it's our turn. Each day has opportunities enough of its own. We can be George Bailey or we can be Mr. Potter. The choice is ours. We can accomplish so much if we can take Jesus at his words; we only need to put them into practice.

We only need to put them into practice.

www.ingramcontent.com/pod-product-compliance
Lightning Source LLC
Chambersburg PA
CBHW071446150426
43191CB00008B/1253